SIEGE OF KHE SANH

SIEGE OF KHE SANH

THE STORY OF THE VIETNAM WAR'S LARGEST BATTLE

ROBERT PISOR

W. W. NORTON & COMPANY
INDEPENDENT PUBLISHERS SINCE 1923
NEW YORK | LONDON

Previously published under the title
THE END OF THE LINE: The Siege of Khe Sanh

First published as a Norton paperback 2002,
reissued with a new introduction 2018

For information about special discounts for bulk purchases, please contact
W. W. Norton Special Sales at specialsales@wwnorton.com or 800-233-4830

Manufacturing by LSC Communications, Harrisonburg, VA
Production manager: Julia Druskin

ISBN: 978-0-393-35451-5 (pbk.)

W. W. Norton & Company, Inc., 500 Fifth Avenue, New York, N.Y. 10110
www.wwnorton.com

W. W. Norton & Company Ltd., 15 Carlisle Street, London W1D 3BS

1 2 3 4 5 6 7 8 9 0

For India Company

SIEGE OF KHE SANH

N
China
North
Vietnam
Hanoi
Gulf
of
Tonkin
Laos
Vientiane
Thailand
Khe
Sanh
1968
INDOCHINA
0
50
100
150
Miles
Cambodia
Phnom Penh
South
Vietnam
Saigon
Gulf
of
Thailand
South
China
Sea

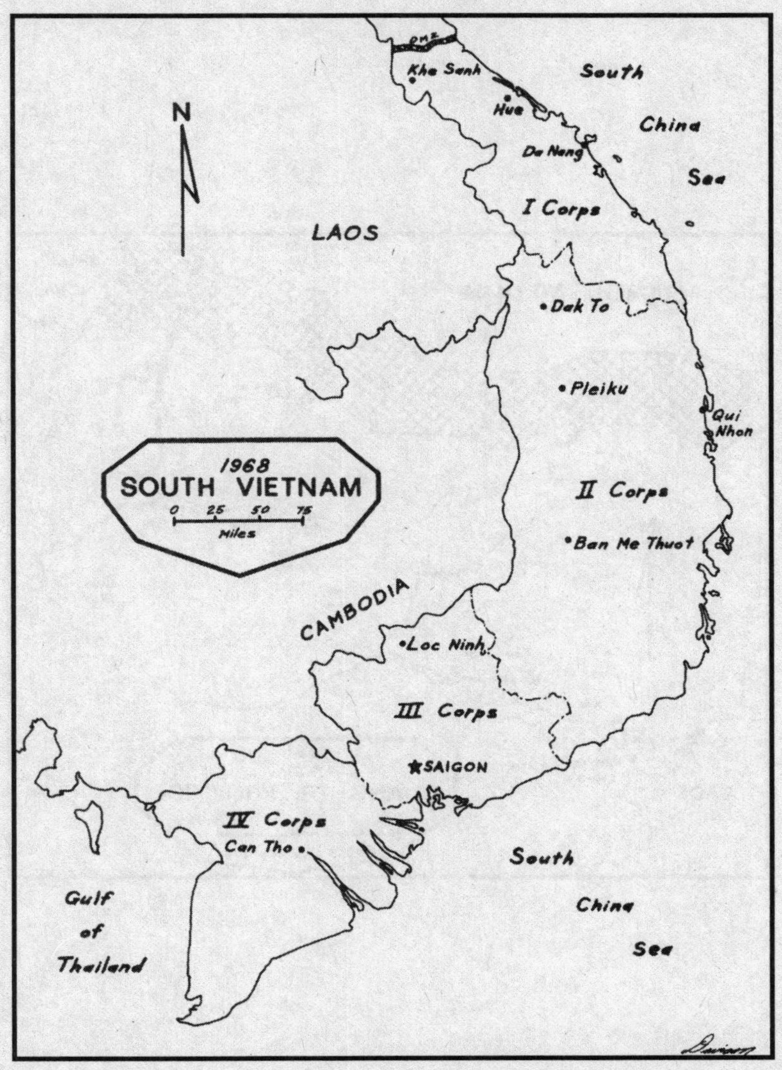
1968
SOUTH VIETNAM
0 25 50 75
Miles
N
DMZ
Khe Sanh
Hue
Da Nang
South
China
Sea
I Corps
LAOS
Dak To
Pleiku
Qui
Nhon
II Corps
Ban Me Thuot
CAMBODIA
Loc Ninh
III Corps
SAIGON
IV Corps
Can Tho
South
China
Sea
Gulf
of
Thailand

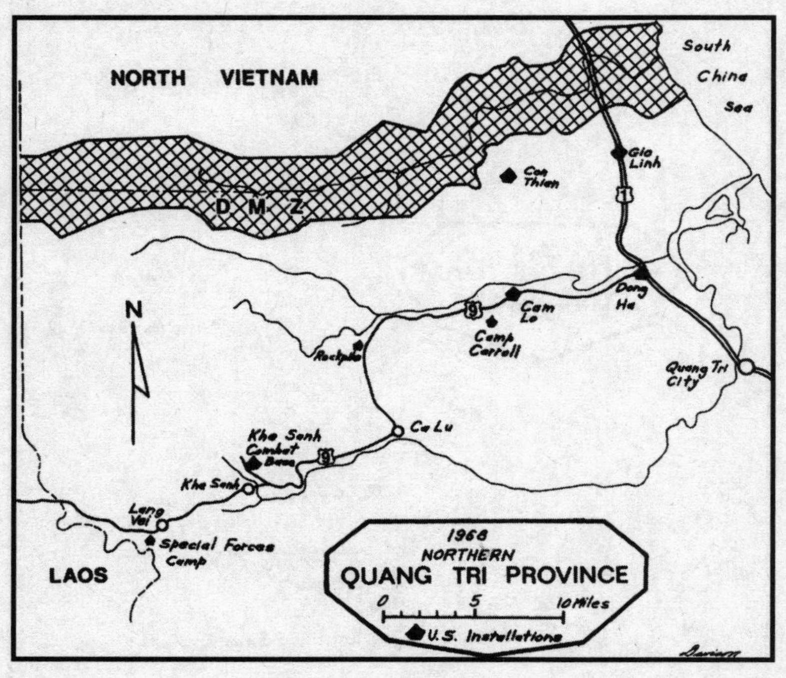
NORTH VIETNAM
South
China
Sea
Gio
Linh
Con
Thien
D M Z
N
Dong
Ha
Cam
Lo
Camp
Carroll
Rockpile
Quang Tri
City
Ca Lu
Khe Sanh
Combat
Base
Khe Sanh
Lang
Vei
Special Forces
Camp
LAOS
1968
NORTHERN
QUANG TRI PROVINCE
0
5
10 Miles
U.S. Installations

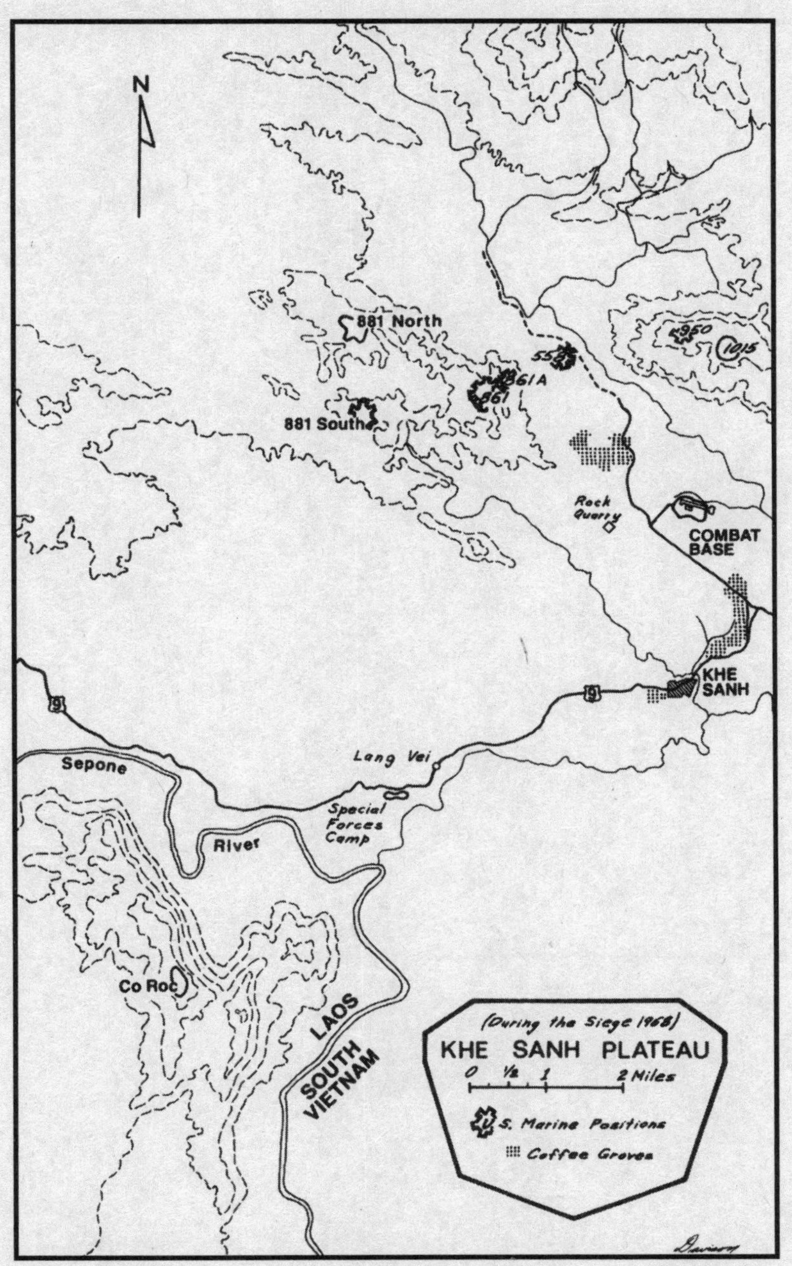
N
881 North
552
861A
861
881 South
950
1015
Rock Quarry
COMBAT BASE
KHE SANH
9
9
Lang Vei
Sepone
Special Forces Camp
River
Co Roc
LAOS
SOUTH VIETNAM
(During the Siege 1968)
KHE SANH PLATEAU
0 1/2 1 2 Miles
U.S. Marine Positions
Coffee Groves
Davison

Contents

MAPS

INTRODUCTION

Mark Bowden

Sometimes one battle in a long war can tell the whole story writ small.

Khe Sanh, the months-long 1968 siege that Robert Pisor recounts in this book, was a staunch American effort to defend one god-forsaken Marine base in the Central Highlands of Vietnam. After a vicious initial engagement near the end of January, the 6,000 Marines dug in waiting for a climactic attack.

At first deemed strategically important for dubious reasons, the base became something more—a point of national pride. Over five-and-a-half months, while the encircled men endured constant shelling, the U.S. military laid waste to the hills and valleys around the outpost, a region of mountain villages, lush jungle, and sprawling coffee plantations. Khe Sanh could not be supplied by road, so its survival depended on airlifts and air power. An estimated 100,000 tons of bombs were dropped and 158,000 artillery shells launched, raining explosives and napalm, more than had been exploded on any comparable space in history, leaving behind, in the words of one military historian, "a red-orange moonscape." The effort displaced tens of thousands of Vietnamese civilians—there is no count of those wounded or killed. Hundreds of American Marines and soldiers were killed and thousands of Vietnamese troops. Then, in the summer of that year, completing the analogy with the Vietnam War as a whole, the United States simply abandoned the position.

As Pisor makes clear in this compelling account, which ranges from the embattled hilltop to the White House and Pentagon, Khe Sanh was less a battle than a symbolic and ultimately meaningless stand. It might as well be known as Westy's Folly, after its architect, General William "Westy" Westmoreland, commander of all American forces in Vietnam. Westmoreland deserves to be remembered alongside Civil War General George McClellan as the archetype for a certain kind of bad generalship.

McClellan was famous for building the Union Army early in the Civil War into a magnificent fighting machine, then refusing to send it into battle. Abraham Lincoln once facetiously asked him if he might "borrow" the army, if the general did not intend to use it. Westy had an entirely different conceit. He was too wedded to his own brilliance to consider anything that contradicted it. So convinced that Khe Sanh was about to be overrun—in a reenactment of the famous French defeat in 1954 at Dien Bien Phu—he diverted enormous resources to the isolated base's defense, and hyped the base's survival into an emblem of the entire U.S. war effort. He promised President Lyndon Johnson that it would never fall. Members of his staff, Pisor reports, reverently passed around copies of Bernard Fall's classic account of the earlier battle, *Hell in a Very Small Place*, sharing their commander's belief that, in effect, it outlined the enemy's intentions.

Dropping sophisticated new sensors into the jungle around the base, Westy's command began collecting evidence of troop movements, upping the estimate of enemy forces there. Eventually certain that as many as 20,000 enemy troops had assembled, Westy, ever the dazzling theorist, spun inventive rationales to explain why. It was crucial high ground athwart the famous Ho Chi Minh Trail, he said. It was a potential launching pad for an American invasion of Laos, just ten miles west. Other generals, notably Maxwell Taylor, didn't see it. He urged President Johnson to withdraw the Marines. But Westy managed to convince the president that Khe Sanh was a test—the ultimate test—of America's will. He was also excited, Pisor notes, by the supposed massing of enemy forces. "The single greatest attraction of the combat base," Pisor writes, "was as a killing ground for North Vietnamese troops." After all, Westy's deep strategy for defeating the Communist effort was "attrition," killing so many enemy soldiers that Hanoi would eventually buckle. At one point, early on, he considered using tactical nuclear weapons, an idea that was quickly abandoned when word of it leaked to the press. The character of the war prior to 1968 had been almost entirely hit-and-run, with American forces searching high and low for enemy troops that tended to melt away after making contact. "The Viet Cong," Westy said, "are uncommonly adept at slithering away." Here, he believed, the National Liberation Front (North Vietnamese regulars and Viet Cong guerrillas) had finally decided to stand and fight. This would be the war's great test of arms, and America had more firepower than any nation in history. It would be a chance for American forces to break the front's back. He would use the unprecedented display of air power—something the French had lacked—to demonstrate the futility of opposing the United States of America.

As often happens in war, the enemy had different plans. It was not, as Westy assumed, wedded to the strategies of the old war. While the attention of U.S. forces remained obsessively focused on Khe Sanh in early 1968—the general sent daily updates directly to Johnson on the number of bombs dropped, weapons and men delivered, and (vastly inflated) estimates of enemy killed—the front quietly amassed tens of thousands of men and arms elsewhere. On the morning of Tet, January 31st, it shocked the world with attacks on more than a hundred cities throughout South Vietnam, and took Hue, not some isolated Marine base but the third largest city in the nation, and the country's intellectual and cultural center.

How did Westy respond? He denied it. And even as his own troops in Hue were engaged in a bloody, bitter, nearly month-long fight to win that city back, with casualties arriving in bloody waves at the field hospital in Phu Bai, the general refused to acknowledge it. While he continued raining fire on the Central Highlands, the enemy was busy in the streets of the old capital, rounding up and executing supporters of the South Vietnamese government and deeply undermining confidence in the regime America was there to defend. Westy dismissed the Tet Offensive, which proved to be the turning point in the war, as nothing but "a diversionary effort" designed to distract attention from Khe Sanh. He continued to believe, plan, and act as if the real attack would come there.

It never did. It turns out that the front never had more than a fraction of the troops thought to be amassed around Khe Sanh. And even as field commanders around Hue reported they were fighting the very enemy units who were supposed to be outside the Marine base, Westy's conviction never wavered.

He had, in fact, been hoodwinked. In my conversations with Vietnamese historians and high-ranking military veterans there in 2015 and 2016 while researching my book *Hue 1968*, they described Khe Sanh as a deliberate diversion. Noted military historian retired Gen. S.L.A. Marshall saw it as such; he called Khe Sanh "a feint." General Lowell English, one of the garrison's Marine commanders, later termed it a "trap" that forced Westy "into the expenditure of absolutely unreasonable amounts of men and materiel to defend a piece of terrain that wasn't worth a damn."

The general's obsession with Khe Sanh, while the real battle raged elsewhere, must have been a deeply satisfying thing to North Vietnam's leaders. And when it became clear that Westy's predicted attack wasn't coming, he declared victory. He never acknowledged, even in his memoirs years later, that Hue had been taken, or that the Tet Offensive had scored anything more than a minor public relations victory. Khe Sanh, he insisted, was his major triumph.

It wasn't. It was a hellish siege, one that over nearly six months accumulated more American casualties than any other single engagement of the war. After a few intense clashes with skilled enemy forces in January, including tanks, the Marines reinforced their perimeter and started digging. They remained on the hilltops of Khe Sanh week after week, month after month, riding out relentless enemy mortar barrages, waiting on edge for the predicted attack to begin, all the while witnessing the greatest display of aerial bombardment in history. Khe Sanh, in the end, was less a battle than a heroic feat of endurance. The isolated men began to look like ragged castaways, bearded, filthy, their clothes in tatters.

Even before this standoff started, Khe Sanh had been a tough assignment. Set on high ground and surrounded by jungle and hills in all directions, it was a choice target. Pisor notes that the Marine rifles had "an etched steel V for a rear sight and a perfect round bead for a front sight. A marksman sets the bead on the shoulder of a deer, or the neck of a squirrel, snugs the bead in the apex of the V, and smoothly squeezes the trigger. To be in the V-ring is to be dead." They took to calling their position "the V-ring."

One veteran Marine general said, "We went through some tough places [in World War II] . . . Tarawa or Peleliu, parts of the canal, Tinian, but I don't think we were ever asked to carry out—day in, day out, no Sundays, thirty-one days a month, twenty-four hours around the clock, 360 degrees of direction—a fight that you were involved in during your whole twelve-to-thirteen-month tour."

During the height of the siege, it was almost unendurable.

"Water was scarce, and most of the Marines wore scraggly beards," Pisor writes. "Few washed regularly. The sleeping bunkers were dank stench chambers, redolent of sweat and urine. Diarrhea and fear, C-ration garbage, vomit, farts, feet, and fungus. Rats ran across the dirt floors, gnawing at shelves and boots and fingers, chittering in fear when the big guns fired and sometimes scratching faces as they raced across sleeping Marines. . . ."

They dug and they dug to escape the constant shelling.

"It gives you the feeling that you're digging your own grave," said one senior officer.

They grew to admire the tenacity of enemy mortar crews, who after absorbing air attacks that seemingly nothing living could survive, would miraculously resume work after the bombers disappeared.

"A North Vietnamese soldier had lugged a .50 caliber machine gun to a spider hole not much more than two hundred yards from the perimeter," Pisor writes. "Every day and night he fired at the Marines or at arriving and departing aircraft. The Marines actually caught glimpses of his face through the scopes of their sniper rifles, but neither marksmen nor mortars nor recoilless rifles could knock him out. Finally, napalm was called in. For ten minutes the ground around the sniper's position boiled in orange flame and black smoke, the vegetation crisping and the soil itself seeming to burn. When the last oily flames flickered out, he popped out of his hole and fired a single round."

Pisor writes that the Marines, buoyed by the solitary man's ability to survive, "cheered him."

They named him "Luke the Gook," and decided to leave him alone.

There were not many light moments. By the end of the first week in February, one of every ten Marines at the base had been wounded or killed.

"When I get back to California, I'm going to open a bar especially for the survivors of Khe Sanh," Lieutenant C. J. Slack of Carlsbad told AP reporter John T. Wheeler. "And any time it gets two deep at that bar, I'll know someone is lying."

The waves of American planes delivering bombs to the enemy and an unending stream of ammunition and supplies to the encircled outpost were hampered by the thick clouds of the rainy season, and targeted by anti-aircraft weapons along approach routes—one C-130 arrived back at Da Nang with 242 holes in its fuselage and wings. During one stretch of six weeks the Air Force was able to deliver only five days of supplies.

Like so many Vietnam vets, the men who survived this ordeal were left to wonder what it had all been about. The Army units that were finally able to relieve them in June arrived almost without contest. The 20,000 enemy soldiers thought to be encircling the base were gone, if they had ever been there at all.

The Johnson administration, under a new secretary of defense, Clark Clifford, grew fed up with Westy's exaggerations and denials. He was kicked upstairs to become Army chief of staff. General Creighton Abrams, his replacement, promptly blew up the fortifications at Khe Sanh and withdrew all American forces. There was no appreciable loss or gain in doing so. The "battle" had, while all too real for the Marines who had weathered it, been in large measure a product of Westy's imagination.

It doesn't detract from their heroism, of course, to say that the entire experience was for naught. Khe Sanh was the Vietnam War in microcosm, a misguided cause, a misunderstood battlefield, and a mistaken and ultimately tragic belief that America had something important to prove by riding it out.

"The disaster of Vietnam was not the result of impersonal forces but a uniquely human failure," concluded H. R. McMaster in his stinging indictment of wartime leadership, *Dereliction of Duty*, "the responsibility for which was shared by President Johnson and his principal military and civilian advisors. . . . The failures were many and reinforcing: arrogance, weakness, lying in the pursuit of self-interest, and, above all, the abdication of responsibility to the American people."

1.

The Curtain Rises

The cold chill of his steel helmet came right through the plastic liner, and Captain Bill Dabney's shoulders shivered for a moment before he willed them still. The Marines of India Company filed past, stumbling, grumbling in the gloom. It was five o'clock in the morning in the northern mountains of South Vietnam.

Dabney stood on the crest of a gnarled thumb of a mountain called Hill 881 South. From this height he could see the bone-shaped scar of an Army Special Forces camp at Lang Vei, the church steeples of Khe Sanh Village, the smokey hamlets of the mountain tribesmen known as Bru, the airstrip and bunkers of the Khe Sanh Combat Base—and even the thick-walled villas of French planters where wrinkled, brown women sorted coffee beans and gracious ladies served crème de menthe on the patio.

All around lay a phantasmagorical landscape, the kind of place where trolls might live. An awesome, sheer-sided mountain of stone called Co Roc guarded the gateway to Laos, the land of mystery and green mountains that flowed gently around Dabney's hill to the south. Tiger Peak loomed large in the hazy far distance, a barrier near the boundary of North Vietnam. Down on the plateau, confusing tangles of thorn and vine and low brush gave way to incredibly dense stands of twelve-foot-high elephant grass. Plummeting mountain streams frothed white against house-sized boulders on the hillsides. Across the valleys, silent waterfalls flashed like sunlit diamonds in the deep, green, velvet lushness of the jungle.

Some of the Marines had caught trout as big as salmon in these rivers. Others hoped for a shot at one of the trophy tigers that stalked this remote, beautiful corner of the earth. This morning, January 20, 1968, the men of India Company were hunting other men; today, they couldn't see five feet in any direction.

A thick fog pressed to the ground, flowing heavily in the hollows and draws, parting and closing as the Marines passed. The point men, lone scouts who probed the thick growth ahead of the company's columns, lurched down the steep hill, pushing at the curtains of mist with their rifles. They knew these trails intimately, but they walked like eyeless men: tense, bent slightly forward, knees flexed, hands outstretched, ears strained, striving for the synaptic millisecond that could give them an edge in the shockingly close combat that marked encounters with the enemy in Vietnam.

The American tunnel rats who squeezed with flashlight and pistol into narrow burrows deep in the earth experienced the same unique, lonely terror that shaped the psyche of point men in this war. Their claustrophobic nightmare—of bats and boobytraps, cobwebs and cave-ins—enclosed them only when a secret tunnel complex was discovered; point men lived with The Fear every day. In a war in which ambush was the enemy's most successful tactic, point men did for the infantry what food tasters did for the Borgias. Just yesterday, one of Dabney's scouts—a volunteer who had explained quite seriously that he *wanted* to walk point because he thought of himself as a gunfighter—had played High Noon with a North Vietnamese Army soldier on Hill 881 North. At a range of less than fifty feet, he had exchanged long, ripping bursts of automatic rifle fire with the enemy and then dropped into the tall grass, shaken but unhurt, as loud cracks and soft whispers clipped leaves and twigs all around him.

India Company, 185 strong, was headed back to the same spot

this morning. The fishing rods had been stowed in the hilltop bunkers. Each man carried twice his normal load of ammunition. They expected to fight today, and for almost everyone it would be the first time in combat.

Rumors of a massive North Vietnamese buildup around Khe Sanh had circulated since mid-December, when India Company and other elements of the Third Battalion, 26th Marines, were airlifted to the combat base on extreme short notice. The commander of all American forces in Vietnam, General William C. Westmoreland, believed that tens of thousands of North Vietnam's finest troops were moving into attack positions around the isolated Marine post. Apprehension mounted as enemy truck traffic on nearby Laotian roads and trails rose from a monthly average of 480 in the fall to more than 6,000 in December.

Then, on January 2, several hours after dusk, six men in U.S. Marine uniforms—one of them as tall and husky as a linebacker—walked up to the western perimeter of the combat base and stood talking, pointing occasionally at strong points. They froze when challenged by a security team, hesitated for too long a second when asked to identify themselves—and died in a hail of rifle fire. A single survivor, bleeding heavily, had been able to collect a map case from one of the bodies and escape into the night, but within hours the Marines were boasting of an important coup: papers on the dead men identified them as the highest-ranking officers of a North Vietnamese Army regiment.

For Westmoreland and Colonel David E. Lownds, commander of the 26th Marines, the incident was the final piece of evidence that Khe Sanh was about to move to the center stage of the Vietnam war. Only for a target of the very highest priority, the American officers believed, would such key leaders undertake the dangerous personal reconnaissance that had ended in death.

The preparations for battle continued with a special urgency.

Cargo planes delivered hundreds of tons of ammunition to scuttling forklifts on the airstrip. Reinforcements hurried to Khe Sanh, including the second battalion of the 26th Marines. For the first time since the terrible fighting on Iwo Jima in 1945, all three battalions of the 26th Marines were operating in combat together. Colonel Lownds told his regimental staff in a hushed briefing that he expected massed assaults to begin before January 20. He ordered the Marines to dig fighting holes next to their sleeping bunkers as well as at their posts on the perimeter. The defenders extended their minefields and added German tape, a twisted rope of razor blades, to the triple coils of barbed wire and bewildering maze of foottraps that ringed the base. General Westmoreland diverted intelligence resources, especially the technological wizardry of the Air Force, to an intensive search for what was now believed to be the largest gathering of enemy forces in the war.

Not a hint of this ominous news trickled down to Captain Dabney and his men on their hilltop four miles to the west. They might not have believed it, anyway. They had humped these hills and ridgelines and stream beds and sawgrass mazes for a solid month, including one grueling, five-day, Christmas-week patrol all the way to Laos. They had patrolled their own hill by day and by night, poked into tangled thickets and bamboo clusters, and plunged into the deep guillies that separated their hill from Hill 861 to the east. They had found nothing—not even a trace of recent enemy activity.

No one doubted that the North Vietnamese *could* be preparing for an attack. The Marines respected the enemy's skill in camouflaged movement. Besides, Dabney's men lived amidst constant reminders of the North Vietnamese commitment to this war. Even now, as the Marines slithered down the steep slope in darkness, they had to dodge the jagged needles of splintered trees and skirt the deep pits of old bomb craters. Melted gobs of plastic, the signature of napalm, hung like taffy in the trees.

For seven days during the previous spring, Marines of another regiment had fought the North Vietnamese for control of this hill and its two neighbors, Hill 881 North and Hill 861. American firepower had finally blasted the enemy troops off the hills. The trees here were so full of shrapnel that combat engineers refused to collect timber for bunkers, complaining that their power saws fouled at the very first cut. When the men of India Company enlarged and deepened their defensive positions on 881 South, they broke into ghastly, putrescent pits that sent them staggering backwards, gagging and cursing at the smell. Nine months underground, these were the corpses of enemy soldiers who had fought and died, and been buried, on the battlefield.

The Hill Fights, as the battles of late April and early May of 1967 had become known, were toe-to-toe slugging matches between the shock troops of two nations. The Marines had shown the "hey diddle-diddle, straight up the middle" spirit that had won them glory in a score of American wars, but somehow the standards had changed for Vietnam. Army doubts about Marine leadership flowered during these battles, and the Hill Fights exposed weaknesses in American tactics and weapons.

The North Vietnamese had been ready, and waiting. Dug deeply into an interconnected system of fighting bunkers with as much as six feet of packed earth and logs overhead, superbly camouflaged and aiming down lanes cut out of the underbrush, the enemy troops had held their fire until the leading Marine units were only a few feet away. The initial volley knocked down scores of young Marines and, as stunned survivors scrambled for cover, enemy marksmen firing rifles with telescopic sights shot radio operators and machine gunners through the head.

Spirited North Vietnamese soldiers shouted, in English: "Put on your helmets, Marines! We're coming after you!"

The Americans fought back, but their new M-16 rifles—received earlier that month—began to break down. As the Marine fire dropped off, signal whistles sounded on the hillside. North Vietnamese squad leaders maneuvered their soldiers out of the bunkers to flank and overrun isolated Marine positions. After the battle, dozens of American dead were found crouched over their rifles, killed as they tried to thread together the three separate pieces of their cleaning rods so they could ram a jammed shellcasing out of their rifles and return to the fight.

The bloodied Marines had pulled back without their dead, a rare concession to enemy might, and then watched, spectators at Armageddon, as waves of B-52 Stratofortresses and fighter-bombers put 3,250 tons of explosives on the enemy positions. The Marine commander in the Hill Fights, Colonel John P. Lanigan, had been awed by the power of bombs and naval gunfire on Okinawa where he had won a Silver Star as a young Marine twenty-three years earlier, but he had never seen more devastating firepower than was brought to bear on the hills above Khe Sanh. In fact, no other target in the Vietnam War had been so heavily bombed.

The Marines waited as heavy artillery and massive airstrikes blasted the vegetation from the hilltops, then waited while more bombs churned the splinters and soil to an ugly brown goo, and then climbed to the top of Hill 881 South to find only silence, "no NVA, no trees, no nothin'."

By the time the third hill was captured and a major enemy counterattack repelled, 160 Marines were dead and more than 700 evacuated with wounds. Estimates of enemy dead, made more difficult by their battlefield burials and disciplined withdrawal, ranged from 558 to 940. The Hill Fights were declared a victory, a successful preemptive attack that had prevented the small outpost at Khe Sanh from being overrun.

The M-16 was strongly defended as a fine assault rifle, and Army officers in both Saigon and Washington suggested in private that Marine carelessness in training and maintenance had been responsible for its breakdown in battle. The chuckle of the day was that the new M-16 was fool proof, but not Marine proof.

Then, on the other side of the world, Congressman James J.

Howard of New Jersey had risen on the floor of the House of Representatives to read a letter from a bitter Marine who had been wounded in the Hill Fights:

"We left with close to 1,400 men in our battalion and came back with half," he wrote, warning his parents not to believe what they read in the newspapers. "We left with 250 men in our company and came back with 107. Practically every one of our dead was found with his rifle torn down next to him. . . ."

The letter, and the new perspective on casualty tolls, tarnished the Marine victory in the Hill Fights. A formal investigation of the new $121 M-16 rifle would find a "serious frequency of malfunctions."

• • •

DABNEY'S MEN WERE eighteen and nineteen years old in January of 1968. Most of them had been in high school during the Hill Fights. They knew little of the sacrifice and scandal that had attended the battles on their hill, but the hard lessons of the previous spring had been a part of their training. It was standard practice in Vietnam now to seek contact with the enemy, then pull back immediately to let airplanes and artillery deliver the punishment. All the M-16s in Vietnam had been recalled, refitted with chrome chambers and a new buffer system to reduce the rate of fire, and provided with a different gunpowder to lessen jamming.

Most of all, Dabney's troops had been warned to respect the tenacious enemy soldier who clearly thought of these hills as his own.

Americans sometimes called the guerrilla soldiers in Vietnam "Charlie" because of the radio initials for Viet Cong: Victor Charlie. Here, near the borders of North Vietnam and Laos, where well-trained enemy troops maneuvered with the support of artillery and rocket and anti-aircraft units, he was known as "Mr. Charles." The North Vietnamese soldiers moving toward Khe Sanh were "well-equipped with the latest weapons, well-uniformed, well-fed, and thoroughly professional."

Dabney's men moved down the slopes of Hill 881 South as though the victory of last spring was still in doubt.

These young Marines were the quintessential American warriors of the Vietnam era, TV sons of *Victory at Sea* and *The Sands of Iwo Jima*, stripped for battle—and loaded for bear.

Each carried twenty or more magazines of ammunition for his automatic rifle, and many had taped two magazines together—back to back, one up, one down. With the taped package, a Marine could double his immediately available firepower from twenty bullets to forty with a flick of his wrist. Only rarely did a U.S. Marine fire all of the eighty bullets he carried ashore with him during World War II—even when the fighting was quite heavy during the first twenty-four hours of battle. The Marines in Vietnam often fired eighty bullets in the first two minutes of combat. In fact, Dabney had already arranged for a pallet of rifle ammunition to be delivered by the first helicopter that came to evacuate casualties.

The men of India Company did not worry about the controversial M-16 because none carried it. Upon arrival at Khe Sanh, they had traded their M-16s for M-14s, heavier, longer rifles that were being phased out but could still be found in support units. The M-14 could reach five hundred meters from ridgeline to ridgeline with power, while the M-16—deadly at close range—couldn't seem to find people beyond three hundred meters.

Each Marine wore leather and nylon jungle boots; baggy, deep-pocketed pants; a long-sleeved shirt; a vest of armor known as a flak jacket; and a steel helmet covered with camouflage cloth. Four small, smooth one-pound bombs, affectionately called "baseballs," hung on every belt, usually beside two smoke grenades. Technology had replaced the heavier cast-iron "pineapple" of previous wars with a thin-skinned grenade that exploded a tightly coiled band of spring steel into a thousand jagged fragments. The new "baseball" increased the circle of death from twenty to thirty meters.

Every man carried a two-foot-long fiberglass tube on a canvas shoulder strap. Called a LAW, this one-shot, disposable rocket launcher was an essential tool for opening enemy bunkers or blasting the roof off a fighting hole. It had been designed as a Light Antitank Weapon, hence its acronym, but there were no tanks here. To the east, toward the U.S. base at Con Thien, Marines carried LAWs because they swore they could hear the ominous clank of heavy treads during night patrols. But the hills around Khe Sanh were a vertical jungle of vines and thorns and thickets, low trees, high trees and higher trees. The very few roads and trails were pitted, potholed, washed out, blocked by landslides and blown bridges. This was difficult terrain for men; it was impossible terrain for tanks.

Four canteens of water, a small shovel, and a first-aid packet completed their gear. There were no ponchos, no bedrolls, no transistor radios, no Polaroid cameras or battery-pack tape decks, no fishing rods or Frisbees, nor any of the other items in the incredible array of personal equipment that Americans often carried into battle in Vietnam. This was to be a fighting day. Even eating and sleeping would wait until their return to the hilltop.

They traveled lighter than usual because they could count on instant fire support from their own hilltop, which would never be much more than a mile away. At that range, the 106mm recoilless rifles on 881 South could fire shells into a garbage can on 881 North. Heavy mortars and three 105mm howitzers on their hill had already fired practice rounds at potential trouble spots on the south-facing slopes of 881 North, and could join the fight in seconds.

The Marines, working their way slowly down the steep hill, were slipping, swearing, shivering proof that the extraordinary technological leaps in electronic warfare had not yet rendered the infantry obsolete.

Somebody still had to go out, look, and report back. This time it was India Company.

An unbelievable variety of highly specialized aircraft had crossed and recrossed the skies above Khe Sanh for thirty miles in every direction for the past month. Some planes snapped thousands of high-speed still photographs, and some sniffed the air with electrochemical analyzers to detect men who dared to sweat or urinate in the jungle below. Some planes looked sideways with radar to detect movement, and some peered at the double and triple tiers of foliage with infrared eyes to "see" the hot spots of cooking fires of bivouacked troops. An air-conditioned electronic laboratory packed with technicians circled high above Khe Sanh, listening to the clicks and beeps of hidden sensors.

By late January, this unprecedented concentration of intelligence assets included "all the resources of Navy, Marine Corps, and Air Force reconnaissance and electronic warfare aircraft, and all ground intelligence-gathering activities" as well as extensive use of the still highly secret sensors.

The intelligence-gathering effort ranged from computer analysis of sensor signals to the hand-crumbling of elephant feces by long range patrols. Still, Colonel Lownds had no exact idea where the North Vietnamese were or when they planned to attack. He shared Westmoreland's conviction that a concentration of 20,000 or more enemy soldiers would be the single most spectacular bombing target of the Vietnam war—but he also knew that his 5,000 Marines risked a fatal surprise if the enemy could approach Khe Sanh undetected.

And so Lownds sent men out, in patrols and platoons, to walk the hillsides, to comb the grassy seas, to listen beside the plateau trails. Teams of eight, their faces smeared with black and green paint and their equipment heavily taped to muffle metallic rattles, jumped from hovering helicopters to undertake dangerous reconnaissance missions many, many miles from the combat base.

Lownds was a fisherman standing in midstream but unable to see beneath the glare reflected from the water's surface. He cast his lures first into the likeliest spots, the pool below the plunging falls, the eddy beneath an overhanging bank, the quiet edge of a swift-flowing current. When each cast came back empty, he began to try the unlikely places, the broad ripple in midstream, the too-shallow rill, the darkness beside a drowned stump.

On January 17, there was a quick swirling of the green water and a sharp tug on Lownds' line. Enemy troops ambushed a reconnaissance team on the south slope of Hill 881 North. The team leader and the radio operator were killed, and the wounded survivors pulled back calling for emergency help. By chance, one of Dabney's platoons was patrolling on the same hill. Tom Brindley, a twenty-four-year-old second lieutenant from St. Paul, ordered his men to shed their bulky flak jackets and packs and then led them, on the run, carrying only rifles and grenades, to the rescue. Brindley found the recon team, organized a helicopter evacuation of the dead and wounded, and returned to the packs without a shot being fired. Only three months in Vietnam, Brindley felt pretty good about his platoon's successful mission.

Yesterday, January 19, Dabney had sent a platoon under Second Lieutenant Harry F. Fromme back to the ambush site. The Khe Sanh Combat Base had ordered a careful search to find the recon team's lost radio and, more importantly, the plastic-wrapped package of shackle cards—sheets of radio codes that provided security for Marine communications. The platoon was still short of the ambush site when its point man, the boastful young gunslinger, had his showdown at fifty feet. Fromme estimated from the sound of rifles that his platoon had brushed against twenty-five or more North Vietnamese, but he didn't wait to count them. Calling on the 81mm mortars to cover his withdrawal, he returned to the hilltop.

Captain Dabney knew nothing about the 20,000 enemy soldiers who were believed to be closing on Khe Sanh, but he was growing concerned. The two shooting incidents on 881 North could indicate an enemy buildup. His little hilltop fortress bristled with barbed wire and mines and machine guns and mortars and recoilless rifles and even three 105mm howitzers. Hundreds of Claymore mines, pocket-sized packages of death, stood on bipod legs, pointing their seven hundred steel balls at likely approach routes. Here and there in the tangles of wire were fifty-five-gallon drums of *fougasse*, a brew of aviation fuel, chemical thickener, and plastic explosive. If a breakthrough seemed imminent, Dabney could spill homemade napalm down the hill. In the most extreme case, he could pull people from the secret radio-intercept equipment and from the big guns and put nearly four hundred rifles on the line. It would be a very, very dedicated enemy soldier who climbed the steep slopes of Hill 881 South to assault these defenses, but Dabney knew it was not impossible—especially with surprise. He needed to know more about the developments on the hill to his north, and he asked the combat base for permission to take his entire company on a reconnaissance-in-force. Lownds approved the mission, and flew 100 men to the hilltop by helicopter to hold the defensive positions while Dabney was gone.

• • •

IT WAS 9 A.M. when the fog finally lifted. It had taken four hours to cover what the map said was only five hundred yards. Now, India Company had eyes, and the men moved forward with more confidence.

Dabney could feel the change in mood, and he shared in it. Leading an infantry company in combat is an essential course in the education of a career military officer. Dabney had set his goals very high. Educated in the private Episcopal schools of rural Virginia and North Carolina, he had attended Yale University on an academic scholarship—only to lose his grant to low grades at the end of his freshman year. He promptly moved from the campus at New Haven to the grinder at Parris Island, a willing recruit for the Marines.

Dabney served three years in the ranks, finishing his enlisted tour on Okinawa. He applied for admission to the U.S. Naval Academy, and was accepted, but he decided to seek his degree at the Virginia Military Institute because VMI would credit his year at Yale—and because three of the last four commandants of the Marine Corps were VMI graduates. Dabney's goals were very high.

He achieved all the necessary scores as a student and young officer, but some of his peers placed special significance on Dabney's marriage to the daughter of Chesty Puller. Lt. Gen. Lewis B. Puller was the most decorated man in the history of the Marine Corps, a legendary warrior whose name alone could lift a thousand combat veterans to their feet in lusty cheers. Like his father-in-law, Dabney was an exacting officer with a special affection for enlisted men. Dabney in Vietnam could read "Eat the apple; Fuck the Corps!" scrawled on a Marine private's flak jacket—and laugh. He'd been there himself.

Almost a third of the men in India Company were draftees, a jolting departure from the traditional volunteers-only policy of the Marine Corps. Captain Dabney had been keeping charts on his men's performance, reliability, and other measures of competency, and he'd decided there was not a dime's difference between volunteers and draftees. A veteran gunnery sergeant might hawk and spit at such a conclusion, but a lot of old gunnies were dead—or had decided to get old by retiring early. Vietnam was proving to be a hard war for the Marines.

India Company, however, was in unusually good shape. Freed from the heatstroke temperatures of the lowlands and rigidly dosed every day with anti-malaria drugs, the unit was near full strength—a rarity in a war that hospitalized American soldiers with fever and fungus five times as often as with combat wounds. Dabney required his platoon leaders to line up the men each morning, place a dapsone anti-malaria pill and a swallow of water in each mouth, and then stand, waiting, "until his Adam's apple bobbed."

The Marine captain had several tasks today, beyond a renewed search for the missing radio and code sheets. He was to seek out the enemy force that had suddenly appeared on Hill 881 North, and he was to cloak the placement of a new recon team on the hill. The helicopter had proved to be both a curse and a blessing for the reconnaissance trade. The agile craft could reduce a recon team's march to a target from months to minutes and, like an angel of the Lord, it could snatch the team out of almost hopeless situations. But the helicopter was a noisy herald for a furtive mission, and it always marked the time and place of a team's arrival in enemy country. In recent weeks, the 26th Marines' long-range reconnaissance patrols had required emergency extraction almost every time they went hunting. Today, an eight-man recon team—helilifted to Dabney's hilltop from the combat base the night before—would tag along until India Company ended its search, then melt into the jungle to stay behind on 881 North.

Dabney did not know that he might meet two North Vietnamese Army divisions, one of them distinguished by its discipline and courage in the Hill Fights of last spring and the other a veteran of the historic battle of Dien Bien Phu. He walked cautiously anyway. Ninety percent of all combat casualties in Vietnam were inflicted on company-sized units—usually in the first few minutes of battle. "In other words, they bag 'em," was the blunt explanation of Lieutenant General John A. Chaisson, a Marine from Maine who commanded Westmoreland's Combined Operations Center in Saigon.

Putting his men into the tiger's mouth was not a part of Dabney's plan for January 20, 1968. He divided the company into two mutually supporting columns with his most experienced platoon leaders at the front. Lieutenant Brindley, who had covered this ground three days earlier on his rescue mission, was leading the right-hand column up a treeless ridgeline toward the summit of 881 North. The new recon team and a section of light mortars trailed his platoon. On the left, on a nearly parallel ridgeline, Lieutenant Fromme led a stronger column that included Dabney's small command group and a reserve platoon of forty-five men under Second Lieutenant Michael H. Thomas.

It was not a quiet march.

High explosive shells from the 105mm howitzers marked the path to the top. Stealth and tactical finesse, traditional assets of the infantry, were often sacrificed to reconnaissance by fire in Vietnam in the hope that the falling shells might trigger an enemy ambush prematurely. Some officers compared the practice to whistling past a graveyard, but a heavy majority employed it whenever possible. Pocket radios blaring Beatles' songs, frequent visits by helicopters with mail or hot food or curious battalion commanders, the loud whacking of machetes, and the constant *How's-it-going?-Seen-anything-yet?* radio chit-chat of units in the field had pretty much eliminated stealth as an American tactic, anyway.

As Brindley moved forward on the right, enemy troops suddenly opened fire on his platoon with automatic rifles, heavy machine guns, and shoulder-fired rocket grenades. The point man fell in his tracks, mortally wounded. Caught on the open ridge with only waist-deep grass for concealment, Brindley's men sought the cover of folds in the hillside as the enemy fire grew more intense.

From his vantage point on the left ridge, Dabney could see Brindley's platoon pinned on the grassy hillside. He ordered the lieutenant by Radio to call for more artillery while Fromme moved up to outflank the enemy positions.

Fromme had hardly begun his dash up the left ridge when a single deafening volley of automatic rifle fire scythed through his platoon, dropping twenty men in less than thirty seconds, many of them with severe leg wounds. Fromme called in a medical evacuation helicopter only to see it shot out of the sky by a heavy machine gun on a ridgeline even farther to the west. With flames streaming from the engine cowling, the stricken aircraft careened over the lieutenant's head and crashed. A crew chief leaped from the burning helicopter, breaking his leg when he fell near Fromme. He was carried inside friendly lines.

Over on the right, Brindley added 155mm howitzers to the explosives he was directing at the enemy positions. The ninety-five-pound artillery shells rose from the combat base more than five miles away, hurtled high overhead, then rushed out of the sky to slam the ridgeline with incredible force.

Brindley waited until the huge earth hammers subdued the enemy fire and then rose to his feet, shouting to his men. Zigzagging up the ridge, urging his men forward in the face of fire, the young lieutenant led a textbook infantry assault against the small knob of ground that blocked his path to the summit. With a final surge, his men broke into the North Vietnamese positions in a killing rage.

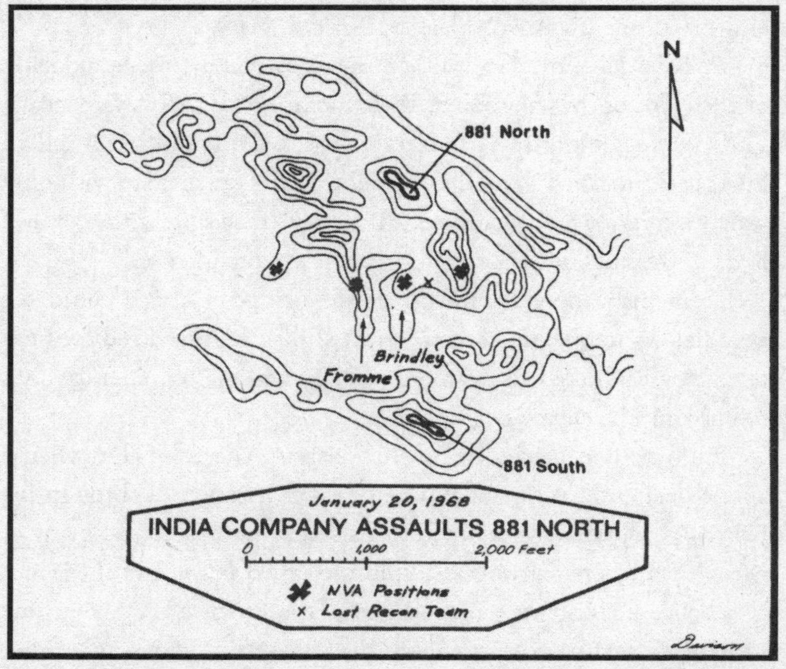

They grenaded the most stubborn defenders, and loosed whole magazines of M-14 fire at the survivors, who reeled away to the east.

The brave charge over open ground, launched while shock waves from the artillery shells still rippled on the hillside, had cracked a superior enemy force and driven it from the field.

It was classic—and costly.

Tom Brindley was killed on the hilltop. The platoon sergeant and the squad leaders had fallen in the assault. The recon team, which had joined the charge up the ridge, had vanished. Sniper fire and steady bursts of a .50 caliber machine-gun fire beat around the Marines as they tumbled into the enemy's fighting holes and old bomb craters. Brindley's radio operator, a corporal, told Dabney by radio that he was the senior man still fighting. The captain sent his executive officer running for the ridge to take command of the platoon. Within minutes, he learned that the unit had suffered heavy casualties—too many to evacuate wounded and still prepare for a counterattack that was already forming on the ridge to the east.

Now it was Second Lieutenant Thomas' turn to get into the fight.

With the eagerness that characterized many young American officers in Vietnam, he moved his reserve platoon quickly into action. Thomas had already organized the evacuation of Fromme's wounded, led a rescue party to recover the crew in the downed helicopter, and helped to prepare Fromme's defensive positions on the left ridge. With Dabney in his column, Thomas moved the reserve platoon back down the ridge, across five hundred meters of low ground, and up the right ridge to reinforce Brindley's battered unit.

Lieutenant Thomas darted from hole to hole on the small knob, urging the men to dig deeper and directing their fire toward the enemy-held ridge to the east. Then he joined Dabney in a shell hole which, because of the command group's radio antennas, was attracting heavy fire. The captain had already hoisted his helmet on a stick—and seen it pierced by a high-powered rifle slug. Crouched in the hole together, the two officers learned that the missing reconnaissance team had been spotted in a brushy saddle between the captured knob and the major enemy strong point to the east.

The spine of the ridge had separated the recon team from Brindley's platoon during the wild charge up the hill. The eight men had veered right and down the slope into a thick stand of brush and elephant grass. When the strong North Vietnamese force was driven from the ridge, it withdrew to the east—and rolled right over the tiny team. In a brief, savage close-quarters fight, all the team members had been killed or wounded. Under the guns of the enemy, they now lay dying in the saddle between the ridges.

Retrieving wounded comrades from the field of fire is a Marine Corps tradition more sacred than life. Lieutenant Thomas organized a rescue party, climbed over the lip of the crater, took two long strides down the ridge—and was killed instantly when a bullet hit him in the face. His platoon sergeant, Daniel Jessup, followed him over the crest and crawled down the slope under heavy fire. He located the lost team in the tangled brush, hoisted the most seriously wounded man on his back, and staggered back up the ridge. Gathering a half dozen volunteers, Jessup returned to the saddle to evacuate all the dead and wounded, then went back a third time alone to collect the team's radio and rifles.

Captain Dabney had become the conductor of a great orchestra of death. From a shell hole, with a backpack radio for a baton, he cued a score of the big guns at the Khe Sanh Combat Base to join the heavy mortars, recoilless rifles, and artillery pieces that blasted the ground around him from the platform atop Hill 881 South. Now, he added the authoritative shriek of jet fighters, the boiling red-black roar of napalm, and the staccato thunder of cluster bombs to the cacophony on 881 North. Tumbling silver canisters of liquid fire had splashed on one enemy counterattack, melting the khaki-clad enemy troops like soft lead soldiers. Marine jets literally blasted the top off the enemy-held ridge to the east with five hundred-pound bombs.

This great storm of steel and fire explained why 185 men could set out to look for 10,000. This was the Götterdämmerung of firepower that was the hallmark of the U.S. military in Vietnam. Infantry captains in this war were as much the coordinators of supporting arms as they were the leaders of men. Dabney now crouched in a landscape that bucked and heaved and burned at his every gesture.

The official Marine Corps history pictures Dabney at this moment as a feisty, impatient field commander calling for reinforcements to roll up the chain of enemy defenses that had been broken by Brindley's assault. The order to withdraw, says the history, "hit him like a thunderbolt" because it ruined the opportunity for a breakthrough.

Dabney remembers it differently.

The captain looked at his watch when the order came, and he was stunned to discover that it was five o'clock in the afternoon. India Company had battled the terrain and the North Vietnamese for twelve hard hours. Seven of his men were dead, including two platoon leaders, and thirty-five were wounded. Brindley's riddled platoon was no longer effective. Fromme, who had not been engaged since the initial volley halved his platoon, was still isolated on the western ridge. Despite the bombs and shells and napalm, enemy fire was building all across his front. Grass fires ignited by napalm and tracer rounds had burned away much of the thin cover on the knob he held—and night was only hours away.

Saddened by their losses but satisfied with the hurt they had put on Mr. Charles, the men of India Company pulled back down the ridge carrying their dead and wounded, and began the steep climb to the bunkers and barbed wire on Hill 881 South.

Captain Dabney had no way of knowing that his Marines had just fired the opening shots in the largest battle Americans would fight in the Vietnam war. It would become a siege, a seventy-seven-day test of firepower and hand-to-hand combat that would utterly rivet the attention of the U.S. military command.

India Company counted almost 200 men present on the morning roster of January 20; only 19 would answer the roll call when the battle was over.

The looming struggle would cause General Westmoreland to weigh the use of "a few small nuclear weapons."

It would drive a deeply worried President to the war room beneath the White House to stand in slippers and robe and sleepless fear, pawing through cablegrams from Saigon and praying he would not be fated to relive the dread thrills of the manly myth of his Texas childhood: the Alamo.

The battle would open raw sores in Army-Marine relations.

It would send ferrets of fear slipping into the sleep of American military professionals everywhere—sharp-edged dreams that echoed with shouts, the crash of hand grenades, the cries of desperate men. The fall of flags.

Dabney had lifted the curtain on the greatest stage play of the American war in Vietnam: the Siege of Khe Sanh.

2.

WESTMORELAND

When news came that battle had been joined at Khe Sanh, General William Childs Westmoreland permitted himself a deeper crinkling of the creases at the corner of his eyes, a twitch of the muscles that tightened the joining of his lips, a faint flaring of the wings of his patrician nose. This was the tight, satisfied smile of a professional. In Westmoreland, it was exultation. He had been preparing this battlefield, a honeyed bait at the very doorstep of the enemy, for almost six months, and now it seemed the North Vietnamese were going to take it. Perhaps Vo Nguyen Giap, the North Vietnamese commander who was acclaimed a genius even in the Western world, was not so brilliant after all.

Trim, erect, surely born to his collar of stars, Westmoreland seemed like a man without nerve endings. He stood, sat, listened to peasants, briefed Presidents, viewed the dead and played tennis with a stiff, handsome, forceful air that he had practiced from a time before his teens. American military professionals call this aura "command presence," and they value it above all other attributes in an officer. Westmoreland's ambiance of authority and assured self-control and, most of all, a carriage that announced command, had moved him smoothly and swiftly past West Point classmates who had outscored him in every other test of leadership. He had paid for his primacy with a loss of spontaneity—a quarter-second delay before he laughed at a well-told story or turned to rebut a critic; his impulses always stopped on the road to expression to check with the Command Presence.

Westmoreland was at the pinnacle of a distinguished military career. His sense of place and pride of achievement showed in the glittering white uniforms and viceregal posture he wore to formal receptions in the Presidential Palace in Saigon, and in the glossy combat boots, and perfectly faded, tailored, and creased khaki fatigues he wore in the field. Even at his ease he stood with his chin lifted, his deep-set eyes focused intently, his head cocked *squarely,* his shoulders set, his back straight, his neck and knees locked firmly, his weight forward the faintest fraction—balanced, poised, ready, a man waiting to be photographed.

He had been First Captain of his class at the U.S. Military Academy, a signal honor that recognized his unique leadership potential and placed him in the elect company of Robert E. Lee, John J. Pershing, and Douglas MacArthur. He had won the Pershing Sword, West Point's symbol of first rank in military proficiency.

Now, thirty-two years later, he commanded an American field army of a half million men, "the most mobile, best-equipped, highest-firepower army in the world—under any flag," and directed a multinational force larger than the United Nations Army that had fought in Korea. His everyday decisions rippled the social and economic fabric of an entire nation, and he spent long, serious hours pondering South Vietnam's problems with agriculture, sanitation, ancestral piety, education, and transportation. He possessed, and exercised, the power of life and death in a land of sixteen million people whose language he neither spoke nor understood.

He was indeed an American viceregent in Asia. *Time* magazine had proclaimed him "Man of the Year." He had addressed a joint session of the Congress, and had sat at the right hand of the President. Cabinet secretaries, senior senators and renowned foreign generals sought him out, respectfully, and film stars, football heroes, Broadway singers, politicians, businessmen, journalists, and Saigon passers-through amused and bemused him seven days a week with foolish flattery and earnest ignorance. The South Carolina legislature had saluted him with standing ovations last year, and friends and influential leaders in his home state had urged him to consider a campaign for the presidency.

His inevitable promotion to Chief of Staff of the United States Army, scheduled for next summer, would be a distinct anticlimax. Combat leadership is the apotheosis of a military career—not the backbiting and bumsitting of Washington. Westmoreland's calling was war. The test of his life of training was battle, and like the very good soldier that he was, Westmoreland moved reflexively toward the sound of heaviest fighting.

It wasn't that Westmoreland would not be good at budgets or bureaucracy. He had already proved himself in previous Pentagon tours, and he had demonstrated during a year at Harvard's Graduate School of Business that Command Presence worked as well in boardrooms as it did on battlefields. Awed classmates later said he had so impressed the 166 business leaders in his seminar that he could have had a dozen top executive posts "at the snap of a finger." He counted the most senior members of the House and Senate armed services committees—Democrats all—as his angels, and his friendship with House Republican Leader Gerald Ford had been forged high over Newfoundland in the hold of a transport plane that reeked of monkey shit.

He was, in fact, the first perfect model of America's post–World War II "compleat general, excelling not only as a combat leader, but a diplomat, technocrat, scholar, executive, and manager."

Handsome, church-going, square-jawed, straight as a ramrod, a recruiting poster of a general, Westmoreland would do very well at stroking congressmen and steeling Presidents. Stepping back from battlefield leadership in the midst of war, however, would be hard.

Khe Sanh would be the capstone of his combat career.

In a war that frustrated traditional analysis or easy measurement,

Khe Sanh would be the single, dramatic blow that would cripple the North Vietnamese beyond any question or doubt. It would be the definitive victory, the perfect finishing stroke for his generalship in Vietnam, and he had prepared it painstakingly.

Westmoreland had personally walked the ground at Khe Sanh. He had rehearsed the aerial resupply of the combat base, lengthened and improved the runway, tripled the size of the garrison, diverted intelligence assets to its environs, and moved the U.S. Army's largest field guns into support range. At his fingertips, he had a stupefying abundance of aerial firepower which he had personally code-named Niagara "to evoke an image of cascading shells and bombs."

Within the past few weeks, Westmoreland had completed a massive amd complex movement of American troops into I Corps, the northernmost military region in South Vietnam. Using the code name Checkers for security, Westmoreland had begun last November to pull brigades and then divisions from around Saigon and out of the Highlands and jump them north. Now there were nearly fifty U.S. battalions in the north—half of all the American combat troops in Vietnam. Including the crack Marines of the Koreans' "Blue Dragon" brigade and two of the very best South Vietnamese Army divisions, Westmoreland had a quarter million Free World Forces braced for battle in I Corps.

In the last forty-eight hours, Westmoreland had moved his kings onto the board: 12,000 veterans of the 1st Air Cavalry Division and 5,000 paratroopers of the 101st Airborne Division. Even now they were deploying in base camps only thirty minutes by helicopter from Khe Sanh. The northern end of I Corps had been the exclusive preserve of the U.S. Marines since the first days of the war, but for this climactic moment Westmoreland wanted the Army's finest shock troops on hand.

Westmoreland wanted this battle. He had planned it and prepared it. He had willed it.

This was the week before Tet, the Vietnamese celebration of

homecoming and thanksgiving that on January 30 would mark the end of the Year of the Goat and inaugurate the Year of the Monkey. Westmoreland planned for 1968 to be the Year of the Hammer. Khe Sanh would be his anvil.

The general would have preferred a bolder finish to his years in Vietnam. He longed for a war of movement, of multidivisional thrusts into the enemy heartland. In just two days, Westmoreland would send to Washington a detailed proposal for the invasion of North Vietnam, a "daring amphibious hook" à la MacArthur, with Marines assaulting the beaches and Army troops leapfrogging ahead by helicopter to bypass enemy strong points, capture hidden guns, and destroy supply caches. Westmoreland was also reviewing his plan for a three-division strike deep into Laos to cut enemy supply routes, with Khe Sanh as the jumpoff point. He had dreamed of such a raid for four years. Now, with the 26th Marine Regiment as the spear point and the First Cav and 101st Airborne for mobile muscle, he had assembled the offensive striking force he wanted for the mission.

The fact that American policy prohibited ground operations outside of South Vietnam neither slowed nor deterred Westmoreland's preparations. He dismissed Washington's phobia about Chinese intervention as "chimerical." There had been many, many prohibitions when he arrived in Vietnam four years ago, and Westmoreland had removed them one by one. It was simply a matter of careful planning and persuasion, of demonstrating to reasonable men that certain military actions were absolutely essential to the successful prosecution of the war. The barriers fell more slowly than Westmoreland wished, but they did fall. The "can do" general had not come to Vietnam to be undone. Westmoreland had survived, and even triumphed, under burdens that might have crushed lesser men.

Three days after he arrived in South Vietnam in early 1964, a group of generals had deposed the generals who had deposed and murdered the country's president a few months earlier. Coup followed coup. The "leaders" came and went every few months, or weeks, a carousel of colonels, a jumble of generals and civilians and singsong syllables, Duong Van Minh, Nguyen Khanh, Nguyen Xuan Oanh, Tran Van Huong, Phan Khac Suu, Phan Huy Quat, Lam Van Phat, Tranh Thien Khiem, Nguyen Cao Ky, Nguyen Van Thieu. . . . Westmoreland never even learned to pronounce their names before they were gone. He always seemed most comfortable with Duong Van Minh, "Big Minh" as he was called. The American general could find moments of peace at Big Minh's villa, playing tennis perhaps, or sitting for an hour and talking as Minh tended his rare orchids and chattered affectionately with exotic pet birds.

Westmoreland discovered that the Army of the Republic of Vietnam (ARVN) was paralyzed by politics and riddled with corruption. The South Vietnamese specifically excluded from service their country's most experienced battlefield commanders, the tough veterans who had led the Viet Minh fight against the French. The best-trained, best-equipped ARVN units—elite paratrooper and Marine brigades—were rarely used in battle. Military coup leaders kept these troops under their personal command, tucked in close around Saigon, with the primary mission of discouraging new coup attempts.

Westmoreland sometimes found entire ARVN divisions standing down from military operations while their commanding officers, weary of war, retired to the mountain resort of Dalat "for a rest." The American general, a highly motivated officer who had risen by achievement to the top of a demanding profession, now dealt with division commanders in their twenties, with corps commanders who had been table waiters in Paris, and with generals who vaulted to command through well-placed uncles. Seven thousand ARVN soldiers walked away from their units every month.

American confidence in ARVN was stored in pressurized tanks in Westmoreland's headquarters in Saigon. The general, worried that his elite ARVN honor guard might bolt in the face of enemy attack, or even *join* an enemy attack, had fitted his rooms with hidden nozzles that could fill the building instantly with clouds of disabling gas. Only Westmoreland and his immediate staff knew where to find gas masks. Westmoreland soon replaced his ARVN guards with Nungs, slender, dusky-skinned ethnic Chinese who had fled North Vietnam and who now fought for money in South Vietnam. Many tribes and nations served the Americans as mercenaries in this war; the Nungs were considered the toughest, and the best-paid.

Buffeted by coups and corruption and incompetence among the people he had come to assist—"like trying to push spaghetti," he complained—and baffled by the glottal song of their language, Westmoreland sought every opportunity to escape Saigon. He reveled in the more familiar truths of combat, and he wanted to get a feel for the pitch of the hills, the heat of the lowlands, the thickness of the jungle, the mood of his soldiers, and the skill of the enemy. He talked for long hours with Sir Robert Thompson, the acknowledged British expert on anti-guerrilla operations, and he even flew to Malaysia to see for himself the terrain on which the British had mixed police and military operations to quell a jungle-based Communist insurgency. He read Sun Tzu, a seminal thinker in Chinese military philosophy, and he analyzed the French military effort in Indochina.

Westmoreland diplomatically consulted with Vietnamese military commanders during the early months of 1964, but his attention was clearly focused on Americans. Even before he took command, Westmoreland had decided that only American troops could save Vietnam; the Vietnamese were obviously not up to the job.

He never hesitated to go to the most isolated or dangerous outposts in his search for first-hand information. During his familiarization tour, enemy machine gun bullets had ripped through his plane as it lifted from the runway at A Shau, wounding both pilots and four of the passengers. Westmoreland did not believe, however, as do some generals, that Command Presence confers immortality.

He would not walk erect on the field of fire, nor foolishly land his helicopter in the midst of battle.

He knew that one of the risks of his profession was death, and he accepted it, without bravado. He believed in showing himself to his men, in sharing the hardships of combat duty, even if only for a few minutes in a mostly symbolic way. He gave his trust to new commanders, he recognized the faces of old comrades, he listened attentively to lieutenants—and he remembered their names at second meetings, weeks later.

Westmoreland first visited Khe Sanh in his earliest months in Vietnam. Centered on a sturdy concrete bunker built by the French, Khe Sanh was then a tiny outpost defended by a dozen U.S. Army Green Berets and several hundred Montagnard tribesmen. The wind from Laos sighed in the groves of coffee trees and rippled the nine shades of green that clothed the hills and flatland. He was tremendously impressed by the place:

"The critical importance of the little plateau was immediately apparent. . . . Khe Sanh could serve as a patrol base for blocking enemy infiltration from Laos; a base for [secret border-crossing] operations to harass the enemy in Laos; an air strip for reconnaissance planes surveying the Ho Chi Minh Trail; a western anchor for defenses south of the DMZ; and an eventual jumping-off point for ground operations to cut the Ho Chi Minh Trail."

This was bold vision in early 1964, when ARVN was crumbling like a cookie, and a scattered 16,000 American soldiers were restricted to advice and support.

The war was different then. The senior United States military advisers in Saigon worked nine-to-five in those days, water skiing on the Saigon River in the bright afternoons of summer, weekending on the white sand beaches of the South China Sea, or relaxing in the colonial ambiance of the Cercle Sportif, an aging tennis and swim club near the Presidential Palace. And in a deadly game that applauds a sudden knee to the groin, there were even "rules": American planes were prohibited from bombing enemy troops unless the planes had South Vietnamese student pilots on board—thus qualifying the bombing runs as "training flights."

Westmoreland's teenage son, nicknamed "Rip," led packs of his pals on spirited motorbike chases through the streets of Saigon. Once a week, all the American kids in the neighborhood gathered at the Westmoreland villa to watch movies flown in from the States. The general's vivacious wife, Kitsy, began to organize a social schedule that reflected the imminence, and eminence, of his Command.

It was all a mirage, and none knew it better than Westmoreland.

South Vietnam was falling apart. It might not last long enough for Westmoreland to complete the logistical buildup he was planning. He was already thinking of support for more than a million troops, of sandbags and survey equipment, tons of concrete and megatons of ammunition. The books he carried into meetings with Secretary of Defense Robert S. McNamara that spring and summer included numbers on the miles of cable that were needed, recommended troop levels, bombing proposals, new airfields and ports, even BTUs of air conditioning. He outlined his needs carefully, buttressing them with facts and figures, and stripping the requests of any hint of emotion. He had learned well the lessons of politics and management, and he wanted there to be no misunderstanding about his plans for the war. His careful preparation and attention to detail, his *readiness* for every contingency, were the very strengths that had propelled him to high rank.

Another asset was his obedience to the code of American generals: "conform, avoid error, shun controversy, forego dissent." Westmoreland listened impassively when Gen. Paul D. Harkins, the commander he would soon replace, told McNamara that another six months should pretty well wrap up hostilities in Vietnam. Westmoreland knew it would take longer than that to deliver the cement he would need to build the ports that would be necessary to support the Army that would have to be fielded if this war was to be won. It wasn't necessary to correct or criticize the general; it was enough to get the job done properly.

Westmoreland took command in June of 1964.

By July, U.S. troop levels had climbed to 21,000 men and Westmoreland's civilian flank in Saigon had been secured by Maxwell D. Taylor, the new American ambassador to Vietnam. Taylor was a former chairman of the Joint Chiefs of Staff, a paratroop commander who had won the admiration of his country for both leadership and literacy. Not incidentally, he was a friend and mentor who had helped shape Westmoreland's military career. Taylor had looked up from his own guns during the 1943 battles in Sicily and seen an eager, aggressive artillery officer who was willing to scout enemy positions personally and who kept his guns in first-class condition. Impressed, he later offered Westmoreland a colonel's eagles as executive officer for the 101st Airborne Division's artillery. In the years since, Taylor had been generous with career advice, key assignments, and supporting words in important Washington councils.

In August, Westmoreland stood stiffly, a lodgepole pine of pride as Ambassador Taylor on one side and his wife Kitsy on the other pinned a fourth star to his squared shoulders. Now, he was truly *General* Westmoreland, Commander, United States Military Assistance Command, Viet Nam. COMMUSMACV. It was a unique professional achievement, and it confirmed his preeminent place among American military leaders. Westmoreland privately regretted that he did not possess absolute control of all U.S. naval, air, and even State Department assets in the Pacific, but he was mellowed enough by his ascendancy to remark that sharing power "was not a thing for which I was going to fall on my sword."

Three days after Westmoreland's ceremony of stars, American fighter bombers roared out of the rising sun to blast North Vietnam's harbor facilities and destroy its tiny navy. It was a piece of cake, like banging a toad with a stick. Many of the planes made several bombing runs before turning back toward U.S. Navy carriers in the Tonkin Gulf. It was announced as a punishment raid, an eye-for-an-eye reply to the torpedo boats that had attacked U.S. Navy destroyers operating innocently in the Gulf. Outraged at such Communist effrontery, the U.S. Senate had extended war powers to President Lyndon Johnson with only two dissenting votes.

The rest of 1964 was a catalogue of disaster.

Coups and counter-coups paralyzed the government and the armed forces of Vietnam. The primitive people of the mountains, the Montagnards who were abused and exploited by the Vietnamese even in the midst of war, declared themselves "neutral." U.S. Army Green Berets, who relied on these people for soldiers and reports on enemy movements, struggled to win them back. Enemy mortars blasted a huge airfield near Saigon, destroying American planes. University students and Buddhist monks and nuns clogged the streets with demonstrators to protest South Vietnamese war policies and growing American influence. On Christmas Eve, the Viet Cong exploded a bomb at the front door of the Army's Brink Hotel in downtown Saigon, killing two Americans and wounding fifty-eight. Tile-roofed, treelined Saigon was changing, and Kitsy and the kids joined the exodus of American dependents.

In the last week of 1964 the Viet Cong 9th Division captured a town east of Saigon, then ambushed and all but annihilated two separate relief columns. The government's control slipped to a dwindling third of the population, and the first intelligence reports came in with word that North Vietnamese troops might enter the war to hasten its end.

Still, the South Vietnamese seemed more intent on barracks politics than battlefield peril. Westmoreland spent many valuable hours trying to find out who was in charge, and more hours pleading with malcontents not to kill the current incumbent. A teetotaler, he repressed disgust while applauding the imaginative American junior officers who helped preserve a semblance of order by drinking putative coup leaders under the table.

General Harkins had dealt with these frustrations by not seeing the problems, a common defense mechanism in Indochina. Later in this war, Cambodian Prince Norodom Sihanouk would pretend that the North Vietnamese were not building military bases in the regions of his country nearest South Vietnam, and then he pretended that the United States was not bombing these areas. The North Vietnamese couldn't complain because, after all, they were pretending they weren't there.

Westmoreland had not come to Vietnam to pretend.

In January 1965, he junked the restrictive "rules" that forced his bomber pilots to carry South Vietnamese air cadets.

In February, he insisted on the immediate deployment of the first American combat units in Vietnam. "The strength, armament, professionalism, and activity of the Viet Cong have increased to the point where we can ill afford any longer to withhold available military means," he declared; only American combat troops could turn the tide of battle.

Admiral Ulysses S. Grant Sharp, the Honolulu-based commander of all U.S. forces in the Pacific, and General Earle G. Wheeler, chairman of the Joint Chiefs of Staff, strongly endorsed a proposal to ship three combat divisions (about 50,000 soldiers) to Vietnam, but Westmoreland more accurately sensed the uneasiness in Washington. "I hope[d] to keep the number of U.S. ground forces to a minimum," he said, winning approval for "only two battalions."

In March, just before two battalions of Marines waded ashore to the whirr of TV cameras and the giggle of bikinied girls, Westmoreland cabled a more detailed request to Washington. He urgently needed, he wrote, more planes, more helicopters, more engineers and logistics people, 50,000 *foreign* troops to bolster the sagging South Vietnamese, and most urgently, seventeen new battalions of U.S. combat troops.

In April, Westmoreland won approval for his seventeen combat battalions, a force of 80,000 men in all—including the U.S. Army's new 1st Air Cavalry Division and some of South Korea's toughest troops. These were the best of the best. It was an excellent beginning, he felt.

Westmoreland was even more pleased by an important change in the "rules." No longer would American troops be restricted to defensive positions around major airfields and bases. Now they could strike at the enemy first, disrupting his attacks before they could be launched. It was the only proper role for infantry—and for a commanding general whose slogan was "Every Man A Tiger!" This was the kind of restriction that might have prompted Westmoreland to resign, but the issue was never drawn. Once the simple truths of combat and maneuver were explained, even the most pacific civilians could understand. Westmoreland never doubted his ability to make these truths self-evident.

Now, he renewed his request for B-52 bombers and for the Army's biggest guns, 175mm artillery pieces that had never before been used in combat. Western generals for more than two hundred years had believed that the best test of Asian troops was "a whiff of the grape." The innocent phrase camouflaged carnage: the firing of cannonsful of lead balls, steel fragments, and junk metal—grapeshot—into massed troops at close range. It had come to mean, more generally, the application of massive firepower to enemy infantry. The big 175mm guns could fire shells over the horizon and the B-52s, flying so high that onboard computers considered the speed and direction of the turning of the earth to assure accuracy, could deliver twenty-seven tons of bombs. Each.

In the first week of June, Westmoreland requested forty-four combat battalions, coolly warning his civilian superiors that these 200,000 soldiers would only provide a "stopgap" force—even with the B-52s. "We must be prepared for a long war which will probably involve increasing numbers of U.S. troops," he said.

Westmoreland now had the feel of his command, an understanding of his unique prerogatives. No military leader of consequence was closer to the action in Vietnam than Westmoreland, and none was prepared to question or criticize his judgments—not when young Americans were fighting and dying. The civilians in Washington, though occasionally seized by what Westmoreland sniffingly called "field-marshal psychosis," knew the limits of their understanding of combat. General Taylor reported through State Department channels from the ambassador's office that the war was being lost. Admiral Sharp in Honolulu and the Joint Chiefs of Staff in Washington supported Westmoreland's every request. Defense Secretary McNamara asked hard questions, but went right to work when he received quick, straight answers. Westmoreland knew now that he could ask for ten thousand tons of plastic explosive or a dozen chromium widgets and the answer would not be *Why?* but *How soon do you need them?*

If there was a voice for deliberation in this torrent of men and supplies, it was Westmoreland's own. "Full speed ahead types would be helpless in Vietnam," he said. He had not yet completed the logistical base necessary to support a huge American force, and he shared President Johnson's concern that the American people were not yet ready to commit themselves to war. He hoped for some form of national mobilization but opposed a call-up of National Guard or Reserve forces because he believed public support was critical to success in Vietnam. He had always invested some hours in building civilian-military rapport in every post where he had held command, and he once proposed a course for the Army War College on "The Influence of Public Opinion on U.S. Military Posture."

Even his superiors listened intently now, for Westmoreland had become "a forceful player who knew what he wanted, how much to ask for, and how much not to ask for."

When his request for forty-four combat battalions was approved, Westmoreland asked for twenty-four more. The American investment to date, he said, could only keep the war from being lost. To move from a holding action to "the win phase" of his strategy, he would need 275,000 U.S. combat troops.

By the late summer of 1965, Westmoreland could look back on twelve months of remarkable progress and compare himself favorably, not with General Harkins, but with Eisenhower and Bradley. Hardly more than a year ago, a few thousand U.S. advisers had watched helplessly as the ARVN suffered weekly routs. American firepower had been leashed by rules that made a mockery of war. Now, 200,000 soldiers and Marines were in the Pacific pipeline or already ashore, poised for operation in the interior. Fighter bombers flailed the enemy homeland six hundred times a week and B-52 Stratofortresses filled the mountains with the thunder of bombs. Fifty-one thousand *civilian* contractors earned oilfield wages to build, faster than they had ever been built before, seaports and warehouse complexes and airfields and power plants and satellite communication systems. Westmoreland would grumble in retirement that "gradualism" had hobbled American power in Vietnam, but right now he could reflect that he had put his troops ashore in less time than it had taken the United States to enter the war against Hitler. In a single year, he had personally transformed the Vietnam war from a feeble losing struggle to the largest test of American arms since Korea.

Westmoreland was utterly confident that American combat troops would do the job.

It was not difficult to find American soldiers and officers in these early days, and later, who believed that racial superiority assured victory, who spoke with "a Caucasian arrogance about the Vietnamese ability," who believed "that when pitted against American troops, the Vietnamese would have to give in. . . ."

Westmoreland was not one of them. He knew the Viet Cong to be a tough and dedicated enemy, and it had been during his military maturation that Western armies had bowed in battle to Japanese, Korean, Chinese, and Vietnamese arms. No, Westmoreland's confidence was rooted in richer soil: the absolute certainty that American troops would go into combat with overwhelming, unconquerable superiority in "firepower, mobility, and flexibility." All of his planning and preparation focused on guaranteeing these advantages to U.S. forces in Vietnam.

Enthusiasm about the arrival of "the first team" was infectious. American military officers shared an outspoken confidence in the outcome, and so Admiral Sharp was being dutiful, not doubtful, when he called Westmoreland from Honolulu to inquire about plans for the 1st Air Cavalry to move into the Highlands, the same region of mountains and jungle and narrow dirt roads that had swallowed an elite French armored unit eleven years before.

Westmoreland was ready. He knew all about Groupement Mobile 100.

A thumbed copy of Bernard Fall's *Street Without Joy* lay on the general's night table, beside Mao Tse-tung's musings on war and the translations of important articles by Vo Nguyen Giap clipped from North Vietnamese military magazines. Fall's fine book about French military woes in Indochina was must reading for thoughtful American officers, and Westmoreland had studied the dramatic account of Groupement Mobile 100.

Americans had written the first chapter in the story of the fated French unit. France had been able to spare only a single battalion for the United Nations forces in Korea because of its own costly war in Indochina. Fighting beside the U.S. Army's 2nd Division, the battalion had "covered itself with glory" in the heavy battles at Chipyong-ni, Wonju, and Arrowhead Ridge. Very professional, very cool, seasoned with Algerian veterans, the battalion had once held the line against a Communist Chinese division for four days.

At two o'clock one winter morning, with temperatures far below zero, the battalion shivered in foxholes hacked out of frozen rice paddies near Chipyong-ni. Suddenly, Chinese assault troops rushed across the creaking snow to the sound of bugles. Someone in the French lines cranked a World War II hand siren into a screeching yowl that obliterated the signal trumpets. A single squad of French and Algerian troops waited until the Chinese closed to within twenty yards, then leaped from their holes with long bayonets flashing at the end of their rifles, shrieked like madmen, and charged—a Berber banzai.

The Chinese stopped in shock, turned, and fled back into the icy darkness. The French "went back to smoking and telling jokes."

After the fighting in Korea, the battalion moved to Saigon where it was greatly expanded by the addition of reserves, an armored cavalry squadron, an artillery group, a shock force of jungle combat veterans, and companies of experienced Cambodian, Vietnamese, and other French colonial troops. Rechristened Groupement Mobile 100, the force numbered 3,498 men, but the steel core of the regiment was the proud Korea Battalion.

The Viet Minh welcomed GM 100 to the Highlands on the first of February, 1954, with an ambush of a strong French patrol. Six months later, minced again and again in bloody roadside ambushes, GM 100 had ceased to exist. It had lost all of its artillery, eighty-five percent of its vehicles, and half its automatic weapons. It had even been forced to abandon its dead and wounded. At the finish, only fifty-four men of the Korea Battalion's proud one thousand were still on their feet.

Westmoreland had no intention of repeating French errors.

There was much, much more than a decade of difference between GM 100 and the United States Army's 1st Air Cavalry Division, between the battles of 1954 and 1965. This was going to be an *American* war. It was actually difficult for U.S. officers not to be patronizing when they talked about the French effort.

The French had tried to hold all of Indochina—Laos, Cambodia, and the two Vietnams—with 180,000 troops and limited logistical support. Westmoreland would be working one-fourth of the territory with 1.3 million troops, "a battlefield mobility heretofore unknown," and a cornucopian commitment of supplies.

Westmoreland would have jumped from a plane without a parachute before he would have sent an armored column like GM 100 down a dirt road in the Highlands. He would first defoliate and bulldoze a cleared strip one hundred yards deep on both sides of the road, pave vital sections to make enemy mining more difficult, provide a complete umbrella of artillery, aerial rocket and bomber support and, perhaps, peel back the topsoil and sow the earth with gravel mines and tear gas crystals.

This was the American way of war.

There had been a moment in the dying of GM 100 when a desperate commander, tanks and trucks burning all around him, had pleaded for a helicopter to evacuate his wounded so he could lead the fighting survivors on an attempted breakout on foot. The request so enraged the French zone commander that he went to the radio room himself to shout through the crackling static: "You carry your wounded like everyone else!"

Westmoreland had decided early that one of the absolute guarantees of soldiering in Vietnam, for Americans, would be instant, first-class medical care. The French had a dozen helicopters in their war; the Americans had thousands. They whisked casualties from battlefield to operating room so swiftly that surgeons saved eighty-eight out of every eighty-nine wounded soldiers.

Battle casualties, however, accounted for only seventeen percent of American hospitalizations. The real drain on combat manpower was malaria, and mysterious fevers, and respiratory diseases, diarrhea, funguses, leech bites, poison plants, and infections that flowered quickly in the oppressive heat and humidity.

Disease had drained the Vietnamese people since the birth of the mosquito, but disease had also been an ally. Vietnamese history celebrates epic victories over superior Chinese forces in the tenth and thirteenth centuries—campaigns remembered in Chinese histories mostly for "the perpetual heat and malaria." In 1789, a French expeditionary force marching toward Saigon simply "melted away, succumbing to the climate." The French came again, to Da Nang in 1858, but sailed away eighteen months later after digging a thousand new graves for victims of "the pestilential harbor." A Chinese army, "ravaged by malaria and other diseases," pulled out of Vietnam's northernmost provinces in 1870. Sickness forced two of France's commanders in the First Indochina War to relinquish their commands. Now the beautiful, deadly land was sapping American strength with "the most formidable medical problems . . . in U.S. history."

Westmoreland demanded the most urgent research into medicines for malaria, which was exacting "an unacceptable drain on combat manpower." Within months, his insistence on tougher field discipline, weekly chloroquinine-primaquine pills, and daily dapsone doses cut his malaria losses "to a militarily-acceptable level." New miracle drugs foiled the fungi. To beat the heat, Westmoreland simply enclosed millions of cubic feet of Vietnam's mugginess and cooled it to a comfortable seventy-two degrees with air-conditioning. The temperature was pushed below freezing in another 2.5 million cubic feet so that steaks and other foods from the United States could be kept fresh frozen.

This was the American way of war.

• • •

SOLDIERING FOR THE world's wealthiest and most powerful nation came naturally to Westmoreland. His father, who found banking "a gold mine" even in the midst of the Great Depression, had given his son a seventy-day tour of Europe when he was fifteen years old, a new, green Chevrolet for a high school graduation present in 1931, a personal checking account—with money—for his college years, and a new Oldsmobile to celebrate graduation from West Point.

There were servants in the Westmoreland household, and thus the leisure to sculpt a more perfect Command Presence. In the soft South Carolina summers, the young cadet paddled to the far edge of a quiet lake in the hills and shouted commands at the shore until the authority in his voice made the very trees stand taller. He excelled at polo as a young lieutenant at Fort Sill, and donned a pink coat every Sunday to ride to hounds with the senior officers. Transferred to Hawaii in 1939 as an artillery officer, Westmoreland practiced his logarithms, polished his polo, and surfed from the flawless beaches as Poland and France and Norway fell to German arms. His wedding to an eighteen-year-old Cornell University freshman was so beautiful it made the front cover of *Cosmopolitan*.

Westmoreland's experience in war, like that of nearly all his contemporaries, was in Big War: fleets of ships and landing craft, four-hundred-mile fronts that rocked with the concussion of big guns, tens of thousands of paratroopers spilling from planes in continental assaults, armored columns fighting across the plains of Europe. He had won his first medal by pushing his 155mm guns through mountains and cold rain to help stem the German breakthrough at Kasserine Pass, and he won another decoration for rushing troops across the Rhine to exploit the capture of the bridge at Remagen. As an administrator in occupied Germany, he "oversaw almost every phase of life" among the Germans, sometimes riding regally through his domain in a two-horse barouche.

Westmoreland had actually lived the fantasy of West Point cadets: battle ribbons from North Africa, Sicily, France, and Germany; post-war command of an elite paratrooper regiment; instructor at the Command and General Staff College; secretary of the General Staff; qualified for command in nuclear warfare; student of helicopters; management courses at Harvard; youngest major general in the Army; and three unforgettable years as Superintendent of West Point itself, the shrine of the United States Army.

He kept his body in excellent physical condition, always picked his parachute from the enlisted men's table, kept current with weapons developments, exploited the vast improvements in modern communications, and understood how to tap into the innovative technology of American industry.

He honed these military skills for use against Russia. Westmoreland's generation of generals rehearsed wars with Germany and France and Panama and Egypt, and with Mexico and Canada, too, as part of their contingency planning; the general's art is readiness. Westmoreland himself had twice begun preparations for actual combat missions into Venezuela and Cuba, but these ultimately false alarms never diverted attention from Russia.

It was in Europe, against the Soviet Union, that the textbook and table wars were fought. The problems chosen for study in U.S. military colleges, the forward placement of American strategic stockpiles, the design of weapons and the direction they aim, the focus of intelligence, the destinations of airlift rehearsals, the programs inside the missile computers, and even the psychic justifications for war all centered on the Soviet Union U.S. Navy admirals wargamed with Japan in the 1920s and 1930s but never with such certainty as U.S. Army generals wargamed with Russia.

Westmoreland was nearly killed once during a practice combat assault when a whipping steel buckle knocked him unconscious in his parachute harness. Struggling to his feet, he saw the battle dress and concerned looks on the men gathered around him.

"Are we fighting the Russians?" he asked. His men led him away for hospitalization for a severe concussion.

Vietnam was not the plains of Europe and Viet Cong ambushes were not the same things as Warsaw Pact treachery, but Westmoreland knew only how to give his best. Westmoreland's best would be war the American way.

First, he limited the tour of duty to one year. The same limitation had agitated General George Washington so greatly that he turned in despair to those who made it and cried: "Good God, gentlemen, our cause is lost!" Westmoreland was justifiably more confident in the combat readiness of his troops. *His* concern, even in the earliest days, was popular support for the war: "I hoped the one-year tour would extend the nation's staying power by forestalling public pressure to 'bring the boys home.'"

Each soldier had a Date of Estimated Return from Over Seas that was precisely 365 days after his arrival in Vietnam (except for Marines, who served thirteen months instead of twelve). Americans in Vietnam carried DEROS calendars like talismans, inking them on flak jackets, taping them inside helmets, tucking them in Bibles and tacking them on the walls of bunkers, but DEROS had really been designed as a time-certain guarantee for moms: "Your boy'll be home in less than a year, ma'am."

Next, Westmoreland built a one-week vacation into the tour of duty to break the tedium, or terror, of a soldier's year in Vietnam. Every American soldier could count on a week in Hawaii with his radiant wife and a baby daughter he'd never seen; or seven days of sensuality in the steamed and scented baths of Taiwan; or maybe an awed trip to the countryside of Thailand to see the great Buddhas; or, perhaps, long, languid evenings nuzzling sheilahs on an Australian beach. Ten romantic Asian capitals beckoned the warriors. Every combat battalion had travel agents to handle all the plane and hotel reservations for Hong Kong, Bangkok, Sydney, Tokyo, Manila, Singapore, Taipei, Kuala Lampur, Penang, and Honolulu. U.S. Army advisers groaned at ARVN's inability to account for 7,000 AWOLs every month, but Westmoreland's Rest and Recreation program took 7,000 U.S. soldiers from their units every week.

Westmoreland ordered a generous distribution of medals and decorations and combat badges, because he believed with Napoleon that "a bolt of ribbon wins many battles."

American troops enjoyed nickel beer, a radio station with the latest hit records, telephone calls to home, high-interest savings accounts, and even prime-time TV, but Westmoreland was most satisfied with his efforts to make life easier on the fighting line.

"Combat units knew that mail from home would arrive on a

scheduled basis and could be read while enjoying hot meals," he said. "The men did like it, I'm sure."

Providing these amenities in an undeveloped, tropical country more than ten thousand miles from the United States required an unusually elaborate complex of logistics installations. Westmoreland had found only a single deep-water port and three small airfields when he came to Vietnam in 1964. In a little over three years he built seven deep-water ports with thirty-two berths and eight major airports with fifteen jet runways. The countryside had been smoothed for airfields in many hundreds of places so that men and supplies could be moved quickly to almost any corner of South Vietnam. Eleven million cubic feet of covered storage provided protection from the monsoon rains.

Ships full of hand grenades, corn on the cob, napalm, wristwatches, artillery shells, pigs, plastic explosive, lawnmower engines, rifle ammunition, tank parts, and C-rations were unloading *one million tons a month* by late 1967.

It was expensive. The United States had been spending about a half billion dollars a year in Vietnam when Westmoreland arrived to replace General Harkins; Westmoreland's tab for 1968 would run closer to thirty billion dollars.

The tidal wave of American dollars swamped the Vietnamese economy. Whores earned more than cabinet ministers, and shoeshine boys more than veteran ARVN sergeants. In an attempt to soak up the U.S. dollars before they reached the local economy, Westmoreland stocked post-exchange shelves with an extraordinary range of luxury items:

> It was a stroll down Fifth Avenue, a gaudy combination of Saks, Bonwit Teller, Hammacher Schlemmer, and Abercrombie and Fitch. The shelves were crammed with sheer panty hose, lingerie, imported perfumes, diamonds and rubies, fine china, radios, portable and console television sets, liquor,

mink stoles, sable wraps, and nearly everything the American soldier fighting a tough guerrilla war could possibly require, including Napoleon's favorite brandy, Courvoisier, at $1.80 a fifth.

But firepower, not fine china, was at the center of Westmoreland's philosophy of war. It was the foundation of his tactics in Vietnam, and he came to believe that his particular applications of firepower had established immutable principles of warfare as important as the ones written in Clausewitz. It was because of his confidence in firepower that he looked forward to a North Vietnamese assault on Khe Sanh.

From the bellies and bomb racks of thousands of American planes fell 250-pound bombs, 500-pound bombs, 750-pound bombs, 1,000-pound Swimming Pool Maker bombs, rockets, napalm cannisters, impact-activated Destroyer mines, Cluster Bomb Units that burst open in midfall to scatter hundreds of softball-sized bomblets over a wide area, and the incredible Daisy Cutter—a 15,000-pound leviathan bomb that drifted silently down by parachute to explode with obliterating force a few feet above ground level. Long before Khe Sanh loomed as a battle, bombing tonnages in Vietnam had surpassed bombing tonnages against Germany in World War II.

Westmoreland was also using bullets faster than any previous military commander in history.

The Huey "Hog," a no-passenger helicopter stuffed with linked ammunition for its flexed machine guns and underslung with pods of rockets and belts of 40mm grenades, entered battle "with the most hellish firepower ever assembled on so small a machine." Chopper pilots joked that their ships actually backed up in midair when they fired all guns, but on the eve of Khe Sanh Westmoreland was beginning to replace the Hog with faster helicopters named Cobras that carried seventy-five percent more firepower.

The most spectacular expenditure of ammunition spouted from the side doors of recycled C-47 cargo planes that had been fitted with electric Gatling guns. There was not a soldier in Vietnam who had not stood open-mouthed in awe while watching this plane hose the earth with curving streams of redgold fire—eighteen thousand bullets at a burst. It was called "Spooky."

Soldiers themselves had become firepower machines. The American practice of aimed fire had died in Korea, where analysts discovered that an astounding number of young soldiers never fired their weapons at all—even in life-threatening combat crises. During the last decade, U.S. training procedures had concentrated on encouraging soldiers to shoot, and the recent changeover to the fully-automatic M-16 rifle was one more step in the multiplication of the American foot soldier's firepower.

Westmoreland's way of war was costly, but because it was designed to reduce American casualties it found ready acceptance in Washington. "The thing we value most deeply is not money, but men," said Defense Secretary Robert McNamara. "We have multiplied the capability of our men [with firepower]. It's expensive in dollars, but cheap in life."

If it had been possible, Westmoreland would have removed Americans from the field of fire altogether—and fought the war with technology and firepower. He was fascinated by the potential of the automated battlefield where the enemy was detected by unmanned sensors and destroyed by distant guns; he knew the names and effects of exotic chemicals; and he had a technician's curiosity about new battlefield equipment.

Westmoreland seeded the clouds over Laos to try to make it rain more heavily on enemy road systems. He experimented with the chemical alteration of mud molecules in the A Shau Valley to make the footing more gooey in the enemy's main supply depot. Converted cargo planes flew nineteen thousand defoliation missions for Westmoreland—spraying Agent Orange to denude hardwood trees and mangrove forests, Agent White to clear the underbrush around American bases, and Agent Blue to kill young rice plants. He used nausea gas, tear gas, and pepper gas in fog form to fill enemy tunnels, and in pellet or crystal form to make parts of the countryside uninhabitable.

Battlefield adaptations of space-age inventions gave Westmoreland overwhelming advantages in his search for elusive enemy soldiers. Starlight scopes provided almost daylike vision in the night. Particle detectors tracked invisible carbon trails through the sky to tiny, smokeless, cooking fires. Heliborne "people sniffers" tested the air for concentrations of urine or sweat molecules to find hidden enemy camps. Mountaintop searchlights illuminated the countryside, and acoustic and seismic detectors concealed in the jungle broadcast enemy troop movements to U.S. intelligence. Radio-intercept equipment, of such extraordinary sophistication that it was wired for demolition, eavesdropped on the enemy's most secret conversations.

Aerial photographers snapped night pictures by the light of electronically fired flashbulbs with the power of 4.5 million candles. Photographic analysis was so advanced that good technicians could locate wire antennas from great altitudes. One special film pinpointed camouflage by detecting chlorophyll loss in the cut foliage. Another was so sensitive to heat emanations it could photograph warm truck engines through double thicknesses of jungle canopy. Three million feet of film and prints moved through the development trays in U.S. laboratories in Saigon each month.

Polaroid cameras, tape recorders, Xerox copiers, and printing presses greatly improved American psychological warfare skills. Within hours of the capture or defection of an enemy soldier, psywar experts could print and airdrop twenty-five thousand safe conduct passes to the soldier's comrades—and include a photograph and testimonial about the deserter's fair treatment in American hands. Westmoreland even haunted the dreams of enemy soldiers with airborne tape recordings of children crying for their fathers, and the ineffably mournful songs of Vietnamese war widows.

Westmoreland's way of war—with 300,000 American soldiers—reversed the tide of battle in South Vietnam. In the closing days of 1966, he met with Secretary McNamara and set new goals that would see U.S. troop levels rise to a half million over the next year.

Confident in his growing strength, Westmoreland moved to the offensive in the first days of 1967 with the huge military operations called Cedar Falls and Junction City.

Cedar Falls was aimed at the Iron Triangle, a featureless patchwork of woods, scrub jungle, and paddyland that lay in a fold of the Saigon River just thirty miles northwest of the capital city. It seemed incredible to American civilians that enemy military forces could establish base camps so close to the cities, but American soldiers knew it to be true. Combat troops in the U.S. Army's 25th and 1st Infantry divisions shook their heads from side to side when they talked about The Triangle, as though massaging a bad memory. The woods were honeycombed with tunnels and bunker systems, and the roads and trails rigged with boobytraps and ambush sites. Casualties on Iron Triangle patrols were as predictable as malaria incidence, yet even the most persistent efforts failed to dislodge the enemy. "No one has ever demonstrated more ability to hide his installations than the Viet Cong," Westmoreland said. "They were human moles."

Westmoreland decided it was time to clean house—permanently. He had traveled to New York City before he left for Vietnam to consult with the Army's fallen and fading hero, General Douglas MacArthur. The old general was unhappy about Americans fighting in an Asian land war, and he had told Westmoreland that "scorched earth" tactics might be the only road to victory.

The centerpiece of Cedar Falls was the removal of 6,000 villagers and the destruction of their towns. Westmoreland had finally despaired of establishing rapport with these South Vietnamese people. "Having undergone long foreign occupations, Chinese, French,

Japanese, the people are strongly xenophobic," he explained. Sometimes, "the only way to establish control is to remove the people and destroy the village."

At precisely 8 A.M. on January 8, 1967, sixty helicopters popped up from behind the tall trees of the Cachua Forestry Reserve, thrummed in over the ripples of the Saigon River and spilled 420 heavily armed infantrymen on three sides of Ben Suc.

There was no resistance. The people seemed stunned. The few who did not hear or did not obey the squawked commands from a helicopter-borne loudspeaker were shot and killed. The rest of the villagers shuffled toward an old schoolhouse in the center of town.

Interrogation teams sorted through 5,987 men, women, and children and found 28 they believed might be Viet Cong. The others were loaded on boats with "anything they could carry, pull, or herd" and shipped downriver to fenced compounds where they could be guarded by ARVN troops.

Bulldozers and demolition teams moved into Ben Suc, pushing over the old school and leveling the houses, sheds, stores, and shrines. A tunnel system was seeded with thirty-pound dynamite charges, sealed, pumped full of acetylene gas, and blown up. Ten thousand pounds of explosives were stacked in a crater in the center of the ruined town, covered with earth, and tamped down by bulldozers to cork the blast. A chemical fuse triggered the five-ton coup de grace and "the village of Ben Suc no longer existed."

Engineer units flattened the other three small hamlets and then clanked noisily into the surrounding scrub jungle to scrape the ground clean of cover. M-48 tanks with bulldozers blades ripped through thickets. Huge bulldozers crashed through the woods with a 4,600-pound spiked curl of hardened steel called the Rome Clearing Blade that could splinter the largest trees. The Army would soon employ a 97-ton transphibian Tactical Crusher so huge that it simply rolled over jungle trees, chopping and pulping the debris beneath giant cleated drums it dragged along behind it.

"If the U.S. has its way," *Time* magazine reported, "even a crow flying across the Triangle will have to carry lunch from now on."

"We're winning the war," exulted Brigadier General William DePuy, who commanded the U.S. 1st Infantry Division, the Big Red One. "We're killing Viet Cong, guerrillas and main forces, destroying their bases, destroying their caches of food and weapons. . . . What we need [to win] is more bombs, more shells, more napalm."

More, more of everything, was the essence of Junction City, the gigantic military operation that crashed into War Zone C on February 22. Westmoreland's only admonition to planners had been "Think big!"

Nine U.S. infantry battalions air-assaulted into a horseshoe of blocking position near the Cambodian border about sixty miles northwest of Saigon. Simultaneously, an even larger number of mechanized infantry troops, tanks, and armored cavalry rolled north to complete the seal on one of the Viet Cong's most vital base areas. Thirteen separate artillery bases, the largest commitment of big guns in the war, ringed the operational theater to provide instant fire support.

As a special gesture to COMMUSMACV, Junction City planners included a parachute assault by the 173rd Airborne Brigade. At exactly 0900 on D Day, sixteen C-130 transport planes roared over a drop zone just three miles from Cambodia. When the green light in the lead plane blinked on, Brigadier General John R. Deane Jr., by tradition the first man out, jumped through the open door. In an instant, 845 parachutes blossomed in the sky and the first combat assault by American paratroops in a generation was underway.

This was the American way of war, what the British call the "national style" of the United States.

The great Junction City horseshoe found no enemy soldiers on Day One and, by ill luck, Westmoreland missed the only American parachute assault of the Vietnam war. His command ship had hovered over the wrong drop zone, a victim of mistaken map coordinates.

On Day Two, the largest military operation of the war began to uncover a treasure of enemy supplies, documents, ammunition, and food. Over the next several weeks, the American soldiers who trudged the dangerous cart trails of War Zone C found a sandal factory, commodious underground bunkers and base camps with shower facilities, dining halls, lecture halls, ping-pong tables and volleyball courts, miles of communication wire, extensive tunnel systems, an information office with 120 rolls of motion picture film and numerous still photographs of previously faceless Viet Cong leaders, loudspeaker systems and, just two hundred yards from Cambodia in reinforced concrete bunkers fifteen feet under the ground, two Chinese printing presses with cutting and folding attachments and a capacity of ten thousand sheets an hour. The presses had been built in Shanghai less than two years before.

American soldiers tear-gassed tunnels, dynamited bunkers, burned storage sheds, destroyed hospitals, bulldozed the brush on both sides of the roads, constructed bridges over rivers and streams, and leveled the land for new airfields in the heart of the enemy's base area. Rome plows growled in the undergrowth, clearing square miles of thick jungle.

In the few instances that enemy troops chose to fight rather than run, they were crushed by American firepower.

In the battle called Prek Klok II, for example, two battalions of Viet Cong soldiers tried to attack a wagon train circle of U.S. armored vehicles by charging across ground ripped by heavy machine guns, more than five thousand artillery rounds, and the bombs, rockets, and cannonfire of one hundred Air Force fighter bombers. Helicopters shuttled sixteen tons of fresh supplies to the defenders during the midnight fight, and Spooky arrived to brighten the dark with magnesium flares and to pour molten fire on the Viet Cong. Three Americans died at Prek Klok, and 197 enemy soldiers.

Lieutenant Colonel Alexander M. Haig, commander of the Blue Spaders Battalion in the 1st Infantry Division, provided another firepower demonstration three weeks later. Haig's soldiers were dug deeply in Y-shaped bunkers at Landing Zone George when Viet Cong soldiers attacked an hour before dawn on April Fool's Day—punching a hole one hundred yards wide and forty-five yards deep in the American position. Haig pulled back, but "the Viet Cong walked right through our mortar fire and artillery fire, they just kept coming."

The colonel threw his reserve platoon at the breach at first light, when pilots could see the target clearly. "The main Viet Cong attack began to falter under the heavy volume of fire. Light and heavy helicopter fire teams were firing rockets and mini guns on the woodline . . . artillery was massing fire along the east flank . . . the jets began striking within thirty meters, littering the entire area with enemy dead [including] one string of 29 enemy dead in a line 150 meters long; Cluster Bomb Unit had literally curled them up." Haig's soldiers reported 491 enemy dead.

During Cedar Falls and Junction City, American troops counted 3,748 dead bodies. Psychological warfare teams snapped photographs of the piles of corpses, turned the negatives into leaflets, and airdropped 9,768,000 invitations to surrender. One leaflet, addressed personally to the commanding general of the Viet Cong's 9th Division, was a taunt from the Big Red One's new commander, General John H. Hay Jr:

"[Your] commanders disgraced themselves by performing in an unsoldierly manner . . . [they] failed to accomplish their mission and left the battlefield covered with dead and wounded. . . ."

Westmoreland would complain after he left the Army that he had been "forced to fight with but one hand" in Vietnam, but there were few signs of fetters in these huge search and destroy operations. The numbers of troops committed to battle, the tonnages of bombs and shells, and the heaps of enemy dead approached those of World War II campaigns.

Americans destroyed six thousand structures and bunkers during Cedar Falls and Junction City, captured four thousand five hundred tons of rice, forty tons of salt and dried fish, seven thousand five hundred Viet Cong military uniforms, a half million documents including vital information on enemy organization and plans, more than one thousand weapons, and tens of thousands of grenades, rifle rounds, mortar shells, and rockets. All three regiments of the enemy's 9th Division had been "trounced," and officials of the enemy's clandestine government forced to flee.

Westmoreland was elated. He praised his commanders for a job well done, and he called the operations "a serious defeat" for Vo Nguyen Giap, "a disaster that forces the enemy high command to make basic revisions in his tactics. . . ."

Still, a worm of doubt nibbled at the edge of Westmoreland's confidence. He knew he not truly destroyed the enemy's forces, but merely scattered them to deeper jungle or into Cambodia. The Viet Cong were like Bartholomew's hats; every time he killed one, another sprang up in his place—and sometimes two.

"The ability of the Viet Cong continuously to rebuild their units and make good their losses is one of the mysteries of this war," General Taylor had observed, shortly before he became ambassador. "Not only do the Viet Cong units have the recuperative powers of the phoenix, but they have an amazing ability to maintain morale."

"I never thought it would go on like this," said Secretary McNamara as the enemy body count rose past 100,000. "I didn't think these people had the capacity to fight this way . . . to take this punishment. . . ."

News reporters, politicians in the United States, and even high-ranking officers on Westmoreland's own staff began to question an "official" body count that approached the number of enemy troops believed to be in South Vietnam. The general had no doubts. He had personally visited some of the most sanguinary killing grounds to see the piles of dead for himself. He insisted that his subordinate commanders exert every effort to insure accuracy. "If anything, the count probably erred on the side of caution," he said later. "Any American commander who took the same vast losses as General Giap would have been sacked overnight."

Nevertheless, American commanders found it almost impossible to make the enemy stand still long enough to be destroyed by supporting arms. The megadeath nightmare of every American infantry officer was the sudden arrival on the battlefield of countless Asian automatons in dark uniforms—Oriental fatalists who would sacrifice themselves in human wave assaults for the chance to close with American troops in the field. In Vietnam, the problem proved to be exactly the opposite: it was hard to find the enemy at all.

"The Viet Cong," Westmoreland conceded, "are uncommonly adept at slithering away."

He was *most* frustrated by the difficulty of finding and destroying enemy soldiers in the midst of millions of rural Vietnamese. Killing Viet Cong in large enough numbers to do real damage in this setting meant killing a great many civilians, too. Yet killing sixteen-year-old guerrillas two or three at a time on the mud paths of tiny hamlets was penny ante stuff for an Army prepared to do battle with the legions of Lenin.

The best place to find large concentrations of enemy forces, Westmoreland decided, and the best place to employ his superior firepower, were the jungled mountains near Cambodia and Laos:

"[With] their large airmobile capability, their extensive communications and flexible logistics support systems, [but] above all, with their tremendous firepower, it was vastly more desirable that [Americans] fight in the remote, unpopulated areas if the enemy would give battle there."

Westmoreland planned to force the enemy to give battle there by thrusting huge forces into the very heart of enemy base areas. Otherwise, he believed, the war would go on forever. Seek the enemy aggressively, Westmoreland ordered, hold him in place with aggressive, infantry tactics, and then crush him with firepower. Find him, fix him, *finish* him.

Important American military leaders disagreed sharply.

"Digging the guerrillas out of the populated and fertile lowlands is more important than going into the mountains after big North Vietnamese units," said General Victor Krulak, commander of Marine forces in the Pacific. "It is our conviction that if we can destroy the guerrilla fabric among the people, we will automatically deny the larger units the food and intelligence and taxes and the other support they need. The real war is among the people, and not among the mountains."

A short, round, gruff, bespectacled U.S. Army historian named S. L. A. Marshall questioned Westmoreland's mountain tactics for quite different reasons.

"Rattling around the . . . border held nothing good for our side except in the most extraordinary circumstances where sheer luck or some fluke made things break our way," Marshall wrote. He had just spent several months following the 1st Air Cavalry Division and other troops who were probing the heavy jungle in the Central Highlands.

"The enemy was ever scouting, measuring, and plotting the countryside. He had every possible landing zone tabbed and taped and he knew where to set his mortars to zero in on them. We were literally engaging the Charlies on the maneuver ground where they did their training exercises. Our average line infantry unit was almost as foreign to this countryside as a first astronaut landing on the moon."

Westmoreland knew the difficulties and dangers of operating on the enemy's ground, but he believed that aggressive sweeps of the enemy turf were infinitely more productive than sitting around waiting for the enemy to strike first. It was inconceivable to him that the North Vietnamese should be allowed to operate freely in the mountains.

"Do *that*," he warned, "and you allow [the enemy] to push his base areas ever closer to the centers of population so that in the end you would be fighting among the population you were supposed to protect.

"If we avoided battle, we would never succeed," he said. "We could never destroy the big units by leaving them alone."

Pleased with the success of Cedar Falls and Junction City, Westmoreland met with President Johnson and Secretary McNamara in March of 1967. He described in detail the many achievements of his command—the soaring body count, numbers of villages secured, miles of road opened, Viet Cong base camps destroyed—but then he touched on the real difficulty of smashing an enemy force that had an uncanny knack for slipping away. Unless the Viet Cong would stand and fight, he said, "the war could go on indefinitely."

Johnson and McNamara were old hands in a hard political world, but neither could mask the shock he felt at Westmoreland's words. The President somberly asked Westmoreland to put together a list of what he needed to get the war over in less time than "indefinitely," then McNamara suggested that Westmoreland begin to think about a suitable replacement. Not right away, of course, the secretary said, but soon enough so the new man could be ready to take over in a year or so.

For the first time, Westmoreland had a DEROS of his own. He knew it would be nearly impossible to achieve his nation's goals during his command. It was with a strong sense of urgency, then, that Westmoreland flew to Washington, D.C. in April to give his list of needs to President Johnson.

"I see the possibility, if considerably more American troops can be obtained, of stepping up operations and thereby speeding an end to the American role," he told the President. What he had in mind was an "optimum force" of 670,000 American soldiers—and permission to invade Laos, Cambodia, and North Vietnam.

The greater weight of munitions and the difficulty of defending bases throughout Indochina should grind down the enemy's capacity for war in three to five years, Westmoreland predicted. Whatever the President decided, he added, he should know that a "minimum essential force" of 550,000 American troops would be required to maintain U.S. momentum in Vietnam.

General Westmoreland basked in the warm applause of a joint session of Congress on this trip. The South Carolina legislature greeted him with ovations, and the cadets at West Point sat hushed as he talked to them of war and leadership.

Not all his listeners were so respectful. For the first time, Westmoreland had to consider entering buildings by the back door to avoid protestors. His own children, because they were *his* children, heard angry questions from their college classmates. Campus demonstrations against the war and flag burnings were no longer rare.

Westmoreland told a group of newspaper executives that the enemy continued to fight in the face of terrible losses because the enemy believed the American will to win was fragile, that "our Achilles heel is our resolve." *Westmoreland* believed it. His worst fear, that homefront political pressures might recall his Army at the threshold of victory, was becoming a reality.

The general returned to Vietnam with the certain knowledge that the clock was running. He had one year, perhaps a year and a half, to cripple the enemy, to kill so many Viet Cong and North Vietnamese soldiers that Giap would no longer have the young men, or the heart, to continue.

With more troops in hand and more on the way by mid-1967, Westmoreland increased the tempo of combat. American battalions hacked their way into the border country to disrupt enemy plans. More and more enemy soldiers stumbled out of the jungle, blood streaming from their ears and noses—victims of new detection devices and the hammer of B-52 bombs. Captured documents told of food shortages, malaria losses, and morale problems in the enemy ranks. Viet Cong desertions rose sharply.

These achievements were not without cost.

More Americans began to fall in battle, almost always in the sudden, shocking terror of an ambush. A roadside ambush on Dec. 22, 1961 had claimed the first American soldier to die in Vietnam, Specialist 4 James T. Davis of Livingston, Texas. Now, trying desperately to avoid Westmoreland's terrible swift sword—firepower—the enemy had refined ambush to an art form. With careful camouflage, rigid fire discipline, and proper timing, even small enemy units could inflict heavy casualties—and then run before the bombs and shells arrived.

In early June of 1967, two battalions of the U.S. 9th Infantry Division lunged by boat and helicopter toward a suspected enemy base camp in the Delta, south of Saigon. A Viet Cong force in concrete bunkers held its fire until the point men had actually passed through its lines, then began shooting at a U.S. infantry company mired in waist-deep water and mud. Enemy machine guns killed 50 Americans, wounded 143, and shot down three helicopters.

On June 22, North Vietnamese soldiers lay perfectly still while a company of paratroopers—the same ones who had parachuted into War Zone C during Junction City—walked through their position in the Highlands. On signal, the enemy force opened fire, pinned the unit down, and overran it, killing seventy-six men in the assault.

In July, a weary column of U.S. Marines marched back from a DMZ raid on the same road it had taken on the way in. Sappers detonated a mine under the lead Marine vehicle. When the column paused, North Vietnamese soldiers swarmed out of trenches along the road, chopped the column into pieces, and inflicted nearly 200 casualties before falling back.

A nine-man patrol from the U.S. 9th Division disappeared in a rubber plantation not far from Saigon. It was found two days later, sprawled in death in the eye of an L-shaped ambush.

The hard-luck paratroopers of the 173rd Airborne caught it again in the Highlands, losing twenty-six killed and forty-nine wounded in a few minutes.

Then it was the 1st Infantry Division's turn, and the Army's society of officers winced when the names were posted. Sixty-one Americans were killed and fifty-eight wounded in a brief, savage fight at very close quarters in scrub jungle not far from the Iron Triangle. Among the dead was the battalion commander, Lt. Col. Terry de la Mesa Allen Jr., whose dad had led the Big Red One through the campaigns in Tunisia and Sicily. Major Donald W. Holleder, the executive officer and an Army football hero who made All America in 1955, was killed as he moved forward to take command.

The Viet Cong's 9th Division, battered in Junction City, had answered General Hay's taunting leaflet with a hard slap.

The very *concept* of ambush so deeply offended Westmoreland's sense of professionalism that by his order such actions were announced to news reporters as "meeting engagements." Ambush by dictionary definition meant surprise, and surprise by military definition meant carelessness; therefore, ambushes were not ambushes.

The general constantly prodded his officers on proper field precautions against surprise attack. He printed and issued more than a million wallet-sized cards instructing soldiers how to avoid ambushes. Boot camps in the United States added ambush detection courses to the training of new soldiers. Some units in Vietnam required replacements to attend a refresher school on ambush before going into the field. A number of outfits used tracking dogs to sniff out ambushes, and some tried a backpack model of the "people sniffer." The Marines, and some Army units, swore by Kit Carson Scouts, enemy soldiers who had deserted and now earned top wages by leading American troops into dangerous boobytrap and ambush country.

The enemy countered with a bewildering variety of surprises, and one favorite was the decoy. Two or three soldiers baited the trap by standing innocently in the open, looking off to the middle distance like so many birdwatchers. American soldiers would cut the decoys down, and rush over to see what they had shot. The suicides' comrades waited until they had a cluster of excited G.I.'s in the kill zone.

Aggressive American tactics "lead inevitably to dramatic, costly battles" in the border regions, Westmoreland said, but it was the enemy who paid the highest price. Enemy death tolls rose through the summer of 1967 to record levels. It hardly mattered anymore what statistic was used—enemy deaths, enemy desertions, weapons captured, miles of roadway cleared, canals opened, tons of rice harvested, citizens under government control, percentage of voter participation in free elections, bomb tonnages—the war was going very badly for the Viet Cong.

Westmoreland called senior news correspondents to a briefing in the early autumn. "A sense of despair" pervaded the enemy ranks, he said. "After only little more than a year of fighting relatively sizable numbers of American troops, Communist losses are mounting drastically—with nothing to show for it."

The Army chief of staff, General Harold K. Johnson, predicted that American troops could probably start home in another year and a half. "We are very definitely winning," he said.

Still, Westmoreland's soldiers were growing weary of the "seemingly never-ending searches" in the countryside and mountains. He wanted something decisive, something *crippling,* but he seemed unable to force it even with the most massive search and destroy operations. Grinding down the enemy was working, but it was working too slowly.

Then, in September, the North Vietnamese boldly crossed the DMZ to attack a small, muddy, treeless hill named Con Thien. U.S. Marines were holding the hill as one position in a line of a half dozen strongpoints that stretched from the South China Sea all the way to Khe Sanh. For the first time in the war, the enemy used hidden long-range guns and rockets to support an infantry attack. During one nine-day period, North Vietnamese guns put three thousand shells on Con Thien.

Westmoreland answered with twenty-two thousand *tons* from B-52s alone. "Marshalling the entire spectrum of heavy fire support—B-52s, fighter bombers, naval gunfire, massed artillery and local ground fire," Westmoreland transformed the gently sloping, brushy plain surrounding Con Thien into a tortured landscape of craters and ashes.

The firepower deluge, first proposed by Air Force General William W. Momyer, was code-named SLAM, an onomatopoetic acronym that stood for Seek, Locate, Annihilate, and Monitor. The Marines had earlier removed 13,000 villagers from their homes along the Ben Hai River so the guns could fire without restriction into the DMZ. Of the 830 B-52 flights over Vietnam in September, 790 put their bombs "right in front of Con Thien."

"It was Dienbienphu in reverse," Westmoreland declared, estimating enemy casualties at 2,000 or more. The important lesson of Con Thien, he said, was its demonstration "that massed firepower [is] in itself sufficient to force a besieging enemy to desist."

• • •

AT ONE O'CLOCK in the morning on October 29, the 273rd Viet Cong Regiment emerged from the green sea of rubber plantations seventy miles north of Saigon and overran the government's district headquarters at Loc Ninh. Another large force tested the Loc Ninh Special Forces camp, defended by a dozen Americans and several hundred Montagnards. These "A" camps, as they were known, were heavily armed and fortified because of their exposed placement at the very edge of enemy sanctuaries.

"We killed some of them as they came over the top," said a shaken defender the next day, after the bodies had been cleared. He was hard at work with other Green Berets rebuilding the fort's minefield, restringing barbed wire, repairing breaches in the foot traps and resetting machine guns. Neither he nor any of his comrades had ever seen the Viet Cong press an attack for four and a half hours into the teeth of a firestorm, and they were deeply impressed.

Westmoreland had reacted instantly. While the battle still raged, he ordered combat troops and artillery batteries from the 1st and 25th U.S. Infantry Divisions to move to Loc Ninh. Mercenary troops reinforced the Green Beret camp, and an ARVN battalion prepared to retake the district headquarters. B-52s and fighter bombers were diverted from other targets to work the Loc Ninh perimeter.

The general had lost a Special Forces camp in 1966 at A Shau, a narrow, foggy valley far to the north—near Laos. The weather, the terrain, and panic among the native troops had turned the fort's desperate defense into a disastrous retreat that still rankled. Fewer than half the defenders had made it out.

He had no intention of losing Loc Ninh.

The Viet Cong tried again the next night to take the Special Forces camp. Six U.S. Army artillery pieces at one end of the camp airstrip fired beehive rounds into the flank of the attacking force. Each of these special-purpose shells contains eight thousand winged steel darts called flechettes. They hummed and sang insanely as they sped from cannon mouth to soldier. Here was a true whiff of the grape. When the artillerymen ran out of beehive rounds, they lowered the barrels of their guns and skipped high explosive shells off the runway to scythe the Viet Cong with shrapnel.

The most conservative estimate of enemy dead during the weeklong battles around Loc Ninh was 852. Most American officers believed the true count was 2,000. Never before in the war had the enemy sacrificed soldiers with such abandon—feeding them like cordwood into a furnace.

No one in the American command could understand such madness, but *everyone* was impressed by the enemy's numbers, weapons, and morale.

In the last two weeks, the 271st Viet Cong Regiment had

ambushed a Big Red One battalion, the 88th North Vietnamese Army Regiment had attacked Song Be, and the 272nd and 273rd Viet Cong Regiments and the 165th NVA Regiment had taken the field at Loc Ninh. These were *division*-sized operations by an army that just six weeks before had been described as incapable of military action much above the battalion level.

The Viet Cong entered battle at Loc Ninh with impressive antiaircraft weapons and two of the Communists' largest field artillery pieces, the 120mm mortar and the 122mm rocket.

Enemy troops, pictured as sick and demoralized, pressed their attacks with elan. They had superb equipment, including brand new AK-47 assault rifles, flame throwers, the latest model grenade launchers, and new backpack field radios. They carried full pouches of rice slung over one shoulder, personal medical kits, and even a Chinese version of the vacuum-packed canned combat rations issued to Americans. The enemy soldiers wore canvas field packs, web gear to hold essential equipment, and new green uniforms that still showed creases.

Westmoreland did not care if the Viet Cong attacked in tuxedos, so long as they attacked. He considered Loc Ninh an extraordinary engagement that had shattered the best part of four enemy regiments.

Here, in a little rubber town an hour's flight from Saigon, Westmoreland's army had staged a classic demonstration of the principles of mobility and firepower. Enemy forces had launched their assault at 1 A.M. on Day One against a dozen Green Berets and several hundred Montagnards. At dawn on Day One, two U.S. combat battalions and their artillery air-assaulted into Loc Ninh. Two other battalions moved to a nearby base camp for instant reinforcement. On Day Four, two more American battalions rode helicopters from positions near Saigon to join the battle.

Loc Ninh, a very pleased Westmoreland declared, was "one of the most significant and important operations" of the war.

"I am delighted," he told his commanders. "So far as I can see, you have just made one mistake: . . . you made it look too easy."

It was during this battle that the American command announced it had finally reached the "crossover point," the moment when Communist forces began to lose troops faster than they could be replaced. The Viet Cong and North Vietnamese had lost 60,000 soldiers in the first ten months of 1967, Westmoreland said, and had managed to recruit only 20,000 replacements.

"We see the situation getting steadily better," observed Westmoreland's assistant chief of staff, Brigadier General A. Brownfield. "We've gone into the enemy's base areas . . . burned his rice, captured his weapons and medicine. I have doubts he can hang on."

As Westmoreland's command celebrated the unique success at Loc Ninh, a North Vietnamese Army sergeant walked down from the thickly jungled mountains of the Central Highlands, 220 miles to the north, and surrendered. Sgt. Vu Hong said he came from a reconnaissance unit of the NVA's 66 Regiment, and that he had been selecting firing sites for rocket launchers—to support a major assault on the U.S. Special Forces camp at Dak To. And then, in the most extraordinary detail, he gave "the accurate positions and battle plans" of the largest gathering of North Vietnamese troops in the war: four infantry regiments and a rocket/artillery regiment.

Westmoreland decided to pour it on.

During his first year in Vietnam, enemy troops had nearly hacked the country in half where the mountains reach almost to the sea: the Central Highlands. He had reacted strongly to enemy threats in this region ever since.

"You can ring a bell and General Westmoreland will come out of the corner like a, like a *pug,*" said one of his closest aides, General John Chaisson. "And two of the bells you can ring that get this reaction are A Shau . . . and the Highlands."

A single American battalion worked the hills above Dak To in the first days of November. By mid-month the U.S. 4th Infantry

Division was at Dak To—and the 173rd Airborne Brigade, and the first brigade of the 1st Air Cavalry Division, and six ARVN battalions, and "a myriad" of supply, communications, medical, and fire support units. Engineers dynamited the tops off a dozen mountains to build level artillery platforms, and chemical units bathed the steep slopes with herbicides to strip the foliage.

Helicopters flocked in such great numbers to Dak To that 895,740 gallons of special fuel had to be flown in to slake their thirst. Under the ceaseless pounding of 170,000 artillery shells, twenty-one hundred fighter bomber attacks and three hundred B-52 missions, the green jungle canopy trembled, split open, and finally hung in blackened tatters.

This was the very closest thing to Big War that Westmoreland could devise.

The battles at Dak To were much fiercer than the battles at Loc Ninh and, despite almost perfect knowledge of the enemy's plans and hiding places, not nearly so one-sided.

On November 15, the North Vietnamese rocket regiment hurled its missiles at Dak To's crowded airfield and base camp. Two C-130 cargo planes burned on the runway, and a thousand tons of ammunition exploded in a blast that rolled shockwaves across the valley. "Jesus," said Lieutenant Fred Dyrsen amid the flattened wreckage of the American camp, "it looked like Charlie had gotten hold of some nuclear weapons."

Before they left the field, the North Vietnamese mouse trapped a battalion of the 173rd Airborne Brigade on the steep tangled slopes of Hill 875. This was the same outfit that parachuted into War Zone C without a casualty, and the same that lost 76 killed in a Highlands ambush in June. Now it suffered its most terrible trial. Unable to advance or retreat, cut off from water and early reinforcement, and deeply shaken by an errant five-hundred-pound bomb that landed squarely on the aid station, the paratroopers fought alone for fifty hours. In the battles near Dak To, the airborne lost 124 killed and 347 wounded.

Dak To, a series of sharp engagements over 190 square miles of the most difficult terrain in Vietnam, was the biggest battle of the war. More than 1,200 enemy bodies were counted on the battlefield, and countless others were presumed dead. Two hundred eighty-seven Americans died, 18 vanished, and 985 were wounded.

"An overwhelming success of U.S. arms," the Army concluded.

"In a classic example of allied superiority in firepower and maneuver," the after-battle report declared, "fifteen U.S. and Vietnamese battalions beat the enemy to the punch and sent survivors limping back to their sanctuaries."

Dissenting voices on Westmoreland's own staff asked: "Is it a victory when you lose 347 friendlies in three weeks and by your own spurious body count only get 1,200?"

Even those who believed the North Vietnamese had suffered grievously at Dak To were concerned about pulling U.S. forces from pacification duties among the people and sending them to do battle in the mountains. Westmoreland had stunned Chaisson when he moved the 1st Air Cavalry brigade to Dak To from rice-rich Binh Dinh province, "the keystone of II Corps." Peter Arnett, the veteran Associated Press correspondent, asserted, "The NVA is sucking large American forces away from population centers and bogging them down in . . . mountain fighting."

Some critics pointed at the words of a Viet Cong strategist, framed and hanging on a wall of the U.S. Marine headquarters in DaNang: "The National Liberation Front will entice the Americans close to the . . . border and bleed them without mercy. In South Vietnam, the pacification campaign will be destroyed."

Westmoreland knew these words. He knew the enemy strategy, and reminded himself of it by rereading Vo Nguyen Giap. "The primary emphasis of the North Vietnamese," he said, was to "draw

American units into remote areas and thereby facilitate control of the population in the lowlands [by the Viet Cong]."

But Westmoreland believed he could move his forces to distant battlefields without dropping his guard around the Vietnamese cities. "A unit might be 'lured' to the Highlands," he said, "yet if that was to have any appreciable effect, the lure had to be maintained for a long time.

"A boxer faces problems of both defense and attack," he continued, explaining his tactics. "As he jabs and probes with one hand, he keeps his defense up with the other. Only when he sees a clear opportunity does he attack with both fists. When he does use both hands offensively, he accepts a calculated risk by leaving himself momentarily uncovered."

Using "both fists," Westmoreland had thrashed the enemy at Loc Ninh and Dak To. These border battles weren't diversions, he felt, but *defeats*—massive, bloody, demoralizing setbacks from which the enemy would not soon recover.

Westmoreland returned to the United States in mid-November feeling more optimistic than at any time in the past four years. Indeed, President Johnson was so impressed by his field commander's glowing reports of progress that he had asked him to speak to the American people to ease growing doubts about the war.

"It was easy for me, for we were in fact making substantial progress," Westmoreland said later. "In all three frontier battles, we had soundly defeated the enemy without unduly sacrificing operations in other areas. The enemy's return was nil.

"The war *was* going well [and] I could foresee the possibility of a start on American withdrawal. . . ."

On November 21, Westmoreland told an attentive audience of news correspondents at the National Press Club in Washington, D.C. that "a new phase is now starting."

"We have reached an important point when the end begins to

come into view. I am absolutely certain that, whereas in 1965 the enemy was winning, today he is certainly losing. The enemy's hopes are bankrupt."

The only reason that the Viet Cong and the North Vietnamese continued to fight, he asserted, was "the delusion that political pressure in the United States combined with the tactical defeat of a major American unit might force the United States to throw in the towel." Westmoreland had voiced this same concern in April. It was no delusion. Political pressures in the United States *were* rising.

A month earlier, in October, President Johnson had received a letter from forty-nine young men and women who worked as volunteers in the South Vietnamese countryside. The American style of war, they wrote, specifically mentioning the use of napalm and herbicides and the forcible relocation of the rural population, was "an overwhelming atrocity."

On October 31, the very day that heliborne assault troops from the Big Red One were drubbing the Viet Cong at Loc Ninh, Defense Secretary Robert McNamara had resigned from the cabinet, telling President Johnson that the Vietnam war was "dangerous, costly, and unsatisfactory to our people."

As Westmoreland spoke in Washington, an International War Crime Tribunal chaired by Bertrand Russell began to hear public testimony in Roskilde, Denmark. Among the early witnesses were American soldiers who had deserted, and who told of the torture of enemy suspects and the mutilation of enemy bodies.

Hairline cracks in the Army itself appeared. Respected noncommissioned officers of long service were caught transferring monies from Vietnam clubs to private accounts in Switzerland. Drug addiction was on the rise. American forces in Europe, drained of their best officers and soldiers and equipment, presented a fragile shell to the poised juggernaut of the Warsaw Pact nations.

The United States Senate, which had approved the Vietnam war resolution in 1964 with only two dissenting votes, had scheduled hearings on evidence that the North Vietnamese might not have been the aggressor in the Tonkin Gulf incident.

American casualties had risen from twenty-five hundred in 1965, to thirty-three thousand in 1966, to eighty thousand in 1967. "We are dropping $20,000 bombs every time somebody thinks he sees four Viet Cong in a bush," said Representative Thomas P. O'Neill, a Boston Democrat who was moving from support of the war to opposition, "and it isn't working."

President Johnson's long face told of the burdens he was carrying. His dream of a Great Society for America was coming undone. Black people had torched their own cities in the autumn; Newark, Detroit, Cincinnati, and Atlanta had bled, and burned. Mothers' marches had become mobs, and the President's dreams were haunted by the chants: "Hey, hey, LBJ, How many boys did you kill today?"

On November 28, the President told General Westmoreland that he doubted he could continue to take the pressure; he was considering not seeking reelection.

Westmoreland could see the national will unraveling before his eyes. Everything he had worked for was slipping away.

The general worked to assure that no trace of these worries rippled the perfect surface of his confidence. "A commander is the bellweather of his command and must display confidence and resolution," he said. "Even the slightest pessimism on his part can quickly pervade the ranks. In Vietnam, I *was* confident, so no play-acting was involved in showing this confidence, yet . . . I was sharply conscious of the need to demonstrate it."

The most powerful demonstration of progress, of course, would be a convincing battlefield triumph. Westmoreland was certain that Vo Nguyen Giap was looking for a Dienbienphu style victory—hoping to drive America out of the war as he drove France out in 1954. Why else had he sacrificed his forces at Con Thien, at Loc Ninh, and Dak To?

Westmoreland's eyes ran up the map when he returned to Vietnam, pausing at the tiny dots with strange names, weighing each for its defensive strengths, its reinforcibility, its potential value as a propaganda piece. The last small dot was Khe Sanh. No other outpost in Vietnam looked more inviting. There, the enemy could count on "the advantage of nearby sanctuaries [in Laos], and short lines of communication to plan carefully and to strike with speed and strength." It would surely be Khe Sanh.

Intelligence reports in December confirmed his judgment. The great southward flow of enemy troops and supplies through Laos began to slow, then eddy and pool in the jagged mountains west of Khe Sanh. Westmoreland sent in reinforcements—not enough to scare off the North Vietnamese but enough to ensure the camp's survival. He *wanted* this battle. Khe Sanh would be his Dienbienphu, not Giap's. This time, refining the aggressive tactics of Dak To, he would "lure the enemy to their deaths" and destroy them beneath a Niagara of bombs.

• • •

THERE COMES A moment on the eve of battle when a commander knows that he has done all he can do to prepare for the coming test. Westmoreland made his assessment with complete confidence: "In the face of American firepower, helicopter mobility, and fire support, there was no way Giap could win on the battlefield." His certainty was shared at the highest levels in Washington, where it found expression: "In a few months everybody—even the most cynical and skeptical reporter in Saigon—is going to have to admit that we are definitely winning this war."

Few knew of the general's deep frustrations, or of the effort of will he had made to build U.S. strength in Vietnam, to quietly change his country's policies until he could wage war the American way. These had been hard years, filled with "many frustrations, much interference, countless irritations, many disappointments, considerable criticism."

If these burdens had been a test of his leadership, he had endured. He had built his striking force from two token Marine battalions in March of 1965 to almost 500,000 American fighting men on the eve of Khe Sanh.

Westmoreland kept a quotation from Napoleon beneath the clear glass on his desk top to remind him every day of his duty:

> A commander-in-chief cannot take as an excuse for his mistakes in warfare an order given by his sovereign or his minister, when the person giving the order is absent from the field of operations. . . . It follows that any commander-in-chief who undertakes to carry out a plan which he considers defective is at fault; he must put forward his reasons, insist on the plan being changed, and finally tender his resignation rather than be the instrument of his army's downfall.

Westmoreland never considered resigning; he had worked to change the plan. Now, he focused all of his considerable energies on Khe Sanh which he felt "could be the greatest battle" of the war.

"I had no illusions that Khe Sanh would be a brief fight lacking in American casualties," he said, but he believed it would be catastrophic for the North Vietnamese.

Intelligence reports indicated Vo Nguyen Giap might be committing four *divisions* to this battle. Practiced from his many briefings, Westmoreland knew the 1967 numbers perfectly. The enemy had lost 88,000 slain in battle, 30,000 dead from wounds or forever crippled, 18,000 defectors, and 25,000 sick with malaria or other tropical diseases. Now, in a single stroke, he might be able to kill 40,000 more. It would be the perfect conclusion to his Vietnam years.

Westmoreland had been raised a teetotaler. In his mid-years he trained himself, just as he had trained the muscles of his eyeballs to pass the Air Corps' optometric tests, to drink an occasional beer or watered Scotch—to be sociable, to soften the hard edge of his Command Presence.

He sipped his beer in the late evening, reflectively, when his work was done.

Khe Sanh, he believed, might be the turning point. He went over his preparations one more time. Checkers was done. Niagara was rehearsed. The relief force was in place.

Never, Westmoreland thought as the dark tropical night closed on Saigon on January 20, had he been more ready.

3.

In the Time Before the War

The tiny deer picked its way delicately across the courtyard to lean against Felix Poilane's leg and to stretch its neck for the caress of his fingers. The lean French planter chuckled at his pet's pleading, and he introduced the deer, Bambi, to the American pilots visiting in his home. Madeleine Poilane served the guests clear glasses of mountain water and crème de menthe, a green coolness of a summer drink that perfectly mirrored the fresh greenness of Khe Sanh.

Jean-Marie and Françoise, the Poilanes' young children, played in the garden, where old Bru women raked coffee beans on sun-warmed concrete slabs, turning them gently and drying them evenly.

The pastoral quality of refreshments in the villa courtyard, like Felix's easy laughter, masked real tension in the Poilane household. The Air Force pilots wore battle dress, all zippers and map pockets and sheath knives. The genial conversation was punctuated by the crash of artillery at the combat base, less than a mile away.

Poilane was thirty-six years old. He had spent his life working this land, planting, and nurturing the groves of coffee trees that trembled in a green shimmer beneath the summer sun. The delicate trees, like fine grapevines, need almost a decade of care before they deliver up their treasure. Now, just as he harvested hundreds of tons of rich, red Rubuston and Cherri coffee beans, United States Marines were moving onto his plantation in large numbers, cutting trees for better fields of fire, building mountains of garbage, and harassing his Montagnard workers.

Furthermore, the burgeoning Marine presence had shattered his plan to get the beans to market.

In the time before the war, coffee beans from the Khe Sanh plantations traveled west on Route 9 to Savannakhet, the Laotian market town on the Mekong River. The war in Laos had closed that route years ago. Now, it was impossible to go *east.* The town of Ca Lu was only twelve miles down the road and Quang Tri, the old provincial capital with its moated citadel, was only twenty-five miles beyond that, but these places might as well have been in France.

In early August, enemy troops had ambushed a large Marine truck convoy on Route 9 near Ca Lu, then destroyed the bridges, blocked the passes, and mined the highway to isolate the combat base at Khe Sanh. Supplied quite easily by air, the Marines suffered few hardships—but the cutting of the road was a disaster for Felix Poilane.

He was, after all, a farmer. The years of war had drained his resources. The thick-walled, yellow cement villa was beginning to look shabby. His Montagnard workers had gone without their daily pay—rice allotments—for months; the stability of the civilian economy in Khe Sanh was seriously threatened. Felix Poilane's only hope for income was in the hands of the American pilots in his courtyard. Their huge planes flew empty every day to bases near DaNang and Saigon. And so, he invited them often to his home, generously poured the cool, green drinks, and gave each a small bag of fresh coffee beans as a leavetaking gift.

Felix Poilane was not yet discouraged. Bad times had visited in Khe Sanh before the autumn of 1967. This, too, would surely pass. He had been born in this beautiful place, one of the many sons of a gentleman botanist who had come here from France in the early 1920s.

His father, Eugene Poilane, had discovered a place "like Europe, with small valleys, plenty of water and paths and flowers and hills, [with] land as good, as rich and red as in Tuscany."

With his wife Madame Bordeauducq, a proud woman who insisted upon keeping her maiden name "to look independent," Eugene Poilane had cleared the jungle and begun to experiment with different crops. Sometimes, he vanished into the mountains, walking the narrow trails all the way to China, and Burma, and Siam. He returned with newly discovered plants, each wrapped carefully in moist leaves. Between 1922 and 1947, he sent thirty-six thousand samples to a botanical museum in France. He made coffee grow where it had never grown before, and he planted a garden of such rare variety that botanists came from all the countries of the world to visit in Khe Sanh. He cultivated avocado and jackfruit, and he made oranges bloom beside the fragrant white flowers of his coffee trees.

"He made that plantation entirely himself, loving the land as if he'd been born there," said a visitor. "People who talk about colonialism when it involves people like Papa Poilane make me laugh. He wasn't a colonialist. He was a peasant who cultivated the land."

Wealthy sportsmen from America and France came to Khe Sanh in the early days to seek tiger pelts, and deer, civets, wild boar, bear, and rare panthers for their trophy rooms. They sailed up the Perfume River to Hue, found rooms at the tennis and swim club maintained for French gentlemen, and admired the flame trees and flowered moats that surrounded the thick, brick walls of the old citadel. It was only thirty-five miles up Highway One to Quang Tri, then thirty-five miles west to Khe Sanh.

There, they found warm hospitality in the Poilane villa, a house "like the houses in Tuscany or in Auvergne: with a tower in the middle for the pigeons, and a courtyard in front . . . always full of dogs, cats, and chickens."

Madame Bordeauducq bore five children in Khe Sanh, and managed the plantation when Papa Poilane disappeared. She often spent long, uncomfortable nights perched in a tree, patiently waiting for a shot at the tigers that terrified her workers. Before her hair was iron grey, she had killed forty-five of them.

"I don't like to kill the tigers," Madame Bordeauducq said, "but they eat up my peasants."

The remote valley did not escape World War II. Japanese occupation troops imposed a savage discipline in Vietnam until 1945, then abruptly pulled out. Chinese soldiers from Chiang Kai-shek's armies moved into the vacuum—and behaved like conquerors until the French reimposed colonial rule in 1947.

During these years Papa Poilane invited Madame Bordeauducq to leave his house. He married a Nung woman from North Vietnam, and quickly fathered a new family of five. He could sometimes be found in the misty mornings standing amidst his apple trees, wishing for the impossible frost that would give them fruit.

Madame Bordeauducq moved a thousand yards to the east, cleared the dense brush from the land, and began planting new coffee groves for a plantation of her own. Her son, Felix, joined her, though he often walked next door to consult with his father on farm problems.

New neighbors and new prosperity came to Khe Sanh after World War II. M. Simard and his wife settled on a coffee plantation west of the village, along the highway to Laos. M. Linares, a wealthy Frenchman of Spanish descent, settled with his Vietnamese wife and numerous children on a coffee plantation east of the village, on the road to Quang Tri and the coast. Linares loved his new home "like a woman," and he used to tell visitors that he had asked God for only one thing: "I ask to die at Khe Sanh."

Benedictine brothers from a monastery in Hue carved out a small plantation between the town and Linares.

French soldiers built several military outposts near the village, including a handsome concrete bunker and airstrip about a mile north of Route 9, but the First Indochinese War did not touch the families at Khe Sanh until its final year, 1954. Simard's wife was killed in a Viet Minh mortar attack, and Papa Poilane took a shell fragment in the leg.

The plantations had thrived again after the French war was over. Vietnamese merchants set up shop in the tiny village to do business with the Bru. Papa Poilane had become a legend, "an extraordinary man unusual in every sense" with a long, white beard and "keen, sparkly eyes." He loved the Bru people, and it pleased him to let two of their most ancient elephants—each of whom was addressed respectfully as "Grandfather"—graze on the lawns of his villa.

In 1958, the new South Vietnamese Army sent patrols to Khe Sanh, then up into the mountains to require the Bru to come down and live near the village. The resettlement made it possible for the government to protect the Bru—and to keep them from assisting the North Vietnamese.

The people of the mountains probably numbered two million or more in the years before the war. They were scattered in tribal clusters throughout the Annamite Mountains, from the border with China in the north to the low foothills in the far south. Dark-skinned, primitive, they had developed distinct tribal identities in the thousand years of their mountain isolation. The Bru, a Montagnard tribe of more than thirty thousand, had never known national boundaries. Now they found their lands divided among Laos, North Vietnam, and South Vietnam—and well-armed soldiers telling them where they could and could not live.

More than 13,000 Bru lived in the immediate vicinity—"reachable by road" was the South Vietnamese rule—of Khe Sanh village by 1960. Many had been forced to leave rich mountain hamlets that had small orchards, tobacco plots, and gardens.

The Bru practiced slash and burn agriculture, clearing small patches of jungle to grow rice, sweet potatoes, manioc, and corn. Every adult Bru worked in the rice fields, which had to be moved every two or three years when the soil was exhausted. Fish and game were abundant.

Even after the resettlement, no Bru lived in Khe Sanh. The Vietnamese lived there, and their contempt for the mountain people was blatant. The Vietnamese traders and small farmers routinely cheated the Bru out of the rice they earned on the coffee plantations. The Montagnards *were* naïve, unskilled in business matters, and utterly without guile—but they were not stupid. They knew they were being cheated, and they searched for an understanding of behavior alien to their own culture. The conclusion was unanimous, and it could be heard in every household: "The Vietnamese have two gall bladders."

The Vietnamese Evangelical Protestant Church sent Pastor Bui Tan Loc as a missionary to the Bru. He tried to learn their language, and he became the first outsider to communicate readily with the mountain people.

In January, 1962, John and Carolyn Miller came to Khe Sanh to begin fourteen years of work to learn the Bru language, devise a written alphabet and grammar, teach the mountain people how to read in their own language—and then put into their hands the New Testament, in Bru.

John Miller was thirty when he arrived at Khe Sanh. Born near Allentown, Pa., the seventh of thirteen children, he had served in the U.S. Army during the Korean War. While studying at Houghton College in upstate New York, he had decided to devote his life to unknotting the mysteries of unknown, unwritten languages so that their speakers could know the Bible.

A quiet, shy student, John Miller discreetly courted the college president's daughter by sending her Bible verses through the mail. Carolyn Paine was more than seven years his junior but she knew her suitor was serious when she read: "I thank God upon every remembrance of you . . . because I have you in my heart."

Miller wrote from a jungle training school in Mexico, and then from Vietnam where he had gone in 1959 to work with the Wycliffe Bible Translators. In 1961, Carolyn Paine, her grandmother's hand-stitched batiste wedding gown carefully folded in her luggage, flew to Saigon to meet and marry a man she had not seen in almost three years. They spoke their vows in the yellow stucco French Protestant Church in Saigon and, shortly afterwards, moved to Hue to study Vietnamese and to prepare for their mission. It was in Hue that they first heard about the mountain people called the Bru.

The Millers loaded all their belongings and linguistic manuals into a rented truck, headed out across the Perfume River and up Highway 1, then west on the narrow, winding road that led through the mountains and over plunging rivers to Khe Sanh.

"It always reminded me of Colorado," Carolyn remembered. "It was so beautiful."

They arrived quite late in the afternoon, and drove through Khe Sanh to Lang Bu, a small Bru hamlet a mile and a half past the village on the road to Laos. The Vietnamese truck driver was anxious to get back to civilization. Like many of his countrymen, he feared the climate of the mountains, especially the "poisonous winds" that blew death into the mouth and nose of their victim.

All one hundred families in Lang Bu turned out to carry the books and furniture and crates and clothing down from the road, across a stream, and up a small hill to the hamlet.

"It was like a circus coming to town," Carolyn laughed.

John Miller sat down with the hamlet's elders to discuss his need for a permanent home. The Bru listened patiently until one, Khoi No, stood and said he would sell his home for eight thousand piasters and move in with relatives until he could build another.

Following the custom of barter that was the *essence* of Vietnamese business relations, Miller offered four thousand. The homeowner looked puzzled and turned to his colleagues on the council. After long argument, the hamlet chief rose and spoke:

"Khoi No says if that is all you can afford to pay, he will let you have it for that amount."

Thus the Millers learned their first lesson of the Bru. Open, innocent, anxious to please, they would literally sell their homes for half their true value to accommodate visitors. Vietnamese traders had prospered on this naiveté for years.

The next morning the Bru moved Khoi No's baskets of rice, gourds of rice alcohol, brass gongs, and cooking pots from the house, and moved the Millers in. By afternoon, they were settled in a two-room bamboo and thatch hut built on poles six feet above the ground.

"Those were golden days," Carolyn Miller said. "Our neighbors laughed a great deal at our efforts to learn their language and their ways. But they were proud of us, and our presence seemed to give a certain status to their village.

"Our tape recorder, which sang Bru courting songs and reproduced their musical instruments, was an endless source of fascination."

Slowly, painstakingly, the Millers began to record and transcribe the words of Bru rituals, weddings, burials, legends, myths, the names of kitchen utensils, techniques for hunting, and seasons for planting. Khoi No swept the bare ground beneath their home when he swept his own, kept the house in excellent repair, and screened the unending stream of curious visitors who came to see the Millers. One day John Miller fastened a hand-printed sheet of paper to the bamboo wall of the house. It read in Bru:

"I am standing at the door and calling [Brus do not have doors on which to knock]; if anyone opens the door to me, I will come in."

"Look at that!" neighbors exclaimed as they led curious visitors through the Millers' house. "That's our language!" None of the Bru, of course, could read. Until the Millers arrived, a written Bru language did not exist.

There was little time or opportunity for social affairs among the half dozen Westerners in Khe Sanh. Carolyn Miller met Madeleine Poilane, who was about her age, from time to time but she spoke no

French and Madeleine spoke little English. The two young women conversed awkwardly in elementary Bru and Franglais.

In the late summer of 1962, ten U.S. Army soldiers in jaunty forest-green berets drove up Route 9 from the coast to establish a small military outpost. They broomed the cobwebs from the old French bunkers, filled in the eroded gullies on the small airfield, and began to recruit Bru to lead them on long-range patrols deep into the mountains of Laos.

The passing of the days was measured in long hours of summer sun and the billowing of grey clouds in the monsoon. Margie, the Millers' first child, was born in 1962. Gordie and Nathan would be born during the years at Khe Sanh. In the spring of 1964 Father Poncet, a priest from Paris, arrived in the village. Quiet, ruggedly handsome, his eyes twinkling in a face half-hidden by a black moustache and beard, Father Poncet wore farm clothing and searched out his parishioners on a motor scooter He became immensely popular among the Bru, but he was greeted most warmly during his daily visits to Felix Poilane's plantation, where he played with the children and shared memories of Paris in his pure, rarely heard French.

The idyll of Khe Sanh was shattered in April 1964 when men stepped from the side of the road, ordered Papa Poilane and M. Linares from their car—and riddled Poilane with bullets. The gentle mountain man who had walked Route 9 when it was still a dirt path, the builder of Khe Sanh, the father of two families, was dead.

• • •

NOT UNTIL 1966, when American combat troops began to arrive in larger numbers, was General Westmoreland able to turn his attention to the small outpost at Khe Sanh. He was, in fact, growing concerned about the entire northern region.

Quang Tri Province was only thirty-five miles wide in some places. It was the first barrier to Communist invasion across the De-

Militarized Zone. Apart from the Bru in the western mountains, a few vegetable farmers on the broad piedmont, and scattered fishing villages at the river mouths, *all* of Quang Tri's 280,000 people lived in a narrow band of rich paddyland between Route 1 and the coast. Slogging French soldiers in the First Indochinese War knew this last area, which stretched south into Thua Thien Province to the former imperial capital at Hue, as "la rue sans joie"—an endless series of fortified villages and ambushes, literally "a street without joy."

In the first months of 1966, the northern part of South Vietnam was wracked by anti-government protests. ARVN units ignored orders from Saigon, and actually drew guns on several American units. Soldiers joined Buddhists and students in street marches in Hue and DaNang. The USIS library in Hue was torched. At the height of turmoil, U.S. intelligence learned that Vo Nguyen Giap had decided to place the two northernmost provinces under his jurisdiction; henceforth, the North Vietnamese Army would work this battleground—not the Viet Cong.

"If I were General Giap," Westmoreland said in February, "I would strike into Quang Tri and Thua Thien Provinces for a quick victory."

The general ordered the Marines to "familiarize" themselves with the region—and to take a particularly close look at the western mountains near Khe Sanh.

The Marines sent Lt. Col. Van D. "Ding Dong" Bell, "a tough officer of the old school," to stir up a fight with the North Vietnamese regulars reported to be near Khe Sanh. Bell's battalion of one thousand Marines was set to go on April 5, but had to wait almost two weeks until weather allowed Marine C-130s to land at Khe Sanh. Bell's Marines thrashed around the countryside for two weeks without enemy contact. He marched the battalion home on Route 9; fifty men collapsed with heat stroke, but "not a shot was fired in anger."

Westmoreland remained certain that "trouble was brewing." The

U.S. Army Special Forces team at Khe Sanh boosted its strength to 300 irregulars. An Army intelligence unit called Special Operations Group and "classified higher than SECRET" moved into an old French fort south of Route 9, dubbing their new home "Fort Dix." A U.S. Navy Mobile Construction Battalion arrived to extend the old French runway from fifteen hundred feet to thirty-nine hundred feet, and cover it with pierced metal planks. Vietnamese government officials and Marine officers urged the Millers to move from Lang Bu. They decided to rent an old stone house near Khe Sanh village from the Nung widow, who still farmed Papa Poilane's plantation.

In September Westmoreland asked the Marines to wargame a North Vietnamese invasion from the western mountains. The Marine command staff studied the problem, and decided to pull back to The Rockpile.

"I notice you haven't . . . put a force in Khe Sanh," Westmoreland observed. "What are your reasons for this?"

"Well, we think it would be too isolated. We think it would be too hard to support . . . and we're worried about the weather. The weather shuts down pretty badly there. . . ."

"Nonetheless," Westmoreland said, "I think we ought to have a larger force out there." He recommended a battalion.

The Marines resisted.

"We didn't want a force that size out there . . . because you had to hold those outlying hills with *something*," one Marine general said. The assistant commander of the 3rd Marine Division was less diplomatic:

"When you're at Khe Sanh, you're not really anywhere. It's far from everything. You could lose it, and you really haven't lost a damn thing."

The Marines bowed to Westmoreland's judgment reluctantly, and ordered a battalion to Khe Sanh "just to retain that little prestige of doing it on your own volition rather than doing it with a shoe in your tail."

The first large American unit to arrive at Khe Sanh for an extended stay brought unique pressures to the plateau, and the first to feel them were the Special Forces, who were shouldered out of their snug French-built bunker at the airfield. Marine officers enjoyed this demonstration of the privileges of rank; there was little camaraderie between the Army's "Green Beanies" and the Marines' "grunts."

Crewcut Marine Corps officers thought of the Special Forces as ill-disciplined rabble—bearded soldiers with foreign accents who lived casually with Bru women, drank rice alcohol, ate rats, and had little respect for rank or rules. The Special Forces troopers thought of the Marines as stupid innocents who blundered about in too-large units with too-little understanding of just how tough things could get in the mountains near Laos.

The small "A" team and its Montagnards moved in December from the airfield, west along Route 9 to Lang Vei, a Bru hamlet about four miles west of the Marine combat base.

There were other difficulties.

Marines liked to lean out of the back of trucks and tip the conical hats of Vietnamese peasants. A mortar round hit in the Millers' side yard, exploding clods of dirt against the house. Artillery shells crashed randomly in the countryside as the Marines fired harassment and interdiction rounds into the gathering grey clouds of the monsoon.

The Millers received a formal visit from a delegation of Bru elders who assumed the Marines were a part of the Millers' larger family: "Will you please tell your friends to be more careful when they shoot their big guns. Some are exploding in our fields and villages, and we're afraid someone will be hurt."

The Marines sent medical teams into the Bru hamlets, shared food and clothing with the village orphanage, donated money to the schools and churches, and built playgrounds for the children. They helped buy a new large-type typewriter for the Millers' language classes. The base commander even sent a squad to dig up the mortar shell in their yard. "It won't happen again," he promised. Some Americans, homesick for their own families, stopped by to play with the Miller children; Margie got a very fancy doll from the commander of the Special Forces team.

Contact with enemy forces was rare in the final months of 1966, but one visitor to Khe Sanh looked at the great bustle of activity and construction at the airstrip, and said: "It's like setting out honey to attract flies."

In the first days of the new year, a flight of U.S. fighter bombers appeared over Khe Sanh one morning, circled once to get on the proper line for attack—and then roared in on Lang Vei with high explosives and Cluster Bomb Units. It was a slaughter. American soldiers in the new Special Forces camp across the road tried desperately to reach the pilots by radio, but could not find the frequency. Bru soldiers in the camp cried out as the planes rolled in for a second pass; their families lived in Lang Vei. More than one hundred Bru civilians were killed in the mistaken bombing.

In the last week of April, a Marine platoon lost twelve killed and two missing in an ambush near Hill 881 South. A second platoon that rushed to help was also mauled. The Marines air lifted a battalion to Khe Sanh the next day, and before dark it was locked in combat on Hill 861. Another battalion flew to Khe Sanh, then an artillery battalion.

The Hill Fights were underway.

The North Vietnamese Army's 18th Regiment resisted "with great fury," and the Marines found the going very tough: "The NVA are excellent troops whose marksmanship, fire and camouflage discipline, and aggressiveness are outstanding." On May 1, the battered 18th Regiment slipped away as the NVA's 95th Regiment counterattacked to cover the withdrawal. The vicious fighting drew every eye to the hills four miles northwest of the combat base.

In that moment, North Vietnamese soldiers slashed through

the defensive wire at the new Lang Vei Special Forces camp—and penetrated all the way to the command bunker. The Green Beret commander and his executive officer were killed by satchel charge through a window. The enemy force killed twenty defenders and wounded thirty-six, then retired before dawn.

The Marines withdrew the bulk of their forces from Khe Sanh after the Hill Fights, but sharp clashes continued.

On June 6 the NVA attacked a communications relay station on top of Hill 950. The enemy force knocked out a machine gun in the opening minutes and pushed into the gap. A rocket grenade looped into the radio bunker and killed three defenders. Sgt. Richard W. Baskin rallied the survivors and threw the enemy off the peak, but only five Marines were firing weapons at the end.

The very next day, Marines killed sixty-six enemy soldiers on Hill 881 North, losing eighteen dead.

No single battle during the summer approached the savagery of the Hill Fights, but the Marines' scorecard from mid-May to late July was: 204 North Vietnamese dead, 52 Americans dead, and 255 Marines evacuated with wounds.

On July 21, the Marines at the combat base buzzed about the prediction made by Jeane Dixon, a Stateside stargazer, that 1,200 would soon die at Khe Sanh.

Westmoreland decided it was time to prepare Khe Sanh for its role as the launch point for an invasion of Laos. The airfield had been badly damaged during the Hill Fights—not by enemy shells but by friendly planes. The big C-130s, with a landing weight of almost sixty tons, had pumped water up from the soggy earth as they rolled across the pierced metal planks. The runway had collapsed in a number of places.

On August 17, the airfield closed for repairs. Work crews stripped the old metal plates from the surface while three fifteen-ton rock crushers began eating a small mountain a mile and a half from the base. Trucks shuttled stone from the quarry to the airfield, where bulldozers smoothed the runway. C-130s flew more than two thousand tons of building materials to the base.

General Westmoreland experimented with two aerial delivery techniques during the rehabilitation of the Khe Sanh airstrip—parachute drops and Low Altitude Parachute Extraction—because air was the only way to support the thousand Marines at Khe Sanh. A convoy with 175mm guns that could fire into Laos had set out for the combat base early in August, run into "one horrendous ambush," and turned back to avoid a GM100-style destruction. Route 9 was closed.

Even without the big guns, Westmoreland was ready for a strike into Laos. On September 4, he cabled Admiral Sharp with a proposal for a U.S. assault across the border—to be launched from Khe Sanh.

• • •

THE MUTUAL DISLIKE between Marines and Green Berets grew worse through the summer and fall of 1967. The Green Berets had decided to move away from the ghosts of the short-lived camp at Lang Vei, now a litter of blackened timbers, blowing paper, rusting wire, and scavenging rats—with startling sculptures of gleaming, white toilet bowls standing in the ruins. They chose a spot a half mile farther west, atop a long, gentle rise that provided excellent fields of fire and overlooked both Route 9 and the border with Laos.

This time, relying on their fabled scrounging abilities and the professional help of Navy Seabees, the Special Forces built a *fortress.*

"They built the most magnificent bunker you ever laid eyes on," groused Major General Rathvon McCall Tompkins, commander of the 3rd Marine Division and a daily visitor at Khe Sanh.

"There is no lumber like that available in Vietnam," Tompkins said as he watched large helicopters carry cargo nets full of 8 x 8 beams over Khe Sanh on the way to the new Lang Vei fortifications. "It all came from out of country."

The Green Berets built reinforced-concrete bunkers, ringed their new camp with a chain-wire cyclone fence, installed powerful generators and electric lights, and soon sipped Chivas Regal in their club house. The Marines dug holes with their pack shovels, and fought rats in dark bunkers made of sandbags and sagging timbers. Tompkins despaired as he watched locally cut lumber "go to pieces . . . between the rot and the termites and the bugs."

But the dispute between the Marines and the soldiers went deeper than jealousy over building materials. General Tompkins said he thought the hollow-eyed soldiers at the Special Forces camp were "hopped up." That is, drugged. "There was something mysterious about those wretches," he said. "Those wretches were a law unto themselves."

Tompkins knew his Marines would be asked to help if the Green Berets got in trouble. The new camp was seven miles from the combat base on a road that was little more than a series of eroded gullies, potholes and mud ruts, broken occasionally by bits of the old French asphalt. Racing down this road to rescue some wretches, the general believed, would mean "getting a battalion of Marines chopped up for no possible reason."

The Special Forces soldiers were also upset. They survived behind enemy lines because they traveled with Montagnard guides in small columns that could move quickly. Operating beyond the edge of the American artillery umbrella, they *relied* on stealth. Now, they had to hide themselves as carefully from Marines as they did from North Vietnamese because Marines tended to call airstrikes on anything that moved and wasn't wearing Marine green. Hypertense Green Berets threatened to shoot down the next Marine aircraft that circled one of their patrols, broadcasting map coordinates in the clear to the combat base to determine if they were "friendlies."

Didn't the Marines know, the soldiers asked, that the North Vietnamese also had radios?

The combat base showed so many lights at night that the Special Forces troopers at Lang Vei called it Coney Island.

• • •

ENGINEERS COMPLETED REJUVENATION of the Khe Sanh airfield on October 27, and Westmoreland began stockpiling supplies and ammunition for a multi-division strike into Laos.

In November, the American intelligence web trembled with tiny vibrations from the strands that stretched to the west, across the Xepone River. Some of the Montagnard villages nearest the border began to evacuate and move closer to Khe Sanh—a sure sign of increasing enemy pressure. A Special Forces patrol found fresh elephant feces along the river, as well as other evidence to indicate that an NVA pack train with heavy weapons had recently visited the area.

On November 10, Colonel Lownds helicoptered to Hill 881 South for ceremonies marking the 192nd birthday of the U.S. Marine Corps. "We at Khe Sanh are going to be remembered in American history books," he said.

The colonel was deeply frustrated by the tangled underbrush and the meadows of tall, dense grass that blinded his recon teams.

"We don't have our eyes!" he complained to his regimental staff in mid-November. "We must be more alert. The enemy knows where we are; we don't always know where he is."

Snipers began to harass the hilltop outposts more frequently. Perimeter guards at the combat base discovered cuts in the defensive wire that had been fitted back together and smeared with mud to hide the break. SOG helicopters flew deep into Laos and returned with air samples and radio intercepts that could only mean a great massing of enemy troops.

At two o'clock in the afternoon of December 13, General Tompkins picked up the voice-secure scrambler telephone on his desk in Dong Ha and listened to the words of Lieutenant General Robert E. Cushman Jr., commander of all the Marines in Vietnam.

"I'm getting worried about the enemy buildup at Khe Sanh," Cushman said. High-level intelligence reports indicated it might be a good idea to send another Marine battalion to the base.

Tompkins conceded the Marines at Khe Sanh were "pretty thin" as a result of having to defend the airfield and the hills but he thought the Camp Carroll artillery base looked more vulnerable than Khe Sahn—and he said so to General Cushman.

"You'll just have to take my word for it," Cushman said. "Move the Third Battalion of the 26th out there."

Tompkins sensed pressure from higher up the chain of command. "Westmoreland has always been sensitive about Khe Sanh," he thought. "It may go back to that early incident when the Special Forces camp in there got overrun. He was *always* sensitive about Khe Sanh."

The Third Battalion, already aboard helicopters for an assault mission elsewhere, was diverted in midflight. Within five hours of Cushman's order, the battalion was at Khe Sanh.

Never before in the history of warfare had it been possible to move one thousand men and their equipment sixty miles through impossible terrain with such speed—and no casualties at all. In western Quang Tri Province, unfordable rivers appeared where maps showed dry land, unclimbable precipices jutted from the maps' smooth valley floors, and the double and triple layers of jungle canopy trapped the gloom of night eternally. Now, the Marines soared over the whole mess.

The arrival of the Third Battalion sent rumors racing through the combat base: "We're going to Laos!" Westmoreland *was* preparing for such an invasion, but very carefully. He knew how important it was to lead politicians gently toward difficult decisions, and he did not want to force this issue prematurely:

"Frankly, if I had gone in and said: 'I want *x* number of troops to go into Laos—well, it would have rocked Washington and it would have set us back. [We] had to play this thing very delicately."

As the general and the Joint Chiefs of Staff worked to lift the political constraints that leashed an American assault into Laos, heliborne "people sniffers" suddenly detected "many, many groups of North Vietnamese, five soldiers or so [in each group], moving into the Khe Sanh region." The enemy started to jam Marine radio communications. It was possible to click down the dial in the communications room at the combat base and hear the chatter of North Vietnamese military traffic on several frequencies.

"Things are picking up," Lownds said.

• • •

KHE SANH VILLAGE seemed immune to the rising tension. The little town had grown to more than 1,500 people, and it was bustling with preparations for Christmas. Laundries and whorehouses and souvenir shops had sprung up to service the Marines. One entrepreneur had opened a small Vietnamese restaurant on the main street, just across from the district headquarters, and Americans weary of combat rations flocked to "Howard Johnson's" for the excellent soup and noodle dishes. Shoppers in the black market, conveniently located next to the regular market, could find Schlitz beer in cans, and hand grenades, at bargain prices.

There were children everywhere.

The shrill voices of eighty-seven children at the Buddhist pagoda and day school filled the hours of 1st Lieutenant Thomas Stamper, who worked next door in the advisers' office at the South Vietnamese district headquarters. Most of the Vietnamese in town sent their children to Khe Sanh's public school, but thirty had enrolled in Father Poncet's parochial classes. Pastor Loc had dozens of Bru children in his classes at the Protestant compound on the east end of the village.

The July census had counted 8,930 Bru in the Khe Sanh district, but more than 10,000 were crowded into resettlement areas near the village by the end of the year.

Father Poncet had borrowed some of the Millers' new trained Bru teachers and, with some Vietnamese nuns recruited in Hue, opened a school in a Bru hamlet. Zipping along on his motor scooter in an open-necked white shirt and blue bloused trousers, the bearded priest was a familiar figure from the Bru hamlets near Lang Vei to the front gates of the combat base.

Felix Poilane's coffee groves were slowly giving way to the military needs of the Marines. Tanks and bulldozers and heavy trucks rumbled up and down his farm roads; power saws cleared fields of fire. The Marines had already filled one of the gullies on the plantation with garbage, and they were scouting for a second site.

The French farmer could hardly protest. Many Marine officers made it clear that they believed he must have made some "arrangement" with the enemy to be able to live at Khe Sanh.

"Felix would be treated with great respect as a leader and economic mainstay of the whole area," Carolyn Miller said, "but at the flip of the coin he would be regarded with great suspicion—not to say *rudeness*—as being, at best, someone who paying off the Communist guerrillas and, at worst, a spy them."

But the Poilanes—and the Millers and Father Poncet and Pastor Loc and the great majority of civilians in and around Khe Sanh Village—had never seen an enemy soldier.

Madeleine Poilane had lived in Khe Sanh for almost ten years without fear; now she was growing concerned. "The base installed on our concession . . . is certainly very tempting for the Viet Cong," she worried.

Felix Poilane had driven coffee convoys through the mountains

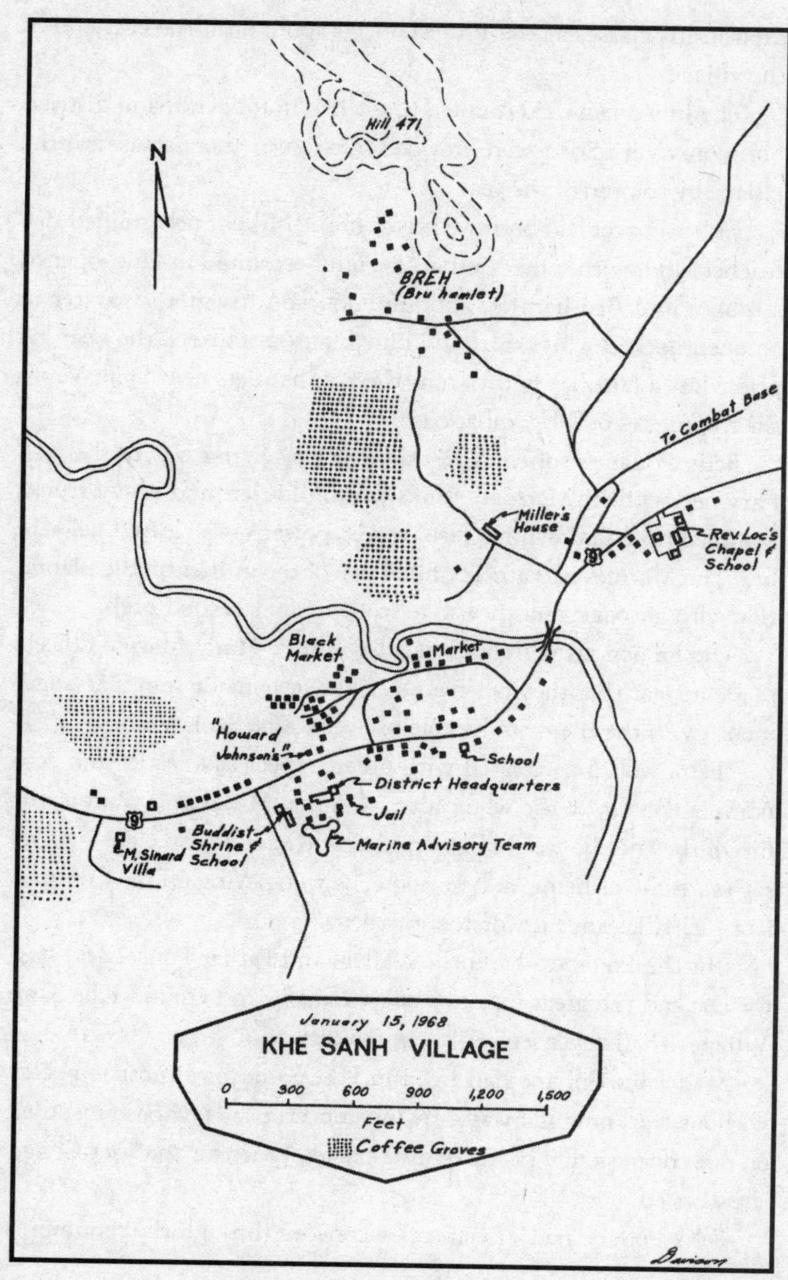
Hill 471
N
BREH
(Bru hamlet)
To Combat Base
Miller's House
9
Rev. Loc's Chapel & School
Black Market
Market
"Howard Johnson's"
School
District Headquarters
Jail
Marine Advisory Team
Buddist Shrine & School
9
M. Sinard Villa
January 15, 1968
KHE SANH VILLAGE
0
300
600
900
1,200
1,500
Feet
Coffee Groves
Davison

of Laos as his father told stories about the hills. He had been born in Khe Sanh, and now he'd labored to build a plantation of his own.

"If I ever had to pay protection money, I'd leave," he declared.

Deeply engrossed in their translation work, the Millers had no time for military concerns. The Marines had finally stopped bringing Bru prisoners to the Miller house for military interrogation. The Millers were rarely home, anyway. They now had six schools operating in the Khe Sanh area, and almost every day they drove their sturdy Land Rover over the rutted roads to deliver new teaching materials or to review class lessons.

Once, they passed through the middle of a Marine combat operation, smiling and waving at the open-mouthed young men who crouched in flak jackets along the sides of the road. "It must be a USO show," one awed Marine said as they drove past.

Marine patrols pushing tentatively along the narrow native trails west of the combat base sometimes came upon Carolyn Miller striding along the same path, a bundle of books under one arm.

Colonel Lownds called on the Millers to scold them in a friendly, but concerned, way—and to deliver a bag of fresh groceries. The 3rd Marine Division's commanding general, Bruno Hochmuth, had been sending food packages to the Millers since August when Route 9 was cut.

"What a treat that was!" Carolyn recalled. "John and I used to laugh that we were probably the only people in the world who had groceries delivered by a Marine colonel."

General Tompkins assumed command of the division in December after Hochmuth became the first American general to be killed in Vietnam when his helicopter exploded in mid-air near Hue.

Two days after Christmas, as Dabney and the new Third battalion scouted an assault route into Laos, Westmoreland cabled Washington with a detailed proposal for a strike across the border.

On New Year's Day, Marine Chaplain Ray Stubbe hitched a

ride from the combat base to town to sample the soup at Howard Johnson's. He walked back, an hour's stroll that took him past the Poilane villa.

The next evening, at 8:30, a sentry dog on the western perimeter of the base stiffened, then alerted his handler to movement outside the defensive wire. A few minutes later six men appeared out of the darkness, stopped, and began talking quietly as they studied the Marine defenses. Second Lieutenant Niles B. Buffington took a squad to investigate and, to his astonishment, found "six men dressed like Marines." When one of the figures reached toward his belt, the Marines opened fire—killing all but one of the intruders. Documents on the bodies identified the dead men as enemy regimental officers.

Extraordinary excitement crackled in the stale air of the Marines' command bunker when Lownds' staff realized who had been killed. These Marines were career officers who had trained and prepared all of their adult lives for battle. They looked at the shattered bodies of their peers and knew the waiting was nearly over.

News of Buffington's score raced up the chain of command to Saigon. Almost immediately, additional evidence arrived to confirm the unprecedented intelligence coup.

Intelligence sources reported that two regiments of the North Vietnamese Army's 325C Division had crossed into South Vietnam about fifteen miles northwest of Khe Sanh and that two regiments of the NVA's 320 Division had crossed the DMZ to take up positions fifteen to twenty miles to the northeast—"within easy reinforcing range." Then came word from the earphoned technicians who listened in on enemy communications: a Front Headquarters had been established across the border in Laos to direct operations of the 325C Division and of a *third* division, the 304.

A photo analyst in Saigon discovered a new road snaking down out of the jagged Laotian mountains to a trail head inside

Vietnam—just fifteen miles from Khe Sanh. Another road was discovered, crossing the border eight miles from the combat base.

To the astonishment of the American command, "hostile units seemed to be materializing all along the line of bases . . . just south of the DMZ."

It hardly seemed possible, yet the evidence pointed toward a major North Vietnamese offensive against Marine positions in South Vietnam at the very instant Westmoreland was preparing a major offensive against enemy positions in Laos.

Westmoreland changed his plans. If the North Vietnamese wanted to belly up to American defensive positions the way they had at Dak To and Loc Ninh, he would be pleased to accommodate them. The massing of enemy forces was "a very real threat to the Marines at Khe Sanh," but it was "an undeniable opportunity to direct concentrated air strikes against known enemy positions on a sustained basis."

On January 5, Westmoreland initiated planning for a massive bombing campaign. Colonel Lownds learned about it, and drove immediately to the Millers' house to urge them to leave Khe Sanh until the battle was over. He had adopted the missionaries after General Hochmuth's death, sent American television crews to film their work with the Bru, and passed the hat in his regiment to buy equipment for their schools. He did not want to see them killed.

On January 6, the concept now clear in his mind, Westmoreland chose Niagara as the code name for the bombardment program.

Very quickly, American intelligence filled in important details on the gathering enemy force. The 325C Division was a veteran of the Hill Fights, while the 304 Division was new to South Vietnam. The intelligence teams' reference books identified the 304 as "a veteran of Dienbienphu." The two infantry divisions, with up to 20,000 men, would be supported by the North Vietnamese Army's 68th and 164th Artillery Regiments and, possibly, armored units. The

320 Division seemed to have settled down north of the Rockpile, but it was within striking distance of Khe Sanh. The 324 Division was working in a supply role along the hidden roads in Laos. The total enemy force that might be available for battle could go as high as forty thousand troops.

The target was so huge, so *alluring* after the long years of empty sweeps and patrols, that Westmoreland on January 8 ordered all intelligence gathering activities to focus on Khe Sanh.

• • •

LOCATING THE ENEMY force proved to be difficult.

Marine patrols kept running into the enemy's counter-reconnaissance screen—a thin row of pickets who quickly detected American scouting parties. Patrolling became "a very hazardous business," and Colonel Lownds often spent great quantities of ammunition and sometimes a helicopter or two to extract hard-pressed recon teams from the field.

A few shells began to fall on the combat base as enemy gunners registered their weapons on the American positions.

"They're going to attack," Lownds told his staff on January 10, "and we're going to inflict a heavy loss on them."

The colonel was increasingly apprehensive about the approaching test of arms. On January 13 he ordered every Marine on the base to begin wearing his flak jacket and carrying his rifle at all times.

Lownds felt thin on the ground. His Marines seemed scattered from hell to breakfast, and he did not relish the thought of ten thousand North Vietnamese crashing into one of his outposts. He did not have all his people tucked into a single, impregnable fortress; the tactical situation *required* him to fragment his forces.

"Both General Tompkins and Colonel Lownds were well aware of what had happened at Dienbienphu when the Viet Minh owned the mountains and the French owned the valley," a Marine staff officer explained. "It was essential that the hills around Khe Sanh remain in the hands of the Marines."

Captain Dabney and India Company, 300 men including radio spooks and artillery units, held the top of Hill 881 South, the westernmost American position in South Vietnam, the end of the line. Lownds would send another 100 men to bolster Dabney's force in the next few days, but India Company was just going to have to make do. The hill was only four miles from the combat base, but there was no realistic chance of overland reinforcement—not through that terrain of twisted liana, clumps of bamboo, thorn trees, thick brush, slippery red mud, and deep grass. Not without grievous casualties. General Tompkins, exploring every contingency, had already thought the unthinkable: that Dabney might have to be sacrificed.

A little closer to the combat base, a thousand yards due east of Dabney, was Hill 861, another dominant terrain feature considered vital to the defense of the airfield. Captain Norman J. Jasper Jr. and 200 men of Company K were dug into its crown, supported by two heavy mortars.

A single platoon of less than fifty men on Hill 950 protected the antennas that relayed Marine messages to Dong Ha.

Lownds felt more secure about the defensive prowess of the combat base, where he had eighteen 105mm howitzers, six 155mm guns, six 4.2-inch mortars and even six tanks that had been stranded at Khe Sanh when Route 9 was cut. One valued item in his arsenal was the Ontos, a squat, ugly vehicle that mounted six 106mm recoilless rifles. Lownds had ten of these highly-mobile, tracked killers—and enough flechette ammunition to pin the entire North Vietnamese Army to the face of Co Roc Mountain.

The colonel could call for covering fire from the sixteen 175mm guns at Camp Carroll and the Rockpile—or he could crook his finger and undam the torrent of aerial firepower that waited in the skies over Khe Sanh.

Nevertheless, Lownds enthusiastically welcomed the arrival on January 16 of another thousand men, the second battalion of his own regiment. The Rao Quang River, which flowed right past the combat base, came down out of the mountains in a deep jungled ravine that could allow a large enemy force to approach Khe Sanh undetected. Lownds sent the new battalion to Hill 558 which overlooked the river valley and plugged the Rao Quang gap. The new position could also support Hill 861.

Westmoreland and his top Marine and Air Force adviser had carefully weighed the addition of one thousand men at Khe Sanh, and finally decided that prudence required reinforcement. The problem was supply. The food and ammunition required to support another battalion would push Air Force resupply capabilities closer to the red line, but it could be done. It had to be done.

The Marines hunkered down to await the onslaught.

"My whole plan for the defense of Khe Sanh [is] to make the enemy come to us," declared General Tompkins, reflecting Westmoreland's concept of Khe Sanh as a bait that would "lure the enemy to their deaths." Major Mirza M. Baig, who coordinated intelligence reports with firepower missions in Lownds' command bunker, explained it best:

"Our entire philosophy [is] to allow the enemy to surround us closely, to mass about us, to reveal his troop and logistic routes, to establish his dumps and assembly areas, and to prepare his siege works as energetically as he desires. The result [will be] an enormous quantity of targets . . . ideal for heavy bombers."

Colonel Lownds studied reports from the Special Forces team at Lang Vei, and matched them to rumors picked up by Marine civic action teams in the Bru hamlets. The U.S. Army advisers in town passed along information they heard in the South Vietnamese district headquarters, and the SOG people at Fort Dix grilled wandering Montagnards for news. Patching it together with the intelligence captured on spy-plane film and radio-intercept tapes, the Marines managed to find twelve targets for large B-52 raids in mid-January, but Lownds still did not know where his enemy hid.

On January 18, Westmoreland decided that the looming battle at Khe Sanh was so important and the detection of enemy movement so critical that he would risk compromising his most-secret intelligence-gathering weapons: seismic/acoustic sensors.

These devices were so highly classified that only one officer in Lownds' entire regiment had ever heard of them. U.S. Senator Barry Goldwater believed the sensors represented "one of the greatest steps forward in warfare since gunpowder."

The sensors had been developed for an electronic barrier system first proposed by Defense Secretary McNamara. Depressed by rising American combat casualties along the DMZ, McNamara had suggested pulling the Marines back from the line of outposts and letting electronic equipment monitor enemy movement. Construction of "McNamara's Wall" had been abandoned by January of 1968—the military did not like the idea and the secretary was on his way out—but the sensors had survived its demise.

Air Force operatives had been using the sensors for months to monitor southbound truck traffic on the network of roads inside Laos known as the Ho Chi Minh Trail. The equipment was so good that Westmoreland had reports on his desk showing that 1,116 enemy trucks rolled past Khe Sanh in October, 3,823 trucks in November, and 6,315 trucks in December.

Planes and helicopters planted the sensor devices by simply pitching them out the door at precisely mapped locations near known enemy trails.

Seismic sensors plummeted down in freefall to stick deeply in the earth on a steel spike. The jolt activated a mechanism which deployed a broadcast antenna. Whenever a truck rumbled past, or a nearby enemy force started to dig bunkers, or five hundred troops marched down the trail, the sensor picked up the vibrations and radioed the information to American intelligence.

Acoustic sensors drifted down by parachute to hang in trees above enemy roads and base areas. Air Force technicians could turn these on by remote control and actually listen to enemy conversations; they had once heard the excited voices of enemy soldiers who had spotted an acoustic sensor in a tree, the sounds of axes, and the agonized scream of someone hurt by the falling tree. A delicate crystal inside the sensor self-destructed if anyone tried to open its equipment pod.

The Air Force sowed 250 sensors around Khe Sanh in a few days and, because there was too little time to train the Marines on the complex equipment, continued to operate the detection system. An electronic laboratory circling over Khe Sanh picked up the signals of seismic sensors on the ground and transmitted them to Nakhom Phanom in Thailand where computers in the Infiltration Surveillance Center compared the incoming signals with previously stored sample signals to determine what caused the sensor to activate. The secret detachment in Thailand then relayed the information to the fire control center at Khe Sanh for an artillery mission against the enemy target.

Almost immediately, the sensors began broadcasting reports of enemy movement west and north of Khe Sanh. The Marines quickly switched from harassment and interdiction fire—to aimed fire at sensor-identified targets.

Lownds still didn't have eyes, but he had *ears*.

• • •

COLONEL LOWNDS WAS convinced the enemy assault would come on January 20. He was listening very carefully to radio reports from Captain Dabney on the twentieth when John Miller, dispatched to safety two weeks earlier, walked in to say hello. Miller had returned to Khe Sanh to pick up some important materials and a skilled Bru assistant who could help with literacy materials while the Millers were away from the village.

Lownds approved the visit, but urged Miller to fly out that day.

As Lownds listened in the radio room, the Marines at Khe Sanh looked at the new movie schedule posted that morning.

There were six places to see movies at the combat base—this was, after all, war the American way and the Marines could look forward to feature films flown in from the States.

The schedule posted on January 20, 1968, read:

Saturday, Jan. 20	Paradise Hawaiian Style
Sunday, Jan. 21	Murderer's Row
Monday, Jan. 22	Beau Geste
Tuesday, Jan. 23	One Spy Too Many
Wednesday, Jan. 24	Gunsmoke

4.

"Here They Come!"

At two o'clock in the afternoon of January 20, Colonel Lownds and his staff paced restlessly in the command bunker listening to radio reports from Captain Dabney's fight on Hill 881 North. The battle had been going on for more than four hours. Repeated airstrikes had failed to relieve the pressure on India Company. Perhaps the battle for Khe Sanh was about to begin.

At that instant, tense Marines on the combat base perimeter spotted a white flag waving in the scrub brush off the eastern end of the airstrip.

An enemy soldier in a green camouflage uniform and bush hat stepped into the open, raising the white flag with one hand and gripping an AK-47 assault rifle with the other. Covered instantly by the rifles and machine guns of thirty Marines, he walked slowly toward the American lines. A pair of Ontos waddled over, grunting and clattering, to train ninety-six thousand steel darts at the first live North Vietnamese Army officer these Marines had ever seen.

First Lieutenant La Than Tonc, which is how he introduced himself, turned out to be the Sutter's Mill of intelligence finds.

Indeed, the deserter's revelations were so extraordinary that at first the Marines doubted him. How could a mere lieutenant know such detail? And he seemed so *eager.*

"I decided that we would accept the information as valid," said

General Tompkins. "We had nothing to lose and stood to gain a great deal.

"I recalled that sometime before—at Dak To in the Highlands—a similar event had occurred. The Army staff tended to believe the information was too good to be true and should be discounted. The commanding general ruled otherwise, and events vindicated his judgment."

La Than Tonc's information was breathtaking: no less than "a detailed description of the forthcoming Communist offensive"—not just at Khe Sanh but throughout all of I Corps.

The first assaults would begin precisely a half-hour past midnight, the enemy officer said. North Vietnamese troops would strike at Hill 881 South, Hill 861, and the combat base itself. After crushing the defenders at Khe Sanh, the enemy tidal wave would roll east and south to capture all of Quang Tri and Thua Thien provinces, finally raising the gold-starred, red and blue Liberation flag in Hue.

Lownds moved on the tactical information instantly.

Captain Dabney was angrily demanding more air support to quell the fire that raked his position on Hill 881 North. At three in the afternoon, as interrogators worked with Lt. Tonc, a medical evacuation helicopter had refused to pick up his wounded because of heavy enemy fire. It would be stupid for India Company to meet a North Vietnamese Army regimental assault in such an exposed position when the company had prepared defenses in depth atop Hill 881 South. Lownds recalled Dabney at once.

The colonel shared his timely news with the Special Forces commander, the American advisers in Khe Sanh village, and General Tompkins. He ordered the Officers' Club and all six movies closed until further notice, and placed the base and the hilltop outposts on Red Alert.

But La Than Tonc had only begun to talk.

With some pride he identified himself as the commanding officer of the 14th Anti-Aircraft Company, currently in support of the 95C Infantry Regiment of the 325C Division. Here was hard information that the cool, tough, professional unit that had hurt the Marines in the Hill Fights was back at Khe Sanh.

But why had Tonc defected? Why betray his comrades?

For fourteen years, the lieutenant said, he had served in the field with an army at war. He had distinguished himself in battle, constantly courting death as he challenged American control of the air. Now his superiors had chosen an officer with less service and, he believed, fewer qualifications, for promotion to captain. Bitterly disappointed, Tonc decided to defect.

The Marine interrogators could understand such disappointment.

It was inconceivable to this generation of American officers that a man could spend fourteen years in service and fail to make captain—especially in an army that had to be suffering heavy casualties in its officer corps. Under Westmoreland's one-year policy, American officers spent six months in the field with a U.S. unit, then six months on staff or advising Vietnamese. The effective service time for most officers, because of casualties, Rest and Recreation leaves, and transfer lags, was about five months, but the program gave a boost to the career of ambitious military men. The Marines who listened to Lieutenant Tonc's tale realistically aspired to be on the list for colonelcy when they had fourteen years of service. They regarded Tonc with genuine sympathy.

The defector described in detail the assembly areas and attack routes of two regiments of the 325 Division. He gave the battle plans of the 304 Division, especially its role in the attack on the combat base.

The 68th Regiment (artillery) was digging into the face of Co Roc for the coming battle, he said, and both the 308 and the 341 North Vietnamese Army divisions had crossed the DMZ in recent days, near Con Thien, and Gio Linh. The 320 Division was poised for an attack on Camp Carroll to silence the big guns that supported

Khe Sanh. The 4th Battalion of the Van An Rocket Artillery Regiment and the Vinh Linh Rocket Battalion were even now crossing the DMZ to attack the Marines' rear bases at Dong Ha and Quang Tri City.

"He willingly gave a wealth of information to his interrogators with more detail than would be expected of an officer in his position," the Marines reported. "He was able to give extensive details of the forthcoming Tet Offensive, the plans for besieging Khe Sanh, and preparations for an imminent attack [on the hilltop outposts]."

Deception, decoys, and misdirection were North Vietnamese trademarks. The Marines struggled briefly not to believe the defector, but Lieutenant Tonc's information dovetailed perfectly with the intelligence gathered by radio intercept equipment. The "materializing" of enemy units all along the DMZ suddenly became real.

Few commanders in history have possessed perfect knowledge of

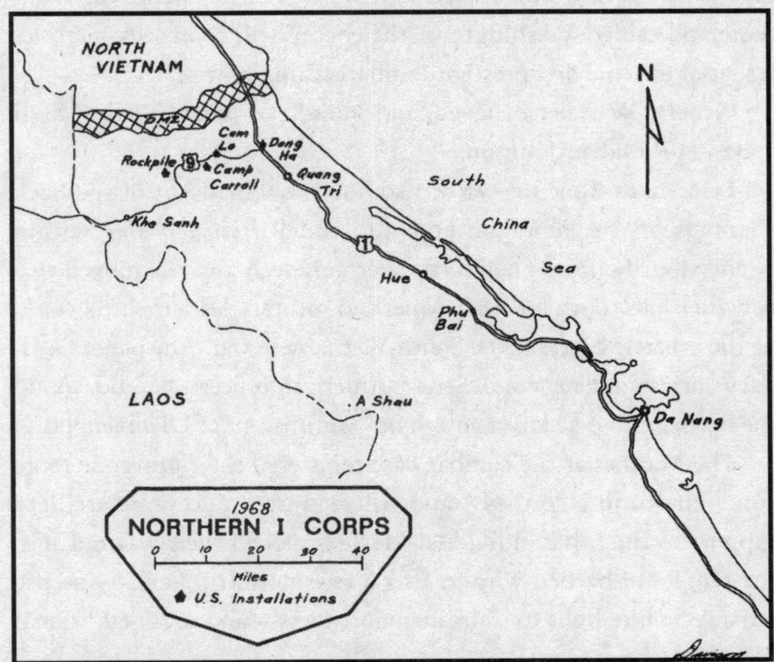

their enemy's plans before battle. In the recorded instances when a commander has received the precise time and route of attack, he has almost always refused to accept the evidence on the grounds that it *must* be false. Russia's supreme commander, for example, knew the hour and strength of Germany's massive assault into the Soviet Union in June of 1941 but refused to believe the information.

Lownds believed.

Lieutenant Tonc was a hundred times more valuable than the five riddled bodies of January 2. The defector's news just might be the most timely and important intelligence of the war. This latest Marine coup *rocketed* up the chain of command.

General Tompkins believed. General Cushman believed.

Westmoreland believed. His intelligence chief telephoned his wife in the United States and told her that "a tense operational situation" made it impossible for him to join her in Honolulu for a planned week of Rest and Recreation. Late on the twentieth, Westmoreland cabled Washington: "the enemy will soon seek victories essential to achieving prestige and bargaining power."

General Wheeler believed, and so did the Joint Chiefs of Staff and even President Johnson.

Lieutenant Tonc's news was so hot it bubbled out of the back channels of the Pentagon and into the *Washington Star* within twenty-four hours. "The North Vietnamese Army has moved two new divisions south for what American military leaders think could be the greatest battle of the South Vietnamese war," the paper's military correspondent wrote. Senior American officers, he said, found the battleground at Khe Sanh to be "reminiscent of Dienbienphu."

The Marines at the combat base registered their guns one more time, fine-tuning so they could deliver instant, accurate artillery support to the hills. Individual Marines picked their way out into the tangles of barbed wire to affix a few more trip flares—intense bursts of white light to illuminate intruders—and to set additional Claymore mines.

As dark closed over the plateau, short bursts of machine gun fire and the hard cracking of M-14 rifles could be heard around every perimeter as the Marines cleared their weapons for the coming battle. They were forewarned, armed, alert, ready.

• • •

AT EXACTLY THIRTY minutes past midnight, North Vietnamese gunners pounded Hill 861 with hundreds of rockets, mortar shells, and rocket-propelled grenades. Heavy machine guns lashed the hilltop, the bullets sometimes clanging insanely inside the open fifty-five-gallon drums that Company K had installed to drain away the monsoon floods.

At one o'clock, 250 NVA soldiers climbed the steep southwest slope of the hill under extremely heavy artillery fire and plunged unhesitatingly into the Marines' "interlocking bands of grazing machine gun fire." The enemy's elite combat engineers, the *dac cong,* led the attack. They breached the defensive wire with Bangalore torpedos and blasted pathways with satchel charges. Some threw bamboo ladders across the wire and leaped into the forward Marine trenches. Assault troops followed them through the gaps.

Captain Jasper was hit once trying to rally his men, then wounded again. A third bullet knocked him down, and his executive officer took command. The company's gunnery sergeant was killed, and the Marines pulled back to a slightly higher piece of ground on Hill 861's crest. Enemy troops overran the helicopter landing zone and began searching through captured bunkers and trenches for Marine survivors. Company K's senior surviving sergeant was still on his feet, but he had to pinch together a gaping wound in his throat to keep from bleeding to death.

Dabney's Marines, waiting their turn in the maelstrom of battle, strained their eyes into the black mists while they listened to the crash of shells and rifles only a thousand yards away. Deep in the command bunker with Dabney were most of the top officers of his battalion. They had helicoptered to the hilltop the previous afternoon to get a good close look at India's fight on 881 North, then been stranded when the weather closed down like wet velvet curtains.

They waited, and waited, and waited.

Not a single mortar shell fell on 881 South that night. Not a single *dac cong* crept forward in the harsh white light of trip flares.

Finally, it was decided to join the fight on Hill 861. Rationing the shells twenty at a time, just in case the enemy did come, India Company's mortars hammered the North Vietnamese over the next few hours with 680 rounds.

Company K hung tough.

The mortarmen on Hill 861 never stopped firing, just tilting their tubes a tad to drop bombs on their own lines after the North Vietnamese overran the trenches on one half the hilltop. Sergeant Stephen L. Goddard found one mortar crew at the height of battle bellowing stanzas from "The Marine Hymn." Captain Jasper's radioman, blinded by an explosion, relayed target coordinates to gunners on 881 South "as calm, cool and collected as a telephone operator in New York City."

At 5 A.M., Company K attacked back down the trenchlines, shouting and shooting. Individual Americans and North Vietnamese grappled and stabbed in "vicious hand-to-hand fighting." Some Marines engaged in brutal, short-range grenade duels, curling up fetally to absorb the blasts of shrapnel in their flak jackets and steel helmets. At 5:15 A.M. the defenders radioed the combat base that they had cleared Hill 861 of enemy soldiers—except for fourteen bodies left behind in the rush to escape.

Colonel Lownds, General Tompkins, and Westmoreland himself breathed more easily when the defensive perimeter was restored.

It had been a near thing. Marine officers believed the battle could have gone the other way if the combat base artillery had not so thoroughly churned the slopes as to make it impossible for enemy reserves to exploit the breakthrough.

Lownds was thinking about getting replacements to the hilltop as soon as the fog cleared, lifting out the casualties, and finding reinforcements to strengthen the position. The battle for Hill 861 had been sobering: several hundred enemy soldiers had actually cracked one of the hilltop fortresses—and their attack plans had been *known*. No great exercise of imagination was necessary to predict the outcome of an assault by five thousand North Vietnamese.

• • •

THE MARINES HAD only a few minutes to celebrate the success of Company K's counterattack.

At 5:30 A.M. a great swarm of rockets ignited on the south-facing slopes of Hill 881 North, streaked almost directly over Dabney's position and slammed into the combat base.

The first of the rockets hit inside an earthen bunker on the eastern perimeter of the base. In a colossal explosion that bathed the Khe Sanh plateau in the glaring white light of Apocalypse, the bulk of Lownds' fifteen hundred tons of stored ammunition detonated.

The shock wave tumbled helicopters like toys, swept away tents and buildings, collapsed the walls of the post office and the PX, curled up steel matting on the airfield and knocked out landing lights and radio antennas.

Tar drums and barrels of aviation fuel ignited, then flooded into the ammunition dump in rivers of flame. Unexploded shells began to cook off in the roaring petroleum fires.

Choking clouds of tear gas, released from the Marines' own stores, swirled across the combat base so thickly that even gas masks didn't work.

The cauldron boiled hottest at the eastern end of the airstrip.

Bravo Company, basking in praise after its live capture of Lieutenant Tonc, was waiting here for the enemy's main assault. Among the many gifts brought by the defecting North Vietnamese officer was the news that the enemy's 304th Division would send an assault regiment at this very place. As chance would have it, this was the sector that included the petroleum-oil-lubricant storage depot and all of the ammunition.

Second Lieutenant John W. Dillon held his platoon in the line, primed for the attack, even though tons of ammunition were going off within fifty yards. Blinding explosions rocked the base, and the eruptions threw up hundreds of unexploded but partially fused or dangerously heated shells. Some exploded on impact. Some hurtled out of the blast furnace and bowled over Marines as they searched for better cover. So many hundreds of artillery shells, half-baked LAW canisters, 106mm recoilless rifle rounds, and mortar bombs cascaded down from the sky that Dillon's trenches literally filled to the brim with unexploded rounds in some places.

Bravo Company's command post moved three times during the morning to try to escape the skittering, tumbling American shells, all the while dodging enemy rockets and shells. After one tremendous explosion, some of Bravo's stunned officers looked down at themselves to discover steel darts sticking in their flak jackets, shirt sleeves—and the skin of their hands and faces. The flechette ammo had blown.

The expected infantry assault never came, but five of the ten men in Bravo Company's command group that night were evacuated from Khe Sanh with "extreme combat fatigue."

At 6:30 A.M., with fire still eating one-hundred-ton chunks out of the ammunition dump, North Vietnamese troops crashed into the western edge of Khe Sanh village.

They cut their way through the defensive wires, penetrated the government compound, and seized the dispensary building. Lieutenant Stamper, who could hear enemy shouts in the schoolyard where children had sung the day before, called Lownds for assistance.

The colonel was dealing with a tactical emergency in his ammunition supplies. He expected the enemy's main assault on the combat base at any minute. It just wasn't possible to send relief force to the village, Lownds told Stamper; he would try to help with artillery.

Working under extremely hazardous conditions, the Marine artillery and mortars had been firing at phantoms in the mist while glowing duds from their own ammo dump rained down all around them.

Every few minutes another enemy rocket or shell would crash inside the combat base perimeter. These were big 122mm rockets, each of them six feet long, weighing more than one hundred pounds, and they hit like the sledgehammer of God. High velocity shells from enemy artillery pieces deep inside Laos screeched out of the sky with such force that no bunker on the base was immune. The 26th Marines' mess hall was demolished.

The Marines ached to answer, but they had no targets.

They could blast the sides of Hill 861 and they could smash the enemy force in the village, but they could not find the enemy guns.

Most of the North Vietnamese mortars were hidden beneath the thick fog blanket of the early morning; some sounded tantalizingly close, but could not be located precisely enough to hit. The enemy artillery was simply too far away in Laos to be reached by anything at Khe Sanh. One of the reasons Westmoreland had wanted the Army's big 175mm guns at the combat base was to answer the enemy's long-range 152mm and 130 artillery in the mountains of Laos. One of the reasons the North Vietnamese had ambushed the artillery convoy in August was to guarantee this weapons overmatch in January.

Desperate for information that could give his guns targets, Major Ronald W. Campbell ran from one fresh shell hole to another to finger the hot fragments, measure the depth of the crater with a practiced eye, and orient the splash of shrapnel on the earth. From these clues he guessed at the caliber, distance, and direction of the enemy weapon, translated the estimates into firing coordinates, then raced to his guns to shoot back down the arc in the hope of silencing the North Vietnamese weapons.

It wasn't much, but it was better than shooting shells into the fog.

On this first morning of the siege at Khe Sanh, the Marine gunners learned a bitter lesson:

"We were never able to silence the heavy artillery and rockets that could bear on the Khe Sanh Combat Base."

• • •

SHORTLY AFTER 8 A.M., Lieutenant Stamper and a few Marines on civic action duty rallied the Vietnamese forces in the village and drove the North Vietnamese out. The victory surprised everyone, especially the ragged force of South Vietnamese regional troops, which was ill-equipped and anxious to avoid serious combat with professional soldiers from the north.

An uneasy calm settled over Khe Sanh. The Marines still battled heavy fires in the ammunition dump, and irregular shellfire plowed the airstrip to discourage landings. At 10 A.M. a half ton of plastic explosive went off with an earth-shaking concussion that almost entombed the command staff of the First Battalion—the chief defenders of the combat base. The blast cracked the timbers in the command bunker, and the beams sagged under the great weight of piled sandbags. Dirt showered down, but the beams held and work continued as new posts were wedged into the bunker to hold the ceiling.

Late in the afternoon, several hundred North Vietnamese soldiers renewed the attack on the government headquarters. This time the defenders held the assault troops in place with heavy machine gun fire and called in one thousand rounds of artillery fused to explode in the air just above the defensive wire. Lieutenant Stamper asked the guns to hit the pagoda, which overlooked his defenses. The Buddhist steeple collapsed with the third volley. An air strike leveled Howard Johnson's. A Marine fighter-bomber came in very low to rip the enemy ranks with explosive shells, claiming one hundred kills. The enemy attack was easily repulsed.

Colonel Lownds decided in the late afternoon to abandon the village. Because he believed the road between the combat base and Khe Sanh might be held by enemy forces, he sent helicopters to pick up the Americans. South Vietnamese government officials and regional troops would have to walk to the combat base. Lownds shrugged; he had too much on his mind right now to practice diplomacy.

The colonel was struggling with serious problems as dark began to thicken in the jungled gorges around Khe Sanh. He had lost ninety-eight percent of his ammunition in the explosion and fires of the morning. In a secret message to Tompkins, he complained bitterly that he had to use his remaining shells to suppress enemy antiaircraft fire—otherwise U.S. pilots refused to deliver urgently needed ammunition. Only six cargo planes landed at Khe Sanh on January 21, bringing in a microscopic 24 tons of supplies. Lownds needed more than 160 tons a day to maintain the status quo—and the status quo was terrible. The ammunition shortage was "critical, to say the least."

The combat base was a shambles.

Fires burned everywhere. Even solid bunkers smoldered fitfully: the Marines had soaked the sandbags in fuel oil hoping it might repel rats. Pools of gasoline flamed in the dark. The base was littered with duds from the ammo dump, ruined building parts and torn tents, pieces of shrapnel and hundreds of thousands of steel darts, everywhere.

Enemy shellfire had reduced usable runway from thirty-nine hundred feet to two thousand feet, and knocked out the landing lights.

Hill 861 needed replacements and reinforcements as soon as possible; the base artillery would not be able to provide the same quality of support if the enemy came again tonight.

Khe Sanh Village was lost.

More than 1,000 terrified Vietnamese civilians had arrived at the gates of the combat base. Felix and Madeleine Poilane were there, too, with their children—and with five nuns from the Catholic school. They pleaded to be let in, but Lownds would let only a very few through the gates; he feared the introduction of a Trojan horse into his battered fortress.

• • •

JANUARY 21 FRIGHTENED the American Command.

The North Vietnamese had committed fewer than 1,000 troops. Their plans had been hopelessly compromised, but the enemy had taken the village, destroyed the Marines' ammunition, and nearly overrun one hilltop. American casualties had not been serious, even in the bitter fighting on 861, but it was now much more difficult to be certain about the outcome if 10,000 or 20,000 enemy soldiers emerged from the swirling fog.

5.

"I Don't Want Any Damn Dinbinfoo"

Captain Larry Budge reached inside his leather briefcase and pulled out a paperback book with a blood red cover: Jules Roy's *The Battle of Dienbienphu*. The only sound in the small, upholstered cabin was the faint clean whine of the engines of Westmoreland's executive jet. Across the aisle, the general was giving numbers to a newspaper reporter while the astonishingly green hills of Vietnam unrolled far below. During these stolen moments in brutally busy days Budge read accounts of one of the most extraordinary battles in history.

The guns had fallen silent at Dienbienphu only thirteen years ago, but the battle had already been accorded classic status.

Captain Budge, who was Westmoreland's personal aide, had already read another brilliant work on Dienbienphu, Bernard Fall's *Hell in a Very Small Place.* This book, too, was covered in red cloth. Like poppies, Fall and Roy bloomed on the khaki bookshelves of every thoughtful officer in the United States military—in the Canal Zone as well as in Saigon. Fall and Roy were textbooks at West Point, and they had been translated into German and Russian and Spanish. When the 304th North Vienamese Army division was first identified near Khe Sanh in early 1968, the intelligence report used a description lifted verbatim from the appendices of *Hell in a Very Small Place.* As soon as Westmoreland's aide finished Roy's book, he planned to read Fall again from the new perspective of *The Battle of Dienbienphu*.

Everyone read and thought about Dienbienphu.

On May 7, 1954, thousands of triumphant Vietnamese had rushed the shattered defenses of an isolated French garrison in the mountains to claim victory on the fifty-sixth day of a terrible siege. Against every prediction and in spite of all thoughtful analysis, Vietnamese General Vo Nguyen Giap had managed to deliver enormous quantities of shells and supplies to the distant battlefield, and to pound 13,000 French defenders into submission. His peasant army had out-generaled, out-supplied, and out-fought France's finest soldiers.

Americans fought today where Frenchmen had failed yesterday. Even the battlefields were the same; Colonel Lownds and his staff at the Khe Sanh Combat Base worked in an old French bunker. Vo Nguyen Giap, the architect of Dienbienphu, still commanded the enemy forces.

Only very stupid military officers ignored these parallels; most thought of little else. Dienbienphu had dominated American planning and tactics from the very beginning. On the day the French surrendered, in 1954, drill sergeants at Quanitco, Va. lined up Marine trainees and announced grimly: "Dienbienphu just fell. Your rifles had better be clean."

Each year in Vietnam on the anniversary of Dienbienphu, American officers doubled the guard and put out extra listening posts and ambush patrols. In 1966, Lt. Col. Henry E. Emerson was sweeping draws and valleys in central Vietnam with a paratroop battalion, but feeling very edgy about being in the field in mid-May. His brigade commander, Brig. Gen. Willard Pearson, was also nervous, and so was Major General H.W.O. Kinnard, the II Corps commander. Again and again Kinnard had been warned, once by the admiral in Hawaii who commanded all U.S. forces in the Pacific:

"Remember, we don't want any Dienbienphus, not one, not even a little one."

It was hardly surprising, then, that American officers began to comment on the striking similarities between Dienbienphu and Khe Sanh, especially after January 21. Never had the specter of siege, and loss, loomed larger.

Every officer knew that if the North Vietnamese had put into Hill 861 and Khe Sanh Village the numbers of troops that the intelligence people had been predicting, both would have fallen. Two hundred Marines would have been snuffed out in a few short, vicious hours of combat.

Professional military men steel themselves for the moment when they might choose—or be forced—to stand and die. It is, after all, the final obligation of a military career. One essential consideration a soldier must make when he considers a life in the service is death in the service.

Westmoreland knew these rules, and so did Lownds at Khe Sanh; so did Dabney, and the great majority of the Marines—volunteers and draftees alike—who manned the hilltop outposts.

They would not choose to die, of course. They practiced the craft precisely to avoid the conditions in which death became inevitable. Still, the hurtling shells and hidden mines and sudden ambushes had made death a companion, and the professionals among them didn't rage when he sat in a friend's place at the table.

The Commander in Chief was not so philosophical. He lay awake at night worrying about a tidal wave of Orientals crashing over boys from Ohio and Virginia and Texas—and of long rows of flag-wrapped aluminum coffins.

Dienbienphu had already burned a place in Lyndon Johnson's mind. In 1954, as a Senate leader and key member of the Armed Services Committee, he had listened to top-secret intelligence briefings about Vo Nguyen Giap's use of thousands of coolies and bicycles to move guns and shells through impossible mountain terrain. He had heard how the Vietnamese, sensing a break point in their long colonial war with the French, had hurled themselves at Dienbienphu with unusual fervor. He had personally argued strongly, and successfully, against American intervention in the French bastion's final hours—and he had seen the photographs of the heaps of dead, the shattered stares of wounded, and the abandoned faces of the losers as they were led away in chains.

Lyndon Johnson knew that his top military advisers envsioned Khe Sanh as a trap to kill 10,000, 20,000, perhaps even 30,000 enemy soldiers in a single stroke. But the President also knew, with the deep certainty of a lifetime in politics, that no quantity of North Vietnamese bodies—not even the highest pile of corpses in the entire war—could offset the loss of the Marine base.

It would not be enough to kill at favorable ratios of six to one or ten to one, or even twenty to one. Khe Sanh could not fall.

President Johnson was tortured by the war in early 1968. The rising costs, the dead, the endlessness of it, had finally broken one of his most steadfast lieutenants, Defense Secretary Robert McNamara. Now the Senate, once his private preserve, was beginning to wonder if the Tonkin Gulf incident might have been an American provocation—and not a North Vietnamese act of war. The President had lost more than thirty points in the popularity polls, he had become insecure, fearful, and unsure about his course, and he had begun to think about not seeking a second term.

The possibility of a battlefield defeat had haunted Johnson from the outset of the war, but he had grown more concerned in recent months. Even before he had fully savored the glowing reports from Loc Ninh and Dak To, he heard from Westmoreland that "the Communists are preparing for a maximum military effort, and will soon try for a significant tactical victory."

In December, his security advisor, Walt W. Rostow, told the President that a newly captured document said the North Vietnamese "intend to reenact a new Dienbienphu." Then came the reports of the enemy build-up around Khe Sanh, and Westmoreland's warning that the North Vietnamese might be willing to make brief, terrible sacrifices for a significant political or propaganda gain.

The President began to make nightly visits to the Situation Room beneath the White House.

Johnson carried the fear with him when he flew to Australia on December 21 to attend memorial services for the prime minister, who had disappeared while swimming alone. Johnson told the Australian cabinet that he expected the North Vietnamese to use "Kamikaze tactics in the weeks ahead, committing their troops in a wave of suicide attacks." He stopped in Rome two days before Christmas, on his way back to the United States, and he told the pope about his fear of "Kamikaze attacks."

After January 21, the President began to demand more detailed information. He wanted to know how many planes were landing at Khe Sanh, how many tons of ammunition had been flown in that day—and how many more were needed. He wanted photographs, and maps, and he badgered his military aides for details on the battle.

JANUARY 22

Thick mists dimmed the dawn at the Khe Sanh Combat Base. Even before the sun burned away the fog at midmorning, however, bombs began furrowing the plateau. Westmoreland had decided that Lt. Tonc's gift of intelligence and the plight of Marines called for the undamming of Niagara.

The general assumed personal control over targeting for B-52s in southeast Asia. He wanted all of his hammer for this battle. His chief of air operations set up a special command post at Tan Son Nhut Air Base near Saigon specifically to orchestrate aerial operations around Khe Sanh. Two of the Army's more gifted tacticians,

General Creighton Abrams and Lt. Gen. William B. Rosson, stood each day over an elaborate sand table model of the Khe Sanh area, studying the ridges and draws and folds in the earth, trying to surmise the enemy's most likely routes of approach, encampment sites and supply points. Based on these thoughtful guesses, Westmoreland dispatched B-52s to Khe Sanh.

At the combat base, the first helicopter slapped the morning air with its blades. Immediately, enemy mortars coughed heavily in the near distance. The pre-aimed enemy scattered the American crews and damaged the ships. It going to be too costly to operate supply helicopters from combat base; from now on, they would fly from Quang Tri or Dong Ha, a half hour to the east.

Fighter bombers, reconnaissance planes, and communication laboratories were stacked past forty thousand feet over Khe Sanh, listening and looking and waiting for holes in the fog, when the first terrified cry for help came in on a radio sideband. Across the border, less than ten miles away, a friendly unit of the Laotian Army was being overrun. Two bomb-heavy B-57s and and a forward air controller went to assist.

Between heavy bursts of static, a Laotian radioman reported that armored vehicles had led a North Vietnamese infantry assault. His unit could hold no longer. The radio crackled with the sounds of panic and gunfire. Hoping for a shot at what might be the first enemy tanks in the war, the American bombers lingered long over the great, grey blanket that hid Laos. The clouds never parted; even million candle power flares winked out in the swallowing mists.

The sideband picked up a last cry for help, a few final blats of static—and the Laotians were gone.

Colonel Lownds was pleading for ammunition. Yesterday's air deliveries had brought in only one-tenth of what he needed, and his need was critical.

General Cushman sat down to rethink an overland push to the

combat base. The Millers used to drive this section of Route 9 in a few hours. Now it would take mine-sweeping, bridge-building, bulldozing—and fighting every foot of the way. Cushman shook his head. "Progress would be too slow," he decided, "and casualties too numerous."

Asking Lownds to march his people out on Route 9 was unthinkable: "Going down Route 9 would have been the Groupe Mobile 100 all over again. There was no way to get the troops out without a guaranteed one thousand casualties—fast."

The Marines at Khe Sanh would have to live by airlift, and it was already proving difficult. The few transports that tried landing in the chaos of January 21 had run gauntlets of enemy machine gun fire. North Vietnamese mortar shells searched the runways for taxiing planes, and tried to catch helicopters on the ground.

As soon as the fog cleared on the morning of January 22, Captain Dabney and his men waved in the first resupply ship. The craft settled on the tiny pad atop Hill 881 South—and two 120mm mortar bombs bracketed the landing zone. Fist-sized chunks of jagged steel killed Marines more than one hundred yards away. The corpsmen found five dead, and fifteen so badly wounded they needed immediate evacuation to hospitals. The only way to get them out was by helicopter, and helicopters drew 120mm mortar fire—every time.

Dabney had lost forty-two men on the twentieth; on the morning of the twenty-second, he lost twenty more.

• • •

General Westmoreland was convinced the North Vietnames were trying to "create another Dienbienphu" at Khe Sanh, and he was beginning to believe that the Marines were not up to the task. For two years he had thought that the Marines routinely underestimated enemy capabilities; now he was certain. The setbacks at the combat base were dangerous, yet General Robert D. Cushman, a Marine and the commander of I Corps, seemed have no thoughtful plan for the Army reinforcements that he was sending north.

Westmoreland was already angry with Cushman.

Several weeks before, as he prepared to concentrate an aerial armada over Khe Sanh, Westmoreland had asked Cushman give up tactical bombers that were not actually supporting Marines in combat. Westmoreland wanted them under centralized Air Force control at his headquarters, available to "go where the targets are" rather than to be reserved solely for Marine support.

Cushman bristled instantly. He was "unalterably opposed," he asserted, "to any fractionalization of the Marine air-group team."

Marine units had fewer artillery pieces than comparable Army units because, in theory, Marines got artillery support from their Navy ships that had carried them to battle. When they got to far inland to get help from the sea, Marines relied on Marine pilots who had trained first as infantrymen. Marine air-ground cooperation in combat was between comrades, not branches of service—and Cushman could not give it up.

The issue had sharpened just a few months earlier, in the tough battles near Con Thien. The Marines had been taking heavy casualties, and they asked the Air Force for help. Afterwards, the Marines bitterly accused the Air Force of a halfhearted effort. General Chaisson, a Marine and the chief of Westmoreland's operations center, actually confronted Air Force General "Spike" Momyer in the hallway in Saigon:

"There is no doubt in my mind. . . that the 7th Air Force is *not* putting the weight of effort in Con Thien it should be putting in there. There is no doubt the Air Force is *not* putting the amount of effort [needed] in there."

Cushman appealed to Admiral Sharp in Honolulu. Sharp was a Navy man, and thus viscerally inclined to Marines, and he was Westmoreland's superior. On January 18, just as he was putting the finishing touches on Niagara, Westmoreland received a cable from Sharp suggesting he withdraw his request for Marine air assets.

On the twenty-second, Westmoreland wired Sharp that he couldn't back off; he needed those planes.

Westmoreland was wearying of the Marines. Back channel reports described the combat base "bunkers" as little more than teetering piles of sandbags. The general had been worried that the Marines had lost initiative in I Corps; now it appeared they were not even prepared to meet an enemy attack. His mind began to turn to the Army for solutions.

The five northern provinces of South Vietnam, I Corps, had been an exclusive Marine preserve just one year ago; now there were more than twenty battalions of Army troops there, and more on the way. Westmoreland began to think about putting the Army in charge in I Corps.

General Cushman sensed the pressure, and he decided to sacrifice Lownds. A dynamic new leader at the combat base might demonstrate a quality of Marine resolve that could cool Westmoreland's rising heat. Lownds kept his job because his division commander, General Tompkins, argued that he "knew the terrain intimately."

Everyone agreed that Khe Sanh needed more troops. Adding defenders would increase the logistical burden, but Lownds couldn't wait for the supply problems to be solved; he needed reinforcements before dark.

Late in the day on January 22, the First Battalion of the Ninth Marines was airlifted from the other end of the DMZ to Khe Sanh. One Nine collected its gear, pushed through the milling crowd at the front gate, put out a point, and marched a mile across the almost flat, scrubby ground west of the combat base to the small hill that had served as a rock quarry.

The thousand rifles of One Nine now blocked the western approaches.

More importantly, the new defensive position put a strong

Marine force on each side of a broad piece of ground that could serve as a drop zone. The defenders at Dienbienphu had lost critically important ammunition and supplies, and sometimes men, when the wind blew their parachutes behind enemy lines. The brooding French could hear the Vietnamese shout and laugh as they opened packages filled with mortar shells and machine gun parts and wine. Westmoreland planned to drop supplies smack on the table; One Nine would make it possible.

More than one thousand Vietnamese settlers and military stragglers, plantation workers, shopkeepers, and children were gathered at the gates to the combat base. They surged fearfully toward the barbed wire every time the bombs fell particularly close, and they parted and closed for the going and coming of military patrols. Lieutenant Stamper had come up the road from the village in late morning, walking beside his South Vietnamese counterpart and helping his unit's walking wounded. Stamper had spent too many days and nights with these amateur soldiers to board a helicopter in the night and fly away; he had brought them out himself.

Colonel Lownds met Stamper near the gate. "We're surrounded by two NVA divisions," he explained. "We couldn't send the [rescue] company. It would have been annihilated."

To reduce the pressure on his perimeter from friendly civilians, Lownds began moving small groups of Vietnamese through the combat base to the airfield to fly them out on the planes that delivered One Nine. The Bru were terrified by the tremendous increase in bombing. When they saw the Vietnamese being lifted to safety, thousands packed their personal belongings and pots and chickens and children and hurried to the front gate, settling in along the dirt paths that led to the combat base, patiently waiting their turn to go.

Lownds was raging. Every time he cleared the ground around the base so that he could concentrate firepower on North Vietnamese assault troops, a couple thousand civilians showed up to screen enemy movements. The top Vietnamese government official for

Quang Tri Province solved Lownds' problem by declaring that only Vietnamese could be airlifted from Khe Sanh; the Bru, he ruled, were ineligible.

The Montagnards, ordered away from the gates, began to move uncertainly back towards hamlets that had already been severely jarred by the first bombs of Niagara. Some drifted east on Route 9, walking the broken road that was impassable to Marines. A few tried for Laos, moving deeper into the mountains, away from the coming fire storm.

It had not been Westmoreland's best day. Only 130 tons of supplies had reached Khe Sanh, and the Commander in Chief wanted to know why. Army reinforcements were on the way, but they were not yet in place. And now, intelligence reports of enemy movements throughout South Vietnam had become so alarming that Westmoreland believed the enemy might attempt a countrywide "show of strength" before Tet.

It was about to get worse.

January 23

Westmoreland woke to crackling radio reports and coded teletype messages that called urgently for aircraft carriers, heavy bombers and cargo ships, and airlifts of troops prepared for combat. The flurry of communications had all the earmarks of war, and the war wasn't in Vietnam.

North Korea had captured the USS *Pueblo* during the night, and American sailors were being paraded through the streets as prisoners and spies.

At the very moment the enemy was poised to strike at Khe Sanh, at the moment of his greatest need, Westmoreland felt his country's attention shift from Vietnam to Korea. Suddenly it seemed possible—even likely—that a significant share of his resources might be taken for action in North Korea.

He couldn't afford it. He felt that he had already stretched himself thin in the Saigon region and the central Highlands so that he could concentrate American forces in the northern two provinces.

Now came worse news. The South Koreans, who had been flattened by a North Korean armored juggernaut in a 1950 surprise attack, had no intention of rolling over this time. They had learned a great deal in the eighteen years since their humiliation, and ROK troops were now very tough soldiers equipped with the finest American weapons. Their government wanted them home, immediately, to deal with the new crisis.

Westmoreland prized the Koreans so highly that he had given them a critical role in Checkers: the securing of Da Nang, the largest military air base and port complex in the northern part of the country. He did not trust the South Vietnamese to do this job. Just two years before, ARVN officers and soldiers in Da Nang had joined students and dissidents in the streets to protest government policies. Americans had risked their lives to confront rebellious ARVN commanders and keep open critical lines of military communication. As he prepared for a showdown Khe Sanh, Westmoreland wanted his vital rear area protect by Koreans—not Vietnamese.

Checkers, a carefully planned, orderly movement of troops to the north, was now a fast-clacking game of great urgency. Pulling the Koreans out would leave a gaping hole in the alignment of pieces; Giap would strike immediately at such an opening.

The strains in the north were beginning to show. The Cavalry Division had been scheduled to fit itself into the defense ring around Hue, a city of considerable symbolic importance to the Vietnamese. The 1st Cav's headquarters had arrived at Phu Bai, fifteen miles from Hue, just yesterday, but Westmoreland now needed the Cav to relieve the Marines at Khe Sanh.

Westmoreland was waging an interservice battle for resources, trying to stir the Marines into a more aggressive stance in I Corps, struggling with serious supply problems at Khe Sanh, wondering at the next move of an enemy who had suddenly become very active—and now it looked as though he might lose his Koreans.

The general grew more intense. A finer pencil now drew the line where his lips joined. He now met twice a day with his intelligence officers, and he began to demand fewer hypotheses and more hard facts. He pushed his staff for innovation. He wanted proposals for action, not plans for reaction. Westmoreland wanted to strike first rather than wait for Vo Nguyen Giap to pick the time and place for battle.

• • •

COLONEL LOWNDS WAS also taking stock. He knew that he was not going to be getting any more Marines. It was going to be difficult to supply the men already at Khe Sanh; it would be impossible to sustain a larger force.

The Marine officers on the hilltops played word games with the combat base during Lownds' census. The radio shackle codes were in enemy hands, captured when the recon team was ambushed on 881 North on January 18, and the Marines had not worked out a new code to secure message traffic. Because they were announcing into an open radio the *exact* number of men in each outpost, officers tried to conceal the truth with tricks. Captain Dabney asked for replacements, for example, by giving cheery reports of robust good health and high spirits—and then whistling the open bars of *Stouthearted Men:* "Give me some men who are stouthearted men, who will fight for the right they adore."

By the end of the day on January 23, Lownds had his head count: 244 Marine officers and 5,528 Marine enlisted men, 21 Navy officers and 207 Navy enlisted, 2 Army officers and 28 enlisted, and 1 Air Force officer.

Half of these men were inside the perimeter of the combat base. A thousand held the Rock Quarry one mile to the west, and another thousand sat on top of Hill 558, plugging the Rao Quang River valley to the north. This last battalion was also supposed to support K Company on Hill 861, but the map readers had missed a rocky shoulder between the two positions. The intervening ridge was discovered on January 21, when K Company was nearly overrun. On the twenty-second, Lownds moved two hundred men from Hill 558 to the ridge, and named the new position 861 Alpha. K Company had been reinforced to a strength of three hundred men, Dabney had close to four hundred on 881 South, and a single platoon—about fifty men—held the peak of Hill 950 to the north.

And that was it: 6,053 men in seven positions, some of them miles apart.

Colonel Lownds did not include in his count the soldiers at Lang Vei, or the 400 troops under U.S. Army control who held the southwest perimeter of the combat base, beside the front gate. This was almost a separate compound within the Marine base; it held Montagnards, Vietnamese, Nungs, hill people from Laos, and other indigenous troops under Green Beret leadership. Lownds was not completely comfortable with this complement of irregulars inside his perimeter. He stationed his six tanks immediately behind their lines.

The Marines were spread thinly on the perimeter of the combat base, and Lownds had fewer than 200 men in his emergency reserve. It didn't seem like enough, but Lownds' role was to draw the enemy in. Supporting arms—B-52 bombers, the circling planes with cluster bombs and napalm, and the long-range Army artillery from Camp Carrol and the Rockpile—would do the killing.

January 24

In the first hours after dawn, the shattered remnants of the 33rd Laotian Elephant Battalion stumbled down Route 9 to Lang Vei. The Lao soldiers' wives and children, camp followers in the long tradition of poor armies in the field, walked along the sides of the road with their men—2,300 civilians in all. They seemed quite pleased to find friendly faces inside the Vietnamese border and, while the battalion commander went inside the Green Berets' fenced camp to consult with the Americans, the women and children pitched tents, drew water from nearby streams, and began preparation of a midday meal.

A few miles to the north, an Air Force fighter bomber took four hard hits, made a half roll to the left, and began shaking itself to pieces. The pilot punched out, and was picked up minutes later by a rescue chopper. It was the third day in a row that an American plane had been shot down over Khe Sanh. Lieutenant Tonc's rival, the new commander of the 14th Anti-aircraft Company, was doing OK.

Shells shrieked in from Laos at odd intervals, smashing buildings at the combat base and punching through sandbags and bunkers like fists through paper. Incoming shells and rockets were counted in dozens, not hundreds, but the Marines began to move in a hunched half-run called the Quick Step.

General Westmoreland, wanting to strike first, proposed to Washington that a force of Marines, paratroopers, and air cavalrymen strike suddenly from the sea at North Vietnam, just above the DMZ. A surprise landing on the enemy coast might disrupt enemy plans for attacks in the south.

President Johnson was meeting with his military advisers to discuss the possibility of war with North Korea. The Joint Chiefs of Staff were deeply concerned about the quality of American units available for combat, and about the tiny reserve of regular troops still left in the United States. A B-52 had crashed the night before in Greenland, and emergency teams were now combing the ice for missing nuclear weapons. Defense Secretary McNamara told the President's inner council that laboratory analysis had identified the powder in the bullets for the M16 rifle as one of the several causes for battlefield jamming incidents. In the next few days, he said, the government would begin to replace the gunpowder used by most American soldiers in Vietnam.

Westmoreland's proposal for an invasion of North Vietnam was considered seriously, but briefly; there were too many other problems to consider expanding the war to a new battlefield at this time.

The Last Days of January

"I couldn't stand it any more. I knew that one of my boys must have been killed. . . . I jumped out of bed, put on my robe, took my flashlight, and went into the Situation Room."

Dreams of Dienbienphu had made an insomniac of President Johnson. He could be found at 3 A.M. in the basement of the White House, reading cables, studying aerial photos, and asking for numbers. The military staff had constructed for him a sand table model of the Khe Sanh plateau and combat base, much like the one in the hangar in Saigon.

He wandered from map to teletype, from message desk to sand table, wondering, worrying, about the Marines.

Every day the President asked the chairman of the Joint Chiefs of Staff about the decision to stand and fight at Khe Sanh, and every day General Wheeler, as confident as Westmoreland, assured the President that Khe Sanh could hold.

The Marine base in these last days of January became the symbol of American determination in Vietnam, just as Dienbienphu had become the symbol of French commitment in 1954. Critics argued that the political and military similarities to Dienbienphu were too great to be ignored, and that the risks were therefore too appalling to consider. Precisely because of such criticism, military tacticians restudied every eventuality, knowing it was imperative that Khe Sanh not fall.

Westmoreland shaped his justifications for the defense of Khe Sanh during these days of debate. He saw many important uses for the remote mountain air strip, especially as the launch point for an invasion of Laos, but the single greatest attraction of the combat base right now was as a killing ground for North Vietnamese troops.

The general had become more politic since the previous spring when, during a visit to the United States, he had rather baldly described his strategy for winning the war. Attrition would do it, he had said, a steady, bloody, grinding-down of the enemy until he quit. "We'll just go on bleeding them until Hanoi wakes up to the fact that they have bled their country to the point of national disaster for generations." Westmoreland had been stung when military critics asserted that attrition was *not* a strategy but rather one of the signs of loss of initiative.

Westmoreland, therefore, used other reasons to support his decision to defend the combat base. "Khe Sanh commands the approaches to Dong Ha and Quang Tri City," he said. "Were we to relinquish the Khe Sanh area, the North Vietnamese would have an unobstructed invasion route into the two northernmost provinces. . . ."

The general knew in late January that thousands of enemy soldiers already were operating in the interior of the two provinces, especially near Hue. In April of 1967, an enemy regiment had slammed into Quang Tri City, spiked ARVN artillery, fought its way inside a moated citadel to dynamite government offices, freed hundreds of prisoners from the provincial jail—and vanished into the night. It was not really possible to think of Khe Sanh as a cork in a bottle because there was, in truth, no bottle. Still, it was one way to describe a difficult war so that Americans at home, with memories of the maps of World War II and Korea, might understand the why of Khe Sanh.

Westmoreland would have preferred to use mobile forces, as he had done at Dak To, but he had nowhere near as many troops available for battle at Khe Sanh as he had at Dak To—and the looming monsoon would immobilize heliborne troops, anyway.

He had already considered the arguments for withdrawal. Weather was foremost: the monsoon mists would make it difficult to get supplies to the Marines, and also hamper close air support. The enemy's supply lines were shortest at Khe Sanh, which was just a few miles off the Ho Chi Minh Trail in Laos, while American supply lines might depend on parachute drops.

It was the enemy's seemingly steadfast commitment to battle that convinced Westmoreland to reinforce—and to fight. "Judging from the size of his buildup, and from his own statements, he was hoping to achieve a military-political victory similar to the one fourteen years earlier at Dienbienphu," Westmoreland said later.

"The question was whether we could afford the troops to reinforce, keep them supplied by air, and defeat an enemy far superior in numbers as we waited for the weather to clear, built forward bases, and made preparations for an overland relief expedition. I believed we could do all these things."

And so did the Marines:

"In the last analysis, Khe Sanh was defended because it was the only logical thing to do. We were there, in a prepared position and in considerable strength. A well-fought battle would do the enemy a lot more damage than he could hope to inflict on us."

President Johnson talked personally with Westmoreland about the decision to defend Khe Sanh. He had been pressing General Wheeler every day for more information, and finally he told Wheeler he wanted to hear the words from Westmoreland himself. It was the only time the Commander in Chief broke the chain of command to Westmoreland. At the end of the conversation, the President said he wanted to be the first to know if Westmoreland decided the Marines had to be evacuated from Khe Sanh.

Johnson was still worried. His political consensus was fraying badly. Democratic Senator Eugene McCarthy had entered the New Hampshire presidential primary, and was trying to make the tiny mountain state a focus for dissent on the war. A week ago, during a formal luncheon in the White House, Eartha Kitt had bitterly denounced U.S. policy in Vietnam, humiliating Lady Bird before friends and guests. The protest marches were getting larger. If he called up the reserves, or began to feed National Guard units into Vietnam, he was certain the nation would turn against the war.

The President asked tougher questions now. He wanted more details about this battle at Khe Sanh, especially reports on the critical shortage of ammunition at the combat base. If one goddam plane landed with six tons of ammo, he wanted to know about it.

A detailed photomural of the Khe Sanh plateau, showing trenches, bunkers, gun positions and ammunition storage areas went up on the walls of the Situation Room. Messages with arcane bits of information about the combat base began to arrive at the White House message desk, sometimes as often as every fifty minutes. Every day, Westmoreland personally prepared a report on supplies and events at Khe Sanh for transmittal to the President.

On January 25, Westmoreland decided he could no longer trust the Marines to do the job in I Corps. He ordered the establishment of a forward post of his own headquarters in the northern provinces—the first step in a transition to Army control.

"Absolutely a slap in the face!" fumed General Tompkins, who was flying by helicopter every day from Dong Ha to Khe Sanh to consult with Lownds. "The most unpardonable thing Saigon ever did!"

Westmoreland pressed ahead. He initiated planning on January 25 for Operation Pegasus, the relief of Khe Sanh. He had decided it would be an Army operation, mounted by the flying horses of the 1st Air Cavalry Division, and he ordered the 1st Cav to move from Phu Bai to Quang Tri City.

Westmoreland's commander in III Corps, the zone that included Saigon, had put together "various bits of tenuous but disturbing intelligence" that the Viet Cong were leaving their sanctuaries in War Zones C and D and moving toward the capital city. He suggested the enemy might attempt some demonstration of strength just before the traditional Tet truce imposed a temporary halt in military operations.

Westmoreland's attention was further diverted when critics noted that the South Vietnamese had apparently been written out of plans for the biggest battle of the Vietnam war. Was this, after all, an American war in Vietnam?

The general was unusually attentive to such political niceties. It was perhaps a sign of his preoccupation with details in this battle that he had overlooked the absence of an ARVN unit in a critically important test of arms.

On January 27, the 37th ARVN Ranger Battalion—all 318 men—was flown to Khe Sanh to be fitted into the defenses. These cocky soldiers, who wore red berets to proclaim their toughness, were marched out to the far east end of the combat base, through the lines of the Marines' First Battalion—to trenches two hundred yards outside the Marine perimeter. The Marines had prepared these positions for the new arrivals; it was an arrangement not unlike the five tanks behind the irregulars in the Green Beret compound.

The weather continued clear over Khe Sanh, and enemy activity dropped off to almost nothing in the final days of January. The airstrip was repaired, and the supply shortages grew less critical. Reinforcements were in place, and a relief force was organizing at Quang Tri City.

Still, President Johnson was near a crisis of confidence with General Wheeler and the Joint Chiefs of Staff. The vulnerability of the combat base was all too clear to him. "I don't want any damned Dienbienphu," the President told Wheeler. He insisted that each member of the Joint Chiefs individually assess Khe Sanh's ability to hold.

On January 29, General Wheeler gave the President a written statement of confidence in Westmoreland's plans for Khe Sanh. It was signed by every member of the Joint Chiefs. The Commander in Chief now had a written guarantee from the nation's highest-ranking military men that the Marines would prevail at Khe Sanh.

It wasn't enough.

That same day, the President asked retired General Maxwell Taylor to go over to the CIA and to make an independent assessment of the intelligence information on Khe Sanh. Taylor's credentials were impeccable: he had preceded Wheeler as chairman of the Joint Chiefs and he had served as ambassador to South Vietnam. He had been friend and mentor to Westmoreland. The general studied the photomurals of Khe Sanh and the secret reports of the Central Intelligence Agency—and he came back worried.

There were haunting similarities between Dienbienphu and Khe Sanh, General Taylor told the President. The bad weather, the difficulty of supplying the Marines, and the possibility that Vo Nguyen Giap might deliver overwhelming artillery support to the battlefield as he had done at Dienbienphu, had convinced the general that Khe Sanh could be placed in jeopardy. Besides, he told the President, it was an adage of infantrymen that a commander can take *any* defensive position if he is willing to pay the price.

It was true that both Khe Sanh and Dienbienphu had been established to lure an elusive enemy to a killing ground, and it was true that both were remote outposts with little obvious connection to areas of strategic importance. Both could be shelled by direct observation, both depended on aircraft for supplies, and both were garrisoned by elite troops who disdained to construct stout defenses. And both had been attacked by troops under the command of Vo Nguyen Giap.

Westmoreland knew all of these arguments; he had been over them again and again. He was resentful that a soldier he greatly admired would second guess his efforts from afar, and he was disdainful of critics who had even fewer credentials.

"None of us was blind to the possibility that the North Vietnamese might try to make of Khe Sanh another Dienbienphu," Westmoreland said, "yet we were aware of marked differences in the two situations, [most notably our] tremendous firepower.

"Lest I overlook any possible peril," he continued, "I carefully studied parallels between Dienbienphu and Khe Sanh."

The French, he decided, had doomed themselves by choosing a valley position with the enemy holding the surrounding high ground. In contrast, the combat base sat on a plateau, with reinforced Marine infantry companies holding key hilltops. The French had no artillery that could support them from the outside, while the Marines could call on the Army's powerful 175mm guns at Camp Carrol. The French position was unusually isolated, with no hope of overland relief, while Westmoreland believed he could reopen Route 9 to Khe Sanh "if it turned out to be essential—and adequate troops were put to the task."

The French had two hundred planes of all types for their battle, and no way of supplying Dienbienphu except by parachute drops. Westmoreland had two thousand attack planes, three thousand helicopters, a fleet of B-52 transcontinental bombers—and a recently rebuilt, crushed rock and pierced steel plate, all-weather airfield at Khe Sanh that could handle even the big C-130 cargo planes.

It was the numbers, the huge numbers, that gave Westmoreland his greatest satisfaction. He had fifty times the mincing power that the French had had at Dienbienphu. He *wanted* the North Vietnamese to attack.

Because of the continuing criticism and doubt in civilian forums in the United States, because of the Joint Chiefs signed guarantee, because of General Taylor's concerns, and because he thought he might learn or relearn an important lesson, Westmoreland decided to order one more formal study. He asked Colonel Reamer Argo, his command historian, to look at Dienbienphu again, and other historic sieges, too, "to discern tactics or methods the enemy might use" at Khe Sanh.

The general was quite confident of Argo's conclusions. He believed with utter certainty that his enormous firepower resources and the helicopters of the 1st Air Cavalry Division gave him the edge that the French never had. "I knew Khe Sanh was different," he said.

Westmoreland met on January 29 with the highest ranking officers in his command to discuss continuing intelligence reports that Viet Cong troops were on the move, and that Saigon itself might be a target. Was it possible the enemy might actually attack Vietnamese cities? Police in Qui Nhon, a large coastal city in II Corps, had captured a half dozen Viet Cong the day before, confiscating tape recordings that called on the Vietnamese people to join in a general uprising.

The general made a few minor adjustments in U.S. deployment and asked the Vietnamese to cancel or reduce homes leaves for Tet, but in the end Westmoreland and his staff rejected as unbelievable a major enemy assault on Saigon and the cities. It would be much too costly: "Why would the enemy give away his major advantage, which was his ability to be elusive and avoid heavy casualties?"

No, it was clearly Khe Sanh and I Corps that faced the greatest threat. It was possible, of course, that Giap was planning something more ambitious, but Westmoreland was now certain that Giap wanted Khe Sanh. He was equally certain that Giap's best opportunity had passed—and that American firepower could destroy any enemy thrust. The mood in Westmoreland's headquarters was clear: "[We] might be able to do at Khe Sanh what the French had tried and failed to do at Dienbienphu."

Westmoreland was *positive* the Marines could hold, even if they wavered. He had absolutely no intention of losing the combat base; he was prepared to use nuclear weapons to save it.

"Because the region around Khe Sanh was virtually uninhabited," he reasoned, "civilian casualties would be minimal." It might be an excellent place to demonstrate American resolve in Vietnam.

"If Washington officials were so intent on 'sending a message' to Hanoi," Westmoreland thought, "surely small tactical nuclear weapons could be a way to tell Hanoi something, just as two atomic bombs had spoken convincingly to Japanese officials during World War II and the threat of atomic bombs induced the North Koreans to accept meaningful negotiations during the Korean War." He understood that nuclear weapons would be so shocking to the world that their use would have to be a political rather than a military decision, but he would have been "imprudent," he said, "if I failed to acquaint myself with the possibilities in detail."

Unknown to Colonel Argo and to most of Westmoreland's staff, a small secret group in the Saigon headquarters was studying the terrain at Khe Sanh, the location of Marine outposts, wind velocities and radiation yields, blast patterns and delivery systems. Westmoreland wanted to be ready.

JANUARY 30

The quality of intelligence, the continuing good weather at Khe Sanh, the lull in enemy attacks, and the smooth transition from Marine to Army control in I Corps had given Westmoreland a feeling of momentum again. The Korean crisis was cooling; his key base at Da Nang would be secure. The forward headquarters he was sending to Phu Bai was even now loading desks and file cabinets and communications equipment onto planes at Tan Son Nhut.

Two of the 1st Air Cavalry Division's most aggressive battalions had already moved west from Quang Tri City, and were hacking out fire bases on the way to Khe Sanh. One whole brigade of the 1st Cav was thrashing through the woods south and west of Quang Tri City, acclimating itself to new terrain and preparing for the push to Khe Sanh. Pegasus was underway.

Now Westmoreland decided to strike the first blow at Khe Sanh. For more than a week, he had personally picked the targets for B-52 raids in South Vietnam, and he had directed most of them to the Khe Sanh region. He decided to concentrate his bomber forces for a single paralyzing blow.

The most famous photograph of Vo Nguyen Giap, familiar to military professionals around the world because it had been taken during the battle at Dienbienphu, showed the North Vietnamese commander standing at a map table in a cave. In recent days Westmoreland's radio spooks had detected heavy radio traffic from a place inside Laos that might be the mouth of a cave complex. The sophistication of the enemy's radio equipment and the great flow of messages convinced Westmoreland that he had discovered "the North Vietnamese headquarters controlling forces around Khe Sanh, if not the entire northern region." It was believed inside Westmoreland's headquarters that Vo Nguyen Giap himself had visited this Front headquarters in Laos—and that he might be there now to take personal charge on the eve of battle.

On January 30, then, thirty-six B-52s—in the largest air strike of the war—came around the arc of the earth, far above sight or sound. One thousand tons of high explosives cascaded out of the sky into the green jungles of Laos. The biggest air raids of World War II had not delivered these tonnages on so small target. After dark, nine more B-52s hit the same place again to catch troops and medical personnel cleaning up after the first raid.

The radio signals ceased.

Westmoreland unlaced his boots on the night of January 30 with a feeling of real accomplishment. He was pretty sure he had destroyed the entire command structure of the enemy force at Khe Sanh. The airfield at the combat base had been reopened to C-130s, and the supply inventory was building in sixteen-ton loads. The 1st Cav was on the way; thank God for the helicopter. If push came to shove, he could put ten thousand very tough soldiers on the plateau in a very short time.

He had even thought to have the jet airfields in North Vietnam nearest Khe Sanh rebombed and recratered to eliminate any chance of aerial surprise over the combat base. A staggering number of planes circled over Khe Sanh waiting for a role in a turkey shoot."

If anything went wrong, he had a secret group working on nuclear weapons.

The weather had been beautiful, absolutely beautiful.

Westmoreland felt very good as he turned out the lights.

There was going to be no Dienbienphu in *his* command.

6.

Giap

When the B-52 Stratofortresses opened their bomb bay doors high over the jungled crags of Laos, General Vo Nguyen Giap was in his command headquarters in Hanoi, hundreds of miles to the north, attending to the final details of the coming General Offensive.

He had been preparing this bold strike into the heart of South Vietnam for more than six months. In just a few hours, the troops would go forward.

The general was almost certain that the Americans would invade his country within the next few weeks—or perhaps strike at the Ho Chi Minh Trail from their forward base at Khe Sanh. Stooped slightly, his rumpled uniform jacket buttoned tightly at the neck, Giap seemed utterly calm. His broad forehead, which had impressed Western visitors as "Beethoven-like," was smooth. He had a fierce personal commitment to his task and he could utterly dominate meetings with his intensity, but Giap preferred to present a placid countenance to the world. The French had negotiated with him, and had nicknamed him "Volcano Under the Snow." It was not a mask, he insisted; it was the outward sign of his readiness, his certainty that he would prevail.

He had prepared his people and his armed forces for invasion. Nearly 300,000 soldiers of the People's Army were at home, arrayed in depth to receive the Americans. Every hamlet and village had dug bunkers, trenches, and fighting positions. Even schoolgirls took bayonet drill.

The enemy's most seasoned troops—Giap was sure that Westmoreland would send Marines and paratroopers—would have to fight first with the schoolgirls and farmers, organized in a million-member Self-Defense Militia, then with regional security forces, and, finally, with the People's Army of Viet Nam and its heavy artillery, armor, anti-aircraft guns, and surface-to-air missiles. Never in the Second Indochinese War had Giap been able to bring the full range of his supporting arms to bear on American forces; he believed he could make an invasion the single most costly campaign the Americans would ever launch in Vietnam.

For now, his attention was elsewhere.

While Westmoreland was moving tens of thousands of American soldiers north in the series of shifts code-named Checkers, Vo Nguyen Giap had been moving tens of thousands of North Vietnamese soldiers south for the most daring gamble of the Second Indochinese War: the Tet Offensive.

The general loved the boldness of the idea—sixty-seven thousand valiant "soldiers of the just cause" against more than one million of the enemy in a surprise attack on a revered holiday—but he was skeptical about the chances for success. He planned to risk only ten percent of his forces in the south; most of the People's Army units would stand by to support the Viet Cong attack on every major city and town in South Vietnam.

Vo Nguyen Giap believed the war with the Americans would be long and difficult. Five hundred U.S. fighter bombers hammered his country every day, the economy was in ruins, the population scattered to the countryside, and the army completely reliant on the fraternal socialist spirit of the Chinese and Russians. He had been at war too long to believe there was a shortcut to victory, especially against a vastly superior force.

He was an ardent student of his country's rich military history and he often sought lessons for the present by reading accounts of the past. He believed it was possible under certain conditions of combat to compress twenty years into a day; he just didn't believe January 31, 1968, was going to be the day.

On the eve of the Tet Offensive, Vo Nguyen Giap was unique in all the world as a military commander. He had personally chosen the first 34 soldiers of the People's Army—and led them into combat carrying two muskets, seventeen rifles, fourteen flintlocks, and a Chinese pistol. Today, twenty-three years later, he was commander in chief of one of the finest, best-equipped fighting forces in the world: 480,000 men, a complete array of modern weapons, and an air defense system more sophisticated than Germany had fielded in World War II.

He had been a scholar, a journalist, and a teacher of history, but he was famed now as one of the world's most gifted military leaders. He had been present at the founding of his country's independence movement, and he had kept the flickering dream alive in the chill rain forests of southern China's fantasy mountains. Now he was minister of defense, third-ranking member of the ruling council—the most influential voice in all the country after President Ho Chi Minh and Prime Minister Pham Van Dong. His writings, and accounts of his battles, were studied in most of the military colleges of the world.

Giap believed victory lay many years in the future. He knew the history of his people, and he had fought French troops, and Japanese troops, and Chinese troops, and foreign legionnaires, and the troops of South Vietnam, and now, for three years, Americans . . . and Koreans, and Australians.

Years of sacrifice would still be necessary, he warned, before the United States withdrew. Sacrifice was both heritage and destiny in Vietnam; few nations of the world have a longer history of invasion, occupation, and wars of liberation.

For Giap, war was a chromosomal memory—a legacy of his race.

Always the enemy had been stronger by ten times, or twenty times, and always the Vietnamese had prevailed. Once, it took a thousand years. The stories of ancient Vietnamese heroes were still told in rural villages. As a graduate student, Giap had matched some of these oral history tales with long-forgotten archeological ruins. As a general, he searched for inspiration in his country's twenty centuries of resistance. Vietnamese partisans had retreated into the mountains to avoid battle with a large Chinese force as early as the 3rd century B.C. "The Viets are extremely difficult to defeat," a report to China stated. "They do not come out to fight, but hide in their familiar mountains and use the jungle like a weapon. . . ." In 111 B.C., the Chinese came in great numbers and reached into the most distant villages to destroy all relics and records so the people of the South, the Viets, could be more thoroughly assimilated into the culture of China.

One hundred fifty years later, in 39 A.D., a young widow outraged by the callous execution of her husband enlisted first her sister and then thousands of peasants in a war of rebellion. The Two Sisters Trung drove the Chinese back for four years, then threw themselves into the Hat Giang River rather than accept defeat. Main thoroughfares in both Hanoi and Saigon commemorate the sisters' courage to this day.

Giap had written studies of ten important insurrections during the thousand years of Chinese occupation, including one in 238 A.D. led by "Dame Trieu." She was a fearless peasant woman whom legend endows with breasts one meter long—a detail still mentioned proudly by farmers in her home province.

The Chinese were finally expelled in a thirty-year war that ended in a brilliancy. The Vietnamese commander retreated up the Bach Dang River in the face of a huge Chinese battle fleet, then attacked at the turning of the tide. The Chinese maneuvered confidently to meet the threat when suddenly their boats were holed or capsized by sharpened, iron-tipped bamboo poles buried in the river bottom before the battle. Fire arrows destroyed the helpless fleet, and the river drank the enemy soldiers.

During the thirteenth century, Kublai Khan, grandson of Genghis, tried three times to reimpose Chinese rule. His Mongol hordes overran an emptied Hanoi in the first campaign, but retreated in the face of "an abundance of tropical diseases." General Tran Hung Dao was the Vietnamese hero in these campaigns. Giap thought his small book, *Summary of Military Strategy*, could be compared with the works of Sun Tzu and Clausewitz. Giap was deeply impressed by Tran Hung Dao's readiness to abandon his capital city ("the importance of not trying to defend 'prestige positions' "), and by his argument that a strong enemy could be weakened by lengthening a war from months to years, from years to decades.

"When the enemy is away from home for a long time and produces no victories, and families learn of their dead, then the enemy population becomes dissatisfied," Tran Hung Dao had written. "Time is always in our favor. Our climate, mountains and jungles discourage the enemy. . . ."

The Chinese came again in 1787. A charismatic Vietnamese leader named Nguyen Hue held his armies in hiding for more than a year, then infiltrated Hanoi on the eve of Tet in 1789—and caught the Chinese in the full relaxation of New Year celebrations. A superior Chinese force was sent reeling back across the border.

Then came wars against the French, the Japanese, and the French again. And now the Americans. "Our history through the centuries," said Prime Minister Pham Van Dong, "is a perpetual struggle with nature and invaders."

War in Vietnam was always bloody. The North Vietnamese maintained a museum in Hanoi that celebrated the sacrifices of national heroes. It was a building filled with drawings and paintings and sketches and poems and photographs of death: beheadings, impalements, suicides, disembowelings, immolations, dismemberings, and boilings in oil. The Vietnamese were imaginative in these matters. An emperor had once submitted a French priest to the Death of a Thousand Cuts—tearing his thighs with five pairs of hot pincers, amputating his eyebrows, hacking off his breasts and buttocks, tearing away the remaining flesh on his legs, quartering the corpse, parading the head—and then grinding the skull to powder and throwing it in the sea.

The Hanoi museum was a record of twenty centuries of warfare and suffering, of betrayal and victory, and the latest exhibitions featured Cluster Bomb Units, rocket fins, airplane parts, and photographs of bombed-out buildings and maimed children. The Americans quickly zippered their dead into opaque body bags; the Vietnamese displayed their dead—the faces twisted in agony, the limbs torn away, the blood still fresh.

It was the history of the Vietnamese people. A perfect understanding of the sacrifices of their forebears could steel North Vietnam's people for the trials to come. They had been driven into the mountains by invaders for two thousand two hundred years; the national slogan since the Americans started bombing had been, simply, "Prepare for the Worst."

• • •

VO NGUYEN GIAP uniquely mirrored the history of Vietnam. He had lived in the mountains for more than ten years, hiding in caves and running from enemy patrols. His iron will had been forged in French jails, years of exile, and terrible defeats on the battlefield.

During the years that his Western military contemporaries moved vast modern armies into textbook battles on the plains of Europe, Giap padded narrow mountain paths in sandals cut from truck tires and puzzled over the problems of supply: if one porter can carry fifty-four pounds of rice fifteen miles a day, or twelve miles a night, then how many porters must begin working and *when* must they begin working to sustain a 400-man combat unit in a ten-day assault on a target 130 miles away? Even now with the duties of minister of defense, he fussed over tactical details, logistics problems and, especially, combat spirit.

Born in 1912 on a small farm in Quang Binh province, Giap was serving a three-year prison sentence for anti-French demonstrations before he was eighteen years old. He had distinguished himself as a student and when the French released him early "for good behavior" he enrolled at the University of Hanoi. He and Pham Van Dong published anti-imperialist newspapers in 1936 and 1937 and, as leaders in Vietnam's tiny Communist Party, came under surveillance by the French secret police. The two-volume study of the role of peasants in Vietnamese history, published under pseudonyms in 1938, was considered by the French to be a guidebook to revolution; the entire press run was seized and destroyed.

Giap won a degree in law and political economics, the highest awarded by France in Indochina. Newly married to the daughter of the dean of the faculty of letters, he began teaching history at the Thanh Long private school in Hanoi in 1938. Ho Chi Minh, the father of the independence movement, had disappeared into the gloomy prisons of Chiang Kai-shek's China; the flame of revolution guttered.

In May of 1940, Giap narrowly escaped lightning police raids on Communist Party activists. His wife was caught and sentenced to fifteen years; she died in prison. His sister was guillotined. Giap hurried toward the Chinese border, jumping from the train to avoid police searches. Near the end of the trip, when he faced the added peril of hostile Chinese patrols, he crossed a river on a bamboo raft.

He was twenty-seven years old when he finally reached the campfires of other Vietnamese refugees in China. He was very slender, hardly five feet tall, with dark eyes and dark eyebrows and dark hair, and so handsome that Ho Chi Minh teased him: "Vo Nguyen Giap is still beautiful like a girl." They shared household tasks in exile—except for Giap, whose cooking was so terrible that he was sentenced to full-time dishwashing.

Giap had been prepared to seek training with Mao Tse-tung's Red Army when Chiang Kai-shek pressed new attacks into southern China in 1941 and he was driven, a seed on the winds of war, to Tsingsi and then Kweilein—just thirty miles from the border with Vietnam. Here he began to study the problems of tactics and strategy, of recruitment and training, of weapons and supplies. He obtained books on Western military thought, and he studied Mao's manuals on people's revolutionary war.

Japan ruled Vietnam during these years. Troops of the Rising Sun had moved into Indochina when France surrendered to Germany.

Giap found young people among the many Vietnamese refugees in the border region, fired them with the spirit of struggle against the Japanese and French, and sent them back into the northern provinces to excite the people with a message of liberation. He trained fifty of these cadre every month, giving them courses in simple tactics and showing them how to organize youths and farmers and women for the revolution.

He worked for three years in his mountain exile, writing training manuals, organizing propaganda teams, publishing a small newspaper with articles on women's organizations and tips on village defense—building an army on hope until he could get guns.

In February of 1944, twenty groups of "Southward Marchers" were represented at Tet celebrations in Giap's headquarters. He electrified the group by announcing that the years of waiting were over: it was time to strike. Ho Chi Minh, gaunt from years in jail, stumbled out of the woods before the offensive could be launched. He reviewed the plans, then criticized Giap for not properly preparing the people or the eager combatants for a long war against a powerful enemy. Only those with a single-minded commitment to the struggle would be able to remain strong, Ho Chi Minh warned.

Giap releashed his cadre, intensified their training, and searched among them for "the most ardent." He believed that soldiers with the highest combat spirit could defeat stronger forces. He wanted soldiers who understood that a war of liberation was a life struggle that could only end in victory or death. From the beginning, Giap prepared his soldiers for hardship.

He planted the seeds for his army in the very first combat operation of the war for independence, in December of 1944. He chose "the most resolute" recruits for the operation, rehearsed them repeatedly on sand-table models—and he picked Christmas Eve for the attack, when the French defenders might be misty with nostalgia or sleepy with drink. This platoon-sized raid against two isolated outposts in the northern mountains is as celebrated in Hanoi as Lexington-Concord is in Boston.

"We forgot we were only thirty-four human beings," Giap wrote, years later. "We imagined ourselves to be an army of steel not to be defeated by any force. . . . Confidence, eagerness, prevailed."

This was the spirit that fired the People's Army of Viet Nam. The commander in chief wanted total commitment—literally ascetic dedication—from his soldiers.

Giap-trained cadre were so scrupulously correct with Thó Montagnards—who lived in the northern mountain region most vital to Giap in the early years—that Thó women came to believe the young men had been "made without cocks." And Laotians who had fought beside the North Vietnamese were amazed their Puritanism. "The Vietnamese are prepared to sacrifice their lives for their duty," one Laotian officer told American interrogators. "They fight with great devotion, never complaining about their problems. They don't drink, and women are against regulations."

There was no one-year tour in this army, no rest and recreation in

Kuala Lumpur, no beer, no mail, no medicine. And no home leave until the war was over.

• • •

BY THE MIDDLE of 1945, Giap commanded several thousand guerrillas by runner—he had no radio—and had established Vietnamese control in five northern border provinces despite the best efforts of the Japanese Army's 21st Division. It was still a rag-tag army—the widely scattered forces carried forty kinds of rifles from eight foreign countries—but when American atomic bombs knocked Japan out of the war, Giap pushed his troops through the night to be first in Hanoi.

He found chaos in the first months after the end of World War II. Demoralized Japanese troops roamed the countryside, some of them killing and looting. The victorious Allies had asked Chiang Kai-shek to restore order in North Vietnam, and more than 100,000 Chinese soldiers had turned away from Mao Tse-tung's growing Red Army to bring typhoid and terrorism to the streets of Hanoi. Floods had damaged rice crops, and serious food problems loomed. The French, aided by a temporary British administration in Saigon, were moving quickly to reestablish colonial rule in the southern part of Vietnam.

Ho Chi Minh did not come down from the mountains. The frail leader of the revolution was sick again, and Giap found him lying on a bamboo cot, weakly sipping a gruel of rice and pulverized roots that had been dug from the jungle floor by a Chinese herb doctor. Ho listened to Giap's report and then said the fight for independence was to continue "even if the Annamite mountains go up in flames."

And so Vo Nguyen Giap, newly titled minister of interior, stood at rigid attention with two of his aides while the flag of liberation was raised, and a free Vietnam was formally proclaimed. Beside him stood a U.S. Army major named Archimedes Patti, one of several

OSS officers who had parachuted into Vietnam late in the war to give Giap American aid in the fight against the Japanese.

Giap set off immediately to assess the situation in the country. As he drove south on Route 1, he mused that the French had a professional army with modern aircraft, warships, tanks, and artillery, while his own forces carried homemade muskets, long and short Japanese rifles, and some 1903 and 1917 Remington rifles from the U.S. And yet, he noted with satisfaction, the French were discovering that the People's Army—the Viet Minh—"no longer scattered like a flock of sparrows" when attacked.

The general visited Hue for the first time since he was a schoolboy, met with Montagnard leaders in the Highlands, talked with young girls in the central provinces who had cut their long black hair to show their commitment to the fight against the French, twice visited battlefields, and once heard "the hissing of bullets" only inches away.

When Giap told Ho Chi Minh about the commitment of the people but the unequal odds in the military struggle, Ho answered:

"Fighting will continue as long as we hold one inch of ground, as long as there remains one citizen."

The chaos in the north was beyond the capacity of the tiny Ho Chi Minh government and its small guerrilla army. Disease and hunger and the roaming troops of four nations had produced near anarchy. The French had already landed 35,000 troops in the south, and were poised to land at Haiphong. The Viet Minh leadership, with no real alternative, agreed to permit the return of French troops during negotiations to establish an independent Vietnam.

News that the French would return drew an angry crowd of more than 100,000 to the square in front of Hanoi's Municipal Theater on the afternoon of March 6, 1946. The mob scented betrayal, but Vo Nguyen Giap's burning intensity worked as well in the open air as it did in a conference room. He explained that the international situation was not favorable to immediate independence, and that resistance offered little prospect of victory—but the certainty of great suffering. He called the agreement with the French "a Vietnamese Brest-Litovsk," comparing it to the truce that Lenin arranged to halt the German invasion of Russia while he consolidated his political revolution. Giap promised the crowd that the fight for freedom would continue; he would personally head the National Resistance Committee while the French were in Vietnam.

A week later Giap went to the Haiphong docks to call respectfully on French General Philippe Leclerc, who was watching the off-loading of high-quality military equipment. Leclerc was eager for this meeting because of what General Douglas MacArthur of the United States had told him:

"If you expect to succeed in overcoming the resistance of your enemy [in Vietnam], bring soldiers and then more soldiers, and after that still more soldiers. But you probably still will not succeed."

Leclerc emerged from his office to meet this unbeatable foe—and found a five-foot-tall, one-hundred-pound "Minister of Defense" in a white duck suit and club-striped tie, wearing a trilby hat. Some military critics believe the French military effort in Indochina never recovered from this first moment of incredulity.

Giap had been deferential in Haiphong—Leclerc was a genuine war hero—but when they met again in Dalat six weeks later to argue military lines of responsibility, Giap was "rough, vehement, and provocative." Ten Vietnamese arrived for the conference, but Giap quickly emerged as the most forceful speaker. He harshly denounced the French for the cruelty of their military operations in the south. He told news reporters about the jailing and death of his wife and the years of struggle in the mountains. Through it all his broad forehead remained smooth. It was here that he was named Volcano Under the Snow.

The rest of 1946 was an ill-concealed race toward war. Ho Chi Minh and Pham Van Dong went to France to try to win guarantees of national sovereignty; Giap and other deputies disarmed non-Communist nationalist groups, closed antagonistic newspapers, arrested leaders of opposition parties, and drove political enemies into exile. It was a time of choosing and Giap did not shrink from spilling blood. In the Delta, south of Saigon, old enemies sent foes "crab fishing"—tying them together in bundles, like logs, and throwing them into the Mekong to float to sea while slowly drowning. In November, the French heavy cruiser *Suffren* fired its big guns into a section of Haiphong and killed more than 6,000 Vietnamese.

The French took over security patrols in Hanoi, and Giap answered by erecting barricades in the streets—and by ordering the people to punch holes in the adjoining walls of their homes and shops so Viet Minh troops could move quickly through the city without using the streets.

Giap sent a note to the French commander on December 19 and proposed an easing of tensions: why not let the French soldiers, restricted to barracks on war footing for more than a week, circulate in the city again? After all, it was only a week to Christmas. By 6 P.M., the bars and brothels and shops of Hanoi were alive again, and lights sparkled on all the main streets of the city.

A Viet Minh demolition team destroyed the electric power plant at 8 P.M., and Hanoi was plunged into darkness. Bands of screaming militiamen threw themselves at army bases, police posts, and civilian compounds in the city. Within hours French soldiers and citizens were defending themselves from attack all across the country. Hue held out until February, when the garrison was finally relieved.

Giap preserved the heart of his army by scattering it again in the northern provinces—"a knotted tangle of 4,000 foot mountains, limestone caves . . . with eighty inches of rain, a protective blanket of fog six months of the year, and rivers and stream everywhere. . . ." Twenty thousand of his soldiers did not yet have weapons, and Giap and Ho Chi Minh needed time to build the army and to prepare the people for a long war. Now was the time for hiding.

The French made daring parachute raids into the jungled mountains of North Vietnam, and once drove Giap into a "last ditch" hiding place. The general counterattacked savagely; motorized Moroccan Colonial Infantry Regiment saved the exhausted paratroopers at the last moment only by smashing through a to-the-death blocking effort by Viet Minh soldiers.

Vo Nguyen Giap spent 1947–1950 in contemplation, studying his enemy and testing tactical ideas, recruiting and training new soldiers, looking always for the "most ardent" cadre. It was a rare opportunity for a military commander at war and, for Giap, an absolutely essential learning period. Just a few years before he had led a thirty-four-man platoon into combat; now he commanded more than 50,000 troops. It would take time to build popular fervor, to organize local guerilla bands and regional militia companies—and to train and equip the large mobile units of his main forces for combat with the French Army.

This was a time for building political strength. In a long war, Giap believed, it was political strength that prevailed—not military strength.

Viet Minh recruits swore an oath "to respect the people, to help the people, to defend the people, . . . to win the confidence and affection of the people, and to achieve a perfect understanding between the people and the Army." And from the earliest days of this army, a political officer shared hardship and responsibility with the military officer in every unit. The political officer organized days of army assistance to the people to plant or harvest rice, to strengthen flood-control dikes, or to improve trails and roads, and his work encouraged the people to open their homes and share their meals with soldiers of the army. Beside every regimental, battalion, and company commander in the People's Army stood a political officer whose permission, support, and assistance were *required* before the undertaking of any military operation.

Giap had strongly emphasized the essential role of the people in a protracted war in a small book he wrote in 1950. A long-term resistance, he wrote, "requires a whole system of education, a whole ideological struggle among the people. . . .

"Without the people, we shall have no information [about the enemy], we shall be able neither to preserve secrecy nor carry out rapid movements. The people suggest strategems and act as guides. They find liaison officers, hide us, protect our activities, feed us, and tend our wounded."

It was imperative, therefore, that the army respect the people. Soldiers had to be *politically* aware as well as militarily adept. "Political work in the ranks is of the first importance," Giap concluded. "It is the soul of the Army."

The Americans would try to wage a war in Vietnam without disrupting the daily routine of American citizens. Giap could not conceive of such a war. From the first tentative guerrilla actions in 1941—indeed, from the beginnings of Vietnamese history in the third century B.C.—success in war had always required the total commitment of the people.

Vo Nguyen Giap husbanded his military resources while the political foundation for the People's Army was laid. The first principle was *doc lap:* independence. The French Army, even in 1950, refused to take him seriously—perhaps remembering the ridiculous little figure in the trilby hat.

In September of 1950, Giap massed his forces at Cao Bang—a provincial capital quite near his own bases and far from French support. The French commander ignored orders to destroy all equipment and force-march his 2,600 soldiers and 500 civilians to Dong Khe. He tried to drive out. Instead of a hard, heartless God-save-the-hindmost dash to the fort at Dong Khe, the Cao Bang garrison pushed a painful, much-ambushed nine miles in the first day. A Moroccan task force of 3,500 men held Dong Khe until the exhausted survivors from Cao Bang arrived, but Giap's hungry legions followed them in. Three French paratroop battalions leaped into the battle in the final days—and vanished like twigs in a fire.

When it was over, on October 7, the French had lost 6,000 soldiers, 13 artillery pieces, 125 mortars and more than 8,000 rifles—enough to equip a Viet Minh division. Giap ruled the northern frontier, and had secured his supply lines to China. The war would continue for four more years, but the initiative was now with the Viet Minh.

Giap learned his trade by trial—and error. Once he left the mountains to try his massed infantry attacks against the French in the open; he lost 6,000 men in a single day. In a 1952 campaign against an isolated but powerful French base, Giap lost 9,000.

Because of these sanguinary tactics, Giap was judged by his Western military contemporaries as "indifferent to heavy losses." Yet these were not appallingly costly campaigns in the annals of war—not even by American standards. During the Civil War in the United States, at Shiloh, on a Sunday and Monday in early April of 1862, more than 13,000 Union soldiers and 11,000 Confederates died in the battle of Pittsburg Landing. McClellan and Lee met in the Seven Day Battles later that year—and 36,000 were killed. The U.S. Marines' 26th Regiment, the one defending at Khe Sanh, had participated in an island assault against the Japanese in 1944 in which the Marines suffered battle losses of 26,000.

Giap parceled his casualties in the early 1950s, slowly building his forces and improving their equipment, stretching out the French defenses with surprise thrusts and distant raids—always probing for an opening where he could strike with effect.

The opportunity came at Dienbienphu. Giap's mobilization order went out on December 6, 1953:

> You must repair the roads, overcome all obstacles, surmount all difficulties, fight unflinchingly, defeat cold and hunger, carry heavy loads across mountains and valleys, and strike right into the enemy's camp to destroy him and free our countrymen. Comrades, forward!

The French intercepted the order, but found it impossible to trace accurately the vast movement of men and supplies toward the distant base at Dienbienphu. Thirty thousand Viet Minh soldiers crossed the Black River on underwater bridges that could not be seen from the air; one regiment marched 250 miles through the mountains. Thousands of porters pushed bicycles hung with artillery shells along narrow paths hacked out of impossible terrain.

"After opening the first breach," Giap had written in his manual on how to assault a fortress, "immediately penetrate into the interior of the enemy's fortified system and hold that penetration to the bitter end. . . ."

After one hundred days of preparation and reconnaissance, Giap stunned the French defenders with an artillery overmatch, filled the sky with anti-aircraft fire—and hurled his People's Army at Dienbienphu. To the bitter end. During the fifty-six-day battle, Giap returned French casualties and refused his own, knowing their agonies would trouble the defenders. The awful scenes and sounds at Dienbienphu gave Fall his title: *Hell in a Very Small Place.* When his losses grew grievous, Giap put thousands of civilian laborers into the front lines to dig trenches to the very face of the French bunkers—"gnawing away," he called it—so his assault troops could literally leap into the defenders' positions.

Dienbienphu fell on May 7, 1954, and France decided almost immediately that Indochina was no longer worth French francs or blood.

General Vo Nguyen Giap, thrust onto the world stage by his spectacular victory, stayed in the mountains until October, when the 308th Division, the spearhead of the Liberation Army, marched proudly into Hanoi. Most of these soldiers had not seen or communicated with their families for eight years—not since the night of December 19, 1946, when they had whispered a quick goodbye and disappeared into the darkness. Giap walked into the Hanoi power station two days later and began discussing technical problems with the French engineers; there was much to learn in the sixty days of transition from French to Vietnamese rule.

• • •

BY JANUARY, 1968, Giap had fought the Americans for three full years. Most of the cities and towns in his country—and nearly all of the masonry buildings—had been bombed to rubble. The Vietnamese, xenophobic in every pore, blamed themselves for some of the early deaths of school children. They had adopted the French style of stately two-story brick buildings for their schools rather than a more modest one-story Vietnamese structure—and the American bombers went for big buildings first.

In the year just past, American bombers destroyed 11,763 boats and barges and sampans, 2,511 rail cars and rolling stock, 5,587 trucks and buses and cars, 30 power plants, and 179 railroad switching yards. The supersonic planes leveled only 3,547 buildings, down from more than 8,000 in 1966 because, outside of Hanoi and Haiphong, there weren't too many buildings left in North Vietnam. And U.S. jets had taken out the thermal plant, a railroad repair shop, and tobacco, soap, and hosiery factories in Hanoi itself.

Yet Giap had increased the flow of men and supplies to the south and, more importantly, the people seemed rock steady One thousand civilians died under the bombs every week, Hanoi was a bleak and cheerless place, and shortages were common. Still, the North Vietnamese seemed to respond to the bombing raids with the same hardy, angry stoicism that had marked British reaction to German air raids. One hundred thousand North Vietnamese worked full-time on bomb damage, another 500,000 worked at bomb repair two or three days a month.

"It is a sacred war—for independence, for freedom, life," asserted Premier Pham Van Dong. "It stands for everything, this war—for this generation and for future generations.

"We are preparing for a long war," he continued. "How many years would you say? Ten, twenty. . . . What do you think about twenty? The younger generation will fight better than we. . . ."

Slowly, Giap had collected the weapons to make the skies of North Vietnam extremely hostile to American bombers. In the bravado of the early days of the war, before Giap had installed eight thousand anti-aircraft guns and carved out more than two hundred surface-to-air missile sites, American pilots liked to carry business cards with their name and rank on one side and these words on the other: "Yea, though I fly through the valley of the shadow of death, I shall fear no evil, for I am the meanest son of a bitch in the valley."

By late 1967, the air defenses in the Red River Valley were awesome. U.S. losses were more than three times as great there as elsewhere in North Vietnam. Two F105 Thunderchief wings had lost more than two hundred planes on the run to Hanoi; in one four-month period, twelve of twenty-two air crews were lost in action. Giap had 125,000 soldiers of the People's Army in air defense roles, and just about every farmer and militiaman with a rifle popped away at the raiders. His surface-to-air missiles had claimed ninety American planes, and last October his new MIGs from Russia had shot down six of the U.S. planes.

Giap's chief deputy, General Van Tien Dung, was certain the Americans would invade out of frustration.

"We would welcome them," Giap said. "They will find themselves caught in people's war; they will find every village a hornets' nest."

The defense minister had issued instructions for the military training of citizens more than a year before. Every village, hamlet, city block, factory, commune and secondary school had a Self-Defense Militia whose members received weapons, light training, and regular assignments in damage repair, camouflage freshening, missile site construction, and even defusing time bombs.

"Every citizen is an enemy-killing combatant," Giap declared. "Every house is a combat cell; every village or factory a fortress."

Twenty-three years earlier, Ho Chi Minh had looked sadly at the French commissioner for Indochina, Jean Sainteny, and regretted aloud that Vietnam and France were on the threshold of war. "If we must fight, we will fight," Ho had said. "You will kill ten of our men, but we will kill one of yours, and in the end it is you that will tire," Ho Chi Minh's mobilization order in 1966. "Prepare for the Worst," pledged a fight to the end: "Johnson and his clique must know that they may send five hundred thousand or one million or more troops, they may use thousands of aircraft to intensify their attacks on North Vietnam. The war may last for five, ten, twenty years or longer. Hanoi, Haiphong and a number of cities may be destroyed but the Vietnamese people are not afraid."

General Giap believed the American political commitment to the war was fragile, and he thought the war was progressing in the manner that he thought it should.

Years before, addressing the political officers of the 316th Division, he had predicted the course of the war with the French—or with any army not prepared for protracted struggle "The enemy will pass slowly from the offensive to the defensive," he said. "The blitzkrieg will transform itself into a war of long duration. Thus the enemy will be caught in a dilemma: he has to drag out the war to win it, but he does not possess, on the other hand, the psychological and political means to fight a long drawn-out war." The people would soon tire of the high costs and useless bloodshed of a winless army, he predicted, and call the army home.

But what might happen, a French television interviewer asked him in 1966, if the Americans used firepower instead of manpower? Giap had arrived before the camera in an open-necked khaki shirt, relaxed and joking. When the French director asked him to sit differently, Giap had retorted, laughing, "I'm the one who usually gives the orders around here." Now his face grew hard, and his voice took on a harsh, forceful edge.

"Whatever methods the Americans employ, they will never be able to change this irreversible truth . . . our liberation war is a just war. We will win!"

He raised his fist to slam the table, but was restrained by the director who feared the tape recording might be distorted by the bang.

Giap had learned an important truth about the Americans by 1966: "they overestimate their strong points." Even with 500,000 troops in South Vietnam, it was a rare day when as many as one-tenth of them aggressively searched the countryside for Giap's soldiers. The Americans had stupendously large base areas and only small combat units.

For example, the U.S. Marines had put together a major assault force for a 1966 operation in Quang Tri Province, in the rolling, savannah country of the midlands, between Quang Tri City and Khe Sanh. More than 1,500 North Vietnamese soldiers had moved across the DMZ, it was believed, and to meet the challenge the Marines formed Task Force Delta—a regimental headquarters, an artillery battalion, and four infantry battalions—more than 4,000 men on paper.

The task force was formed at Phu Bai, and it flew first to Dong Ha, and then to a fire support base near the target area. One of the infantry battalions was left at Dong Ha to secure the major trans-shipment point for Task Force Delta ammunition and supplies. A second battalion guarded the artillery base and headquarters for the operation. A third battalion air-assaulted into the enemy valley with only three companies because its fourth company had been left to guard the perimeter at Phu Bai. Fifteen Marines were killed and 10 seriously injured in helicopter crashes on the first day, so one of the companies secured a landing zone to evacuate casualties. The other two companies, each down to about 130 men because of malaria, heat exhaustion, combat losses, and vacation leaves, set out to look for the North Vietnamese.

The fourth battalion landed by helicopter a two-day march away. It, too, had left a company at Phu Bai for base security.

Thus Task Force Delta was actually searching for the North Vietnamese with just five companies—hardly 700 men.

One of the American units in which General Westmoreland took considerable pride was the 173rd Airborne Brigade, yet a hard-charging lieutenant colonel decided it was a paper unit: "By the time you subtracted support roles, pizza huts, clubs, headquarters, mess, artillery, and engineers," the 10,000-man force was down to 3,000. Applying the "ass in the grass" test—by counting paratroopers actually on combat patrol—the colonel determined his brigade had fewer than 800 men in the field at any one time.

"His forces remain insufficient," Giap had concluded after a late 1967 analysis of American strengths and weaknesses, "even though they are numerous."

The North Vietnamese general respected U.S. firepower, but he did not hesitate to match his soldiers against the Americans in the field. "We cannot compare our weapons to theirs," he said, "but if we consider the infantry—the principal force determining victory or defeat on the battlefield—U.S. forces are not superior to ours.

"They are greenhorns, not to be compared with the French in their time. They have no idea of jungle fighting. . . . They walk into traps that wouldn't fool a baby."

One of Giap's colleagues on the general staff derided U.S. forces for running from combat if air and artillery were not immediately available, yet another thought the Americans had developed excellent fighting methods against the Japanese and Germans and North Koreans. If the People's Army fought in the same manner, spread across front lines, the Americans would surely win, he said. By choosing a different form of combat, the North Vietnamese had caused the huge American military operations to become "only punches in the air."

"We have forced the Americans to eat soup with forks," he declared.

Because of the many frustrations, Giap said, "the morale of American soldiers is lower than grass." He believed his soldiers were "clearly superior in high fighting spirit and good fighting methods." It was true that Giap's veterans rarely faced experienced American soldiers: the one-year tour and rapid rotation of officers guaranteed rookie Americans in the line in almost every battle.

By late 1967, Vo Nguyen Giap believed he could fight this kind of war against the Americans indefinitely, and he thought he saw strategic and political strains developing inside the United States that would undermine American commitment.

Still, Giap did not expect the Americans to go home soon. "It will be a combination of grueling, protracted war of attrition and morale-shattering attacks on urban centers" that would finally force the United States out of Vietnam, he said. To survive in the American meatgrinder during the years of waiting would take a special quality of commitment:

"We must have not just great determination, but we must . . . have a good fighting method."

In every article, speech, and manual, Vo Nguyen Giap talked about camouflage, deception, surprise, and misdirection, and he reached frequently into Vietnam's past to provide uplifting examples of "few against many" victories. Always he emphasized "high quality," and he and Ho Chi Minh underscored the nation's dependence on soldiers of exceptional quality by attending graduation ceremonies for *dac cong.* These elite soldiers took a year of intensive commando training and learned the many uses of explosives; Ho Chi Minh called them "our answer to the B-52s." *Dac cong* had cracked the defenses on Hill 861 at Khe Sanh on January 21; they would lead infantry assaults in the General Offensive.

Camouflage had special meaning for an army without air cover—especially when the enemy flew a Vigilante reconnaissance plane whose cameras stop the action so dead, even at one thousand knots airspeed, "that you can see the worried expressions on the faces on the ground." Hardly anyone in North Vietnam traveled without first donning a broad hat decorated with leaves and twigs; every moving vehicle was covered with a rope fretwork into which boughs and branches had been woven. Camouflage could be a companion more worthy than a flak jacket; the armored vest might stop bullets or shell fragments, but camouflage could keep the bullets from coming at all.

The constant freshening of camouflage was only one of dozens of differences between the *bo doi*, the soldiers of Giap's People's Army, and their American peers.

The *bo doi's* most important piece of equipment was a thirty-inch straight shovel with a hand-hewn hardwood handle worn smooth and dark from steady use. It was his only defense against B-52s—and his protection from American air strikes and artillery. Walking into an empty enemy field fortification was a revelation for Americans: the straight-sided, well-drained fighting trenches zigged and zagged for blast protection, the bunkers were airy and dry, the regimental cooking stoves carefully shielded to avoid infrared detection from the sky, and not so much as a single shovelful of red earth showing to give away the position. North Vietnamese fighting positions were sometimes invisible until you stood in them; U.S. positions could be seen from space satellites.

The North Vietnamese soldier lived with the land. He farmed its fields, cut his bed and his fighting place into it, walked paths, drank its water, used its leaves to hide his movements, and tunneled in its depths. The Americans bulldozed the land, dynamited it, burned it with napalm, and dosed it with chemicals and pesticides.

Thousands of cans of Hamm's and Coke and 7-Up and steaming kettles of mashed potatoes and gravy and aluminum barrels of peaches so enriched the urine of American soldiers that the needles on "people sniffers" banged the right side of the meter when helicopters flew over U.S. installations; the *bo doi* fought without luxuries, often without necessities, and chemical detection was more difficult.

Giap discussed the special problems of moving an entire infantry division—10,000 men—into an enemy city by breaking it down to squads, moving them into place under rigid camouflage discipline, then reassembling the division moments before the attack. When Westmoreland talked about moving a division he worried about airfields and seaports, miles of paved road and thousands of barrels of aviation fuel.

And, to a much greater degree than American soldiers, the *bo doi* had "an unshakable conviction that their cause was just." U.S. soldiers inked DEROS calendars on their helmets to keep track of the exact number of days remaining in their Vietnam tour; the soldiers of the People's Army painted "For Nation—Forget Self" on their hats.

Giap never believed valor would be enough.

"In a war against the United States, you need time," he said, repeating the word for emphasis. "Time. This isn't a war that you can resolve in a few years. The Americans will be defeated by getting tired, and in order to tire them, we have to go on—to last—for a long time.

"A long time," he said again. "A long time."

All through 1966 and 1967 the top military theoreticians in North Vietnam had struggled with how best to fight the United States. Giap counseled patience—a protracted war—but he was criticized for his "conservative spirit" by younger bloods in the People's Army. Heavy battles with powerful American forces had finally convinced most of the doubters, however, and by early 1968 North Vietnam was settling in for a long, hard war.

The formal decision of the political and military councils was to conduct battlefield operations "that would sustain a credible military threat, [yet] prolong the war until political, military, and psychological factors combined to produce a favorable solution."

Some years later, a declining heavyweight boxer would give the strategy an unpretty name: "rope-a-dope." Facing younger, stronger fighters, Muhammad Ali would fall back on the ropes of the ring, cover his head and abdomen with his gloves and forearms, and absorb punch after punch after punch—an armadillo in Everlast shorts. He used the ropes to drain the shock, as Giap used the jungle to blunt American firepower, and he waited, peeking, planning, taking heavy hits, looking for the first sign of tiring, the first faint opening, and then . . . . . . Bam! He didn't have knockout power, but he impressed the judges with his patience and persistence—and the solid authority of his counter-punches. It wasn't pretty, but it extended Ali's career; he even won some important fights when his foes pounded themselves into weariness.

Giap, of course, could not be limited to fifteen rounds, or fifteen years.

"We are in no hurry," he said.

• • •

VO NGUYEN GIAP reviewed his preparations for the General Offensive. He had not originally endorsed this idea, but no one could accuse him of holding back.

He had spent young North Vietnamese soldiers by the hundreds—by the thousands, according to Westmoreland—to draw the strongest American forces to the border country and mountains. He had hit their bases with artillery attacks across the DMZ, and greatly increased their security problems with his new, longer-range rockets. He had completely reorganized his considerable forces inside Laos, and he felt quite sure an American attack at the Ho Chi Minh Trail could be absorbed—and savaged. Preparations for an American invasion of North Vietnam had been complete for months.

He had sent recruits south to fill the holes in the Viet Cong ranks, so their units would be at full strength for the assault on the cities. He had multiplied the flow of supplies to the Viet Cong by ten times in recent months, and moved artillery/rocket regiments to support the attack. His regular People's Army divisions would not lead the way, but they would be standing by to exploit any Viet Cong breakthrough.

Giap was utterly contemptuous of ARVN, the government soldiers of South Vietnam. Fighting at the side of foreigners would destroy their combat spirit as surely as acid, he believed; besides, the mutual suspicion between American and ARVN soldiers was so great "the puppet army [ARVN] has become impotent."

If Vo Nguyen Giap was concerned in early 1968, it was by his total dependence on the Chinese for rifles and bullets, and by the Russians' diplomatic delays in delivering the most modern war equipment.

Giap had found sanctuary in China during some of the hardest years of his life, and China had generously nourished his army for a quarter century—but China was an historic enemy. The Americans would sooner or later go away; China was forever. Yet without the Chinese, Giap's army would wither and die, and so the general put on his most winning smile and joined toasts to eternal friendship with his neighbor to the north.

The Russians were also generous—Giap's small but fine air force, his forests of anti-aircraft guns and surface-to-air missiles and his sophisticated radar tracking equipment had come from the Soviet Union—but the Russians seemed to be playing some Big Power game with the United States rather than pouring themselves into the fight. The Russians counseled restraint, and transmitted back-channel messages from the Americans, and never would provide the very best equipment until it fit *their* purpose.

Giap could have shot down a great many more U.S. airplanes with the superior third-generation missile called Super SAM, but the Russians could not find enough of them to share until American B-52s rattled the windows in Hanoi. And the deadly Strela, a shoulder-fired, heat-seeking missile that could sweep helicopters from the sky, or the Styx, an over-the-horizon rocket that could sink a destroyer in a single blow, were not available to the People's Army until *after* American helicopters and ships had left Vietnam.

Still, Giap was encouraged by growing signs that the Americans would not stay the course, and by the strains he could see in their military resources.

"If small reinforcements are sent, it will be impossible to remedy the situation," he decided, analyzing what he thought was the American dilemma, "and if large reinforcements are sent, it will greatly influence the American people's political and economic life, and U.S. strategy in the world."

In either case, Giap was prepared to fight on—even if it meant starting again at the beginning. He had already prepared positions in the northern mountains. The stakes were too high to think of bowing to a few more bombs or bullets: "Fighting against U.S. aggression and for national salvation is the great, sacred, historic task of the Vietnamese people," he wrote. "Our soldiers and people are united . . . and fear no sacrifices, no hardships. We are ready to carry on the resistance for five, ten, twenty or more years. . . ."

• • •

GENERAL GIAP HAD grown heavier in recent years, and had started wearing medals and dress uniforms on formal occasions. His forehead still climbed "like the brow of a Roman orator" to a thick mat of black hair high on his head, but now it showed tiny purple blood vessels. Some visitors found him not pleasant to look at, but he could still command a room with black eyes "sharp, shrewd, laughing, cruel . . . two drops of black light that convey utter sureness . . . authority."

And calm.

It would happen, several years later, that Cambodian Prince Norodom Sihanouk would come to visit on the very day that a huge South Vietnamese military force launched an invasion of Laos from Khe Sanh. Sihanouk apologized for keeping the appointment on such a day, but Giap waved him to a chair. The general put a record on the phonograph, and music played as the two shared a leisurely meal and talked about the problems of Indochina. Sihanouk apologized again, and this time Giap assured him that the visit was not an interruption. He had been quite prepared for this thrust at the Ho Chi Minh Trail, he said, and he invited the prince to note the unfolding of events. It was *timing* that was so critical in warfare, he said.

And camouflage. And deception. And surprise.

"Surprise is very important," Giap said. "We must practice the art of catching the enemy by surprise as to the direction, targets and time of attack, and the forces fielded and the forms of combat used by our side. We must use skillful strategems to deceive the enemy, and cause him to make a wrong assessment of our intentions.

"We must create surprise in the most varied ways."

Giap had watched Westmoreland move troops to the north in late 1967 and the first weeks of 1968. Now, on the night of January 30, Giap knew the Viet Cong had successfully infiltrated many towns and cities in South Vietnam.

It seemed unbelievable. The Americans had captured the order for the General Offensive in early January and actually distributed a translation of it to the news media in Saigon. They just didn't believe it was true.

Giap was fifty-five years old now, and he had been at war or on the run for more than half his life. He had prepared carefully for the General Offensive, and he had helped choose the time for maximum effect: the first hours of Vietnam's most revered holiday, Tet.

Giap didn't really think the surprise attack would work and he believed the war would continue for years—but he loved the boldness of it.

7.

The Tet Offensive

General Westmoreland was jolted awake at 3 A.M. by the rocket artillery of three enemy divisions in the suburbs of Saigon. Three thousand Viet Cong soldiers and commando teams were already in the city—striking toward the radio station, the airport, the Presidential Palace, the South Vietnamese military headquarters, the port facilities, and other key targets.

Enemy anti-aircraft guns—big ones, on wheels, with seats for two gunners—jabbed the night sky with green tracers. They had been towed hundreds of miles by hand to be parked at the gates of Tan Son Nhut.

Reports flooded Westmoreland's command center. Hue was under heavy attack—and so were thirty-six of the forty-four provincial capitals in the country. Every major airfield was being hammered by mortars and rockets, and some were fighting off infantry assaults. Soldiers were battling in five of the nation's six autonomous cities, in sixty-four district capitals, and scores of smaller towns. A strong enemy force had hit the Delta city of My Tho, where South Vietnamese President Nguyen Van Thieu was spending the Tet holidays with his family.

The U.S. ambassador had been rushed to a secret hiding place. The U.S. Army's military police, outnumbered and outgunned, were taking heavy casualties in the streets. A Viet Cong sapper team had blasted its way into the U.S. embassy compound, killed four guards, and was now trying to batter down the four-inch-thick teak doors with shoulder-fired rocket grenades.

The shockwaves rippled almost instantly into the Situation Room in the basement of the White House, where President Johnson's assistant for national security affairs, Walt W. Rostow, was giving a late afternoon tour to several *Washington Post* reporters. He had hoped to show them that the war was going much better than the skeptical *Post* was reporting. They were looking at the photomural of Khe Sanh when the first printer chattered out its urgent message. Then another printer spoke, and another. Aides began hurrying in and out. The phone from the Oval Office rang.

The President of the United States wanted to know what the hell was going on.

• • •

WESTMORELAND WEIGHED THE hundreds of reports and juggled his forces—especially to meet the threat on the capital city. But his ear was most attuned for news from the north—from Khe Sanh.

At 9:20 in the morning, the general motored through tense, empty streets to the recaptured embassy compound. A helicopter had put thirty-six 101st Airborne paratroopers on the embassy roof just as MPs and Marines battered down the main gates with a jeep and went in shooting. Nineteen Viet Cong commandos, and three embassy chauffeurs who had waved their identity cards in a futile bid for life, lay crumpled along the wall or beside the round concrete planters on the embassy lawn. The rivulets of blood on the embassy steps were still bright red, and the crump of mortars and swish-BAM of rockets sounded occasionally in the near distance. The embassy compound's high walls offered excellent protection, but even soldiers in the crowd of reporters, MPs, paratroopers, and embassy officials flinched as overrounds and richochets careened overhead.

Westmoreland stood perfectly erect. He was clean shaven, and wore a pressed, starched fatigue uniform with his four stars stitched into the collars. The mud of the scarred lawn was everywhere, but not a mote marred his gleaming boots.

"The enemy has very deceitfully taken advantage of the Tet truce," he said, but even so, "the enemy's well-laid plans went afoul." The attempt to take the embassy had inflicted superficial damage to the building's lobby and left all the attackers dead, he reported. The assault on Tan Son Nhut, still continuing, had caused "no damage of consequence."

The general reported that a large store of aviation fuel and two airplanes had been lost at Bien Hoa airbase, not far from Saigon, and that enemy troops had attacked airfields and cities and towns all across the country to "create maximum consternation."

"In my opinion," he said, "this is a diversionary effort to take attention away from the north, [from] an attack on Khe Sanh."

In the meantime, he was glad for the opportunity to apply maximum firepower to an enemy who had become "more exposed, more vulnerable" by his attack on cities.

"When I left the office yesterday, we had accounted for almost 700 enemy killed over the country just yesterday," Westmoreland said. "My guess is that the death toll today will be comparable."

Westmoreland was certain the attack on the cities was a trick. While there was some very hard fighting going on inside Saigon and eight or nine other cities, the total enemy force didn't look much larger than maybe 30,000 Viet Cong soldiers across the whole country. He had 492,000 American servicemen under his command—325,000 Army, 31,700 Navy, 78,000 Marine, 55,900 Air Force and 500 Coast Guard. He had 62,000 Koreans and Australians—and more than a half million South Vietnamese under arms. "It did not occur to us that the enemy would undertake suicidal attacks in the face of our power," he said. He decided in the earliest hours that the enemy offensive was doomed to failure.

Just about the only place in South Vietnam of any significance that had not been attacked in the Tet Offensive was Khe Sanh; none of the five North Vietnamese Army divisions that had "materialized" in the DMZ region had joined the fighting.

It was now clear to Westmoreland that the enemy's 1967–68 winter-spring campaign would unfold in three separate phases: first, the border battles at Con Thien, Loc Ninh, and Dak To; then a lunatic raid on the cities by the Viet Cong to divert attention; and finally a Dienbienphu-style assault by large North Vietnamese forces against Khe Sanh and other I Corps targets. Phase Two was "about to run out of steam," he told news reporters in Saigon on February 1; the enemy had already suffered more than 6,000 casualties.

News that the enemy's hardest blow was yet to come stunned an already sobered Washington. Simultaneous attacks against one hundred cities was an extraordinary military showing for an enemy force that had been described by Westmoreland in recent months as scattered and demoralized. The general had seen "dismay and incredulity" on the faces of reporters in the embassy yard; and now he discovered that the South Vietnamese leadership was paralyzed by the surprise attack. "The government, from President Thieu down through the various ministries, appeared to be stunned."

Shock was also etched on the faces of Westmoreland's own staff. "Saigon was in desperate trouble," said General Chaisson who, as director of the combat operations center, sat at the nerve center of U.S. military communications in Vietnam. "The enemy was in the city. There were three divisions around the city."

Because enemy sappers failed to destroy key bridges, one American armored cavalry unit was able to rush to Tan Son Nhut through the dark, following flares dropped from a helicopter by its commander. Another deciding factor in the fight at the airport, where both the South Vietnamese and American general staffs were headquartered, was an accident. Two of South Vietnam's best-equipped combat battalions had been scheduled to fly out the night before to augment the quarter million Allied troops in I Corps, but a scheduling error had left them on the runway. Thus a thousand ARVN paratroopers and Marines were able to join the fight.

"By the skin of our teeth," said General Chaisson, "we were able to keep the major enemy elements out of Saigon."

U.S. troops in the Highlands were on "good alert status—with patrols out," but still they were shocked by the enemy assault. "We did not expect to encounter fourteen powerful, highly synchronized attacks" on every major government center and military installation in the region, the II Corps commander said later. The enemy, he conceded, had shown "exceeding cunning and keen deception."

The fighting continued in a dozen cities into the early days of February, and Viet Cong forces launched new attacks in some regions. The estimate of enemy forces engaged now rose to 60,000, perhaps 70,000.

Even though the 7th North Vietnamese Army division and the 5th and 9th Viet Cong divisions were close enough to Saigon to pose a second-strike threat, Westmoreland was more concerned about the unstruck blow in the north, at Khe Sanh.

The apprehension was even greater in Washington, D.C. The story of the Tet Offensive—the rubble and the bodies in the embassy attack, the low-level bombing and raging flames in a score of Vietnamese cities, and especially the sharp increase in American death tolls—dominated the front pages and evening newscasts in the United States. The nation, fed on increasingly optimistic military reports all through 1967, inhaled a collective gasp of astonishment.

And according to Westmoreland's daily report to Washington, the "maximum effort" was still to come.

The Commander in Chief dreaded what the next message might bring.

On February 2, he asked General Wheeler if there was a chance that nuclear weapons might have to be used in Vietnam. Wheeler had pooh-poohed the idea in secret testimony before the Senate

Armed Forces Committee that day, but at the President's request he asked the question of Westmoreland.

"We should be prepared to introduce weapons of greater effectiveness," COMMUSMACV replied. The general was now very concerned about the North Vietnamese Army's uncommitted divisions along the DMZ; he felt I Corps positions were "seriously imperiled," especially if the enemy launched massed infantry attacks as he expected.

"Under such circumstances, I visualize that either tactical nuclear weapons or chemical agents would be active candidates for deployment," Westmoreland told Wheeler.

The highly classified discussion splashed onto the front pages on February 9. Senator J. W. Fulbright, chairman of the foreign relations committee, had asked Secretary of State Dean Rusk about reports that Westmoreland was stockpiling nuclear weapons in South Vietnam for possible use at Khe Sanh—and that four nuclear scientists had recently flown from the United States to Saigon on a secret mission.

Johnson Administration officials flatly denied that the Joint Chiefs of Staff had recommended or requested the use of nuclear weapons, which was an honest evasion of the truth.

Newspaper speculation about nuclear weapons for Vietnam had such profound effects in Congress that General Wheeler called Westmoreland and told him to stop planning for their use at Khe Sanh. COMMUSMACV said he thought it was a mistake, but he disbanded his secret study committee.

The threat in the north consumed Westmoreland.

"It [is] conceivable that the enemy could drive us back in the northern provinces, and it [is] wise to prepare for the worst," he decided. He set up a staff study of surf conditions on the South Vietnamese coast in April; if he was pushed out of the northern part of I Corps in the coming battle, he planned to recapture the lost ground with an amphibious assault—with the Marines securing the beaches and the Army leap-frogging ahead by helicopter and tank.

• • •

WESTMORELAND WAS BECOMING more attuned to the magnitude of the Tet Offensive. The enemy seemed willing to spend thousands—maybe even tens of thousands—of soldiers. Heavy fighting was continuing in Saigon, and Hue, and several Delta cities.

Despite Westmoreland's extensive preparations for battle in I Corps in December and January, the situation in the north was worsening.

On January 24, a South Vietnamese military convoy had arrived at Quang Tri City from Saigon—the first through-trip on Route 1 in years. The achievement was announced as an important step in the struggle to secure the roads from Viet Cong interdiction.

At 3 A.M. on January 31, enemy sappers dynamited twenty-five bridges and eleven culverts on Route 1 between Da Nang and Hue. Teams of saboteurs cut an eight-inch pipeline that carried aviation fuel to the thirsty helicopters of the 1st Air Cavalry Division—and torched a tank farm with fifty thousand barrels of fuel.

American forces in the north needed twenty-six hundred tons of supplies every day, not including petroleum, oil, and lubricants, and another one thousand tons a day to prepare for Operation Pegasus—the relief of Khe Sanh. In a single stroke, the daily disgorgement was squeezed off to a trickle.

The logistics situation turned critical almost immediately.

"Achieving a high measure of surprise," three enemy battalions smashed into Quang Tri City, the capital of South Vietnam's northernmost province and a key transshipment point for Marine and Army supplies. ARVN troops blunted the badly coordinated enemy attack, but the fate of the city was still in doubt in the early afternoon. Heavy fog, or the need to guard enormous quantities of newly delivered equipment, kept nearby American units from joining the fight.

The only U.S. forces immediately available were the two 1st Air Cav battalions pushing toward Khe Sanh. They shut down the firebases they had built the day before, turned their backs on the combat base, and flew back to Quang Tri City—air-assaulting into intense enemy fire. They routed the attackers, killing 900 North Vietnamese.

The fighting was worst in Hue.

Eight Viet Cong and North Vietnamese battalions—probably 3,000 men, many of them in dark combat fatigues—moved into central Vietnam's most handsome and historic city without detection. Emperor Gia Long had built a magnificent citadel there in 1802, diverting the waters of the River of Perfumes to fill the moats and erecting great brick walls—ninety feet thick at the main gates—to mark the boundaries of the capital city, the royal city and, in the heart of the fortress, the Forbidden City.

The French colonial governor had made his home in Hue. The city—off-limits to most American servicemen—had retained a French ambiance, with cream-colored buildings and red tile roofs, a large Catholic cathedral, a Jesuit school, nuns in habit in the hospitals and schools, even a sports club on the banks of the river. Sampans still poled its languid lagoons, and on lazy summer mornings it was possible to hear the thock-thock of tennis matches at Le Cercle Sportif.

Westmoreland had cabled Washington January 22 with a warning that the enemy might attempt a multibattalion attack on Hue, but the people of Hue didn't get the word. U.S. and Vietnamese intelligence officials celebrated Tet with a great feast in the back room of Hue's best Chinese restaurant, and some Americans were singing college songs and drinking toasts to the New Year as Viet Cong soldiers clambered into boats for an amphibious assault on the citadel.

With crack battalions of the North Vietnamese Army's 4th and 6th Regiments leading the way, enemy troops overran the city. The headquarters staff of the 1st ARVN division managed to hold out in the Peaceful Royal Library and a small temple in the northwest corner of the citadel, and a U.S. Army detachment on the south side of the Perfume River successfully threw back enemy attacks through the night. But at dawn, flying from the King's Knight, a 123-foot tower built in 1809 to fly the emperor's colors, was the red and blue banner of the Liberation Army.

The Viet Cong flag flew for twenty-five hard days.

American commanders misjudged the size and determination of the enemy force in the first days, sending small Marine infantry units into Hue. Stunned by the brutal losses that attended close-range fighting in the middle of a city, but glad for an opportunity to "kick some behinds," the Marines pushed into the old imperial capital house by house, block by block, street by street. Later, the bombers would come, and huge shells from U.S. Navy ships in the South China Sea, and heavy artillery. Tanks maneuvered awkwardly in the streets, offering broad targets for enemy rockets—and answering with pointblank cannon fire. World War II veterans compared the battle of Hue with the worst city fighting in Western Europe.

Whole blocks of the city were pulverized. More than 3,000 civilians died in the shellfire and fighting, and 116,000 fled their homes in panic.

The North Vietnamese commander on the south bank of the Perfume River had been killed in the opening minutes of the attack; then an artillery shell killed the commander of all enemy troops at Hue. His deputy asked for permission to withdraw: casualties were mounting rapidly, and pressure from both American and ARVN troops was getting unbearable.

He was told to hold.

The North Vietnamese were ferrying supplies and replacements to the citadel in steel-bottomed boats, motoring in under the cover of darkness on the Perfume River. They had established two logistics lines to Hue, one from the mountains that reached to within five miles of Hue on the west, and one from the *north*, down from the DMZ on dirt roads and tracks between Highway 1 and the sea.

Nowhere else in South Vietnam had the Tet Offensive established so spectacular a foothold in a city. Viet Cong political officers moved through Hue's neighborhoods, with lists of names and addresses, to arrest teachers, clerks, government officials, students, American and German civilians, religious leaders, doctors, politicians, and shopkeepers. More than 2,800 were bound and marched away—to be executed, or buried alive.

Serious logistics problems crippled American response to the enemy capture of Hue. Major General John Tolson, commander of the 1st Air Cavalry Division, complained that fuel shortages had virtually grounded his powerful third brigade. Lieutenant General Creighton Abrams, sent north by Westmoreland to sort out the chaos, immediately limited all incoming supplies to "beans, bullets, and gasoline," declaring: "Anyone who brings in nonessentials is interfering with the conduct of the war." A U.S. Army transportation battalion, with Navy Seabees and a Marine logistics unit, finally established an off-loading facility on the beach east of Quang Tri City, constructed a two-lane road to Highway 1, and began shuttling fuel and supplies and ammunition from ships at sea to the fighting units inland. During the construction of this facility there occurred a military rarity: the logistics lines of two armies at war actually *crossed* at right angles.

Tolson's cavalrymen, hampered by foul weather, air-assaulted into positions north and west of Hue in early February to look for enemy troops.

The brigade bumped into "an unusually-large enemy force" as it tried to close the circle on Hue, then battered futilely at North Vietnamese blocking positions for three weeks. The turning point came with the arrival of clearing weather, which gave bombers and gunships room to work, and of two battalions of reinforcements from the 101st Airborne Division. The force that Westmoreland had assembled to invade North Vietnam was now committed to free the city of Hue. The North Vietnamese fought bitterly to buy time for the defenders in the citadel, but on February 21, 22, 23, and 24, four American infantry battalions moved inexorably forward behind naval gunfire, heavy artillery, and tactical air strikes.

On this battlefield U.S. intelligence officers discovered three enemy regiments—close to 5,000 North Vietnamese soldiers—that were thought to be in the ring around Khe Sanh. The 29th Regiment, for example, was marked on Marine maps as part of the 325C Division besieging the hilltops; the 24th Regiment was thought to be near Khe Sanh Village. Somehow these units, and another regiment from one of the North Vietnamese DMZ divisions, had side-slipped through northern I Corps to join the attack on Hue.

"Their presence in the vicinity of Hue had been previously unsuspected," the deputy U.S. Army commander in I Corps reported.

On February 25, the last enemy position in the citadel was smashed and the Battle of Hue was over. General Westmoreland announced that 8,000 North Vietnamese had died in the twenty-six-day struggle.

• • •

ENEMY FORCES FAILED to establish the same kind of foothold in Saigon, although a thousand Viet Cong were still fighting scattered battles in the capital city on February 7. American bombers and ARVN artillery had leveled parts of some cities in the Delta to drive out the Viet Cong; hundreds of thousands of new refugees were seeking shelter and food. Enemy interdiction of roads and waterways had brought commerce to a halt throughout South Vietnam.

According to prisoners and radio intercepts and captured documents, the enemy forces were preparing for a second wave of attacks.

Whispers of discontent with Westmoreland's leadership surfaced in the Senate Armed Forces Committee on February 5. General Wheeler told the senators that he knew of no plans to replace Westmoreland, and Defense Secretary McNamara asserted "it is quite unreasonable" to suggest that Westmoreland might be relieved "in the near future." Wheeler was so concerned that these expressions of doubt might reach Saigon that he cabled Westmoreland: "You should know that all of us, including the Commander in Chief, repose complete confidence in your judgment."

Through the early days of February, the President prodded the chairman of the Joint Chiefs of Staff to provide whatever support Westmoreland might need, and Wheeler asked Westmoreland almost daily to state his needs clearly. Washington was worried about the still-pending "maximum effort," and COMMUSMACV was invited to ignore the official limit of 525,000 U.S. soldiers.

"The enemy buildup in the north constitutes the greatest threat," Westmoreland wrote on February 11. "In view of the widespread, ongoing enemy offensive against provincial capitals, population centers, and key installations in the rest of the country, future deployment of friendly forces out of these areas involves a risk I am not prepared to accept. . . .

"I am expressing a firm request for troops. A setback is fully possible if I am not reinforced, and it is likely that we will lose ground in other areas if I am required to make substantial reinforcement in I Corps."

One day later Westmoreland cabled Wheeler:

"I desperately need reinforcements. Time is of the essence."

Wheeler dispatched the 27th Marine Regiment and a brigade of the 82nd Airborne Division. These were among the last combat-ready troops in the national reserve; America's military cupboard was almost bare.

The chairman of the Joint Chiefs flew to Saigon February 23 to speak personally with Westmoreland. General Wheeler was very tired when he arrived, and his face and manner mirrored the gloom that pervaded Washington. Just as Wheeler settled into bed, Viet Cong 122mm rockets pounded the city—one of them striking quite near his guest villa. He hurried out to the airport to the MACV command bunker, where Westmoreland had been sleeping since the start of the enemy offensive.

Wheeler learned in the next few days that "the enemy has the capability—most significantly with the forces he has in the Saigon area—for a second wave of attacks." A powerful enemy force was threatening Dak To in the Highlands, the 2nd NVA division was still in position to attack Da Nang, fighting continued in Hue, and no one really knew what might be happening in the countryside, abandoned as allied troops fell back on the cities. Most ominously, five NVA divisions were still poised for battle in Quang Tri province.

Westmoreland emphasized that he saw great opportunity in the midst of "heightened risk." He urged Wheeler to push again for authorization to send American infantry into North Vietnam, Laos, and Cambodia, and he asked for 206,000 additional U.S. troops to carry out the attacks. Westmoreland said he needed only 108,000 of these soldiers right away but that he wanted the other 98,000 "in the rack"—that is, drafted, trained, equipped, and readied for shipment to Vietnam if needed.

With substantial reinforcements and permission to pursue across the borders, Westmoreland said, he could confidently meet any new North Vietnamese attacks—and move quickly to exploit the enemy's terrible losses in the Tet Offensive, which he estimated at 40,000.

General Wheeler drove from the airport to the White House through a dismal, pre-dawn rain to breakfast with the President, Vice President Hubert H. Humphrey, Secretary of State Dean Rusk, Defense Secretary McNamara (in his last day on the job), incoming Defense Secretary Clark Clifford, Director of Central Intelligence

Richard Helms, retired Army General Maxwell Taylor, and the President's national security adviser, Walt Rostow.

The Tet Offensive had been "a near thing," Wheeler reported. "And the major, powerful, nationwide assault has . . . by no means run its course. The scope and severity of the enemy's attacks and the extent of his reinforcements are presenting us with serious and immediate problems.

"We must be prepared to accept some reverses."

Westmoreland had asked for 206,000 more American troops, Wheeler continued, in the belief he could "destroy the enemy's will" by pouring in reinforcements now. It would mean calling up the reserves and the National Guard, the Chairman of the Joint Chiefs conceded, but he thought the President should "seriously consider" the request.

Westmoreland's request for 206,000 soldiers for an end-the-war offensive in southeast Asia, relayed by a general worried about American military commitments elsewhere in the world, arrived in a Washington that was still shocked by the Tet Offensive. American death tolls had reached their highest level in the war in the third week of February, 543 dead and 2,547 wounded. The second highest toll came in the final week of February, 470 killed and 2,675 wounded. On the day Wheeler arrived in Saigon, the Selective Service System issued a draft call for 48,000 young men—the highest draft call in a generation. The general's request was, quite literally, the final straw.

The people of the United States, including some of the highest officials in the Johnson Administration, began a wrenching reassessment of American commitment in Vietnam. It seemed clear now that the United States could not defeat the enemy, and could not even guarantee the security of South Vietnamese cities, without a massive new infusion of troops. New voices joined the chorus of dissent. "A tidal wave of defeatism" was sweeping across the land, lamented S.L.A. Marshall, the military historian.

The Tet Offensive would mark the watershed of American involvement in Vietnam. Within thirty days the President would set the nation on a new course.

But this morning, at the White House breakfast, the focus was still on Khe Sanh. President Johnson took General Wheeler to the side as the dishes were cleared.

"What's happening at the combat base?"

Wheeler told the President that the Marines were tying down two divisions that might otherwise have been thrown into the battles in the cities.

"The North Vietnamese would pay a terrible price to take the outpost," he assured the President. "And General Westmoreland is confident he can hold."

8.

Bitter Little Battles

The first hours of Tet brought a thick, wet fog to Khe Sanh—but no rockets, no *dac cong*, no screaming waves of North Vietnamese infantrymen. The sun burned away the mists in the afternoon, but the grey veils began to rise again from the creek beds an hour before the dark.

Colonel Lownds tucked an extra M-16 clip into his shirt pocket, and every marine settled a little deeper in the firing pits and sandbagged trenchlines. Grenades, their pins straightened for quick pulling, were stacked in small piles near at hand. Still, no attack came.

Cries of grief rose from the forward lines held by the 37th ARVN Rangers. Word had arrived that the Rangers' wives and children were caught in heavy fighting in the town of Phu Loc; until three days ago, the Rangers had been stationed at Phu Loc.

On February 2, an enemy rocket hurtled in from Hill 881 North and plunged through the door of the U.S. Army Signal Corps bunker. The explosion killed four soldiers instantly—and cut the communication link to the outside world. Contact was quickly reestablished, but not before palms went moist in Da Nang and Saigon.

Blinded by the fog, the Marines struggled to make better use of the new sensor devices. The secret sound/tremor detectors had been sown so hurriedly January 18 that their precise location was unknown. Sensor #23, for example, might pick up strange sounds and broadcast them to a circling aircraft for relay to the computers in Thailand, but when the analysis came back—with solid information that the sounds were truck engines, or troop movements, or heavy digging noises—the Air Force intelligence people could not say exactly where to fire for maximum effect.

The Marines resorted to area fire. Fire coordinators at the combat base would arrange for the Marine and Army artillery to fire on a timed schedule so that every shell arrived on target at the same instant. By assigning each gun a slightly different map coordinate, it was possible to rain shrapnel on a wide area. With practice, the artillerymen could produce a "micro-Arc light"—for a target five hundred meters square—in just ten or fifteen minutes; it took closer to an hour to ready the guns for a "mini-Arc Light," which concentrated explosive airbursts on a target a half mile long by five hundred meters wide.

Even with the sensors, much of the targeting was guesswork. So much time elapsed between the sensor report and the big guns' readiness that fire control officers had to estimate the speed and direction of enemy marches—or risk shooting shells into the past.

In the early hours of February 4, several sensors northwest of the combat base started broadcasting urgent signals. A large body of men—soldiers, or perhaps porters—was moving toward Hill 881 South.

That night the sensors came alive again. Marine Captain Mirza M. Baig, sitting in the bunker that housed the Fire Support Control Center at the combat base, decided to believe what the sensors appeared to be saying: that hundreds of enemy soldiers were moving into positions to attack India Company. Baig pictured several NVA assault battalions crossing the border from Laos under cover of dark, then moving in a two-stage march to jumpoff points west and south of Hill 881 South. Officers in the Fire Support Control Center figured out how fast a North Vietnamese soldier might be able to move in the dark in this terrain, how the attackers were most likely to line up for the assault, and where the reserves were most likely to wait. Poring over their maps, the FSCC planners picked a five hundred meter by three hundred meter target box and, on signal, fired five hundred high explosive shells into it.

Nothing happened. No terrified shouts were heard on the sidebands of the radio. No secondary explosions marked a hit on ammunition supplies. Still, Baig thought the preemptive artillery strike had disrupted enemy plans.

When the hands on the bunker clock moved past 3 A.M., Baig and other officers in the Fire Support Control Center cheered, then applauded themselves. The prime hour for enemy attack had come and gone; the artillery strike *must* have scattered the assault forces.

Five minutes later, enemy artillery, rockets, and mortars pounded the combat base and hilltop outposts. More than 6,000 Marines squinted into the thick mists for the first thickenings that would herald the enemy attack.

At five minutes after four, *dac cong* slipped Bangalore torpedos into the barbed wire barricades on Hill 861 Alpha—and blasted pathways into the interior of the Marines' newest hilltop position. The hill was covered with tall, coarse grass but bald of trees, and the 201 men of E Company had been forced to improvise overhead cover. Seven Marines died in the opening mortar barrage.

North Vietnamese soldiers crept through gaps in the wire. Rocket-propelled grenades—fired in volley at single targets—knocked out the Marines' machine guns and recoilless rifles. When the platoon that received the brunt of the assault began to fall back, Captain Earle G. Breeding ordered his men to don gas masks. Seconds later, the hilltop was shrouded in choking clouds of CS gas—but still the North Vietnamese pressed the attack. All of the heavy weapons at the combat base were now firing shells in a tight ring around Breeding's embattled company, but by 5:08 A.M. the enemy had taken one-fourth of the hilltop.

Captain Breeding was now coordinating supporting fires from the 175mm guns at Camp Carroll, the artillery and heavy mortars at the combat base, radar-guided jet bombers, and mortars and recoilless rifles from Hill 558, Hill 861, and Hill 881 South—which alone fired eleven hundred rounds from just three heavy mortars. When the tubes began to glow in the dark, Dabney's mortarmen poured precious drinking water on them, then cans of fruit juice; finally, they stood in tight little circles urinating on the metal to keep it cool.

Breeding fed three-man fire teams into the flanks of the enemy penetration, then launched a counterattack. Shouting Marines followed a shower of grenades into the captured trenches—and discovered the North Vietnamese had stopped to look at magazines and paperback books. One Marine nearly tore the head off a slightly built NVA soldier with a roundhouse right, then leaped in to finish him off with a knife. Another Marine saw his buddy grabbed from behind; he jammed his M-16 rifle between the combatants and fired a whole magazine on full automatic—ripping chunks from his friend's flak jacket but cutting the enemy soldier in half. Using knives, rifle butts, and fists, and fighting short-range grenade duels in the swirling fog and lingering clouds of tear gas, the Marines threw the North Vietnamese off the hill.

"It was like watching a World War II movie," Captain Breeding said. "We walked all over them."

Helicopters lifted 42 replacements to the hilltop in mid-afternoon, while E Company repaired the gaps in the barbed wire barriers, dragged 109 enemy bodies down the slopes to reduce the inevitable stench, reset machine gun positions, and installed more Claymore mines. Steadiness—and enormous firepower—had prevailed, but the Marines wanted to be ready if Mr. Charles came again.

Forty-eight hours later, enemy tanks overran the Special Forces camp at Lang Vei.

• • •

LANG VEI HAD dangled alone at the end of the line since Khe Sanh Village was abandoned on January 21. It was seven miles by road to the combat base, through a town captured by the North Vietnamese, but the Green Berets did not feel unusually exposed; their calling required them to live and work on the edge.

Besides, Lang Vei had stouter bunkers, more defenders, better fields of fire, and more immediately available firepower support than any other Special Forces camp in Vietnam. Captain Frank C. Willoughby, the camp commander, could even summon B-52s.

An attack on the camp seemed inevitable. Patrols from Lang Vei had been the first to detect the growing North Vietnamese presence at Khe Sanh, and now they bumped into enemy forces almost every day. Artillery shells arced in from Laos and from Co Roc at odd intervals. Every night tentative probes triggered flares in the defensive wire or set the pebble-cans dancing on the cylone fence.

On January 30, a patrol discovered a heavy-duty road built into a stream bed less than a mile from the camp. Boulders and stones had been rolled to the edges so vehicles could pass easily while water erased the tire tracks.

That afternoon, a young North Vietnamese soldier walked out of the scrub and surrendered. He said his name was Luong Dinh Du and that he served with a badly hurt battalion of the 66th Regiment, 304 Division. He had participated in the attack on Khe Sanh Village, and now his battalion—down to just 200 men—was preparing to attack Lang Vei. He couldn't take it any more, Luong Dinh Du said; he had decided to quit the war.

On February 6, the day after the attack on E Company, enemy mortars pounded the Lang Vei camp for one hour after dawn. A direct hit wounded eight South Vietnamese Special Forces soldiers, but the heavy log bunkers—especially the reinforced-concrete command bunker—provided excellent cover for defenders. In the afternoon, the North Vietnamese snapped an ambush on a patrol just seven hundred yards from the camp, and an American was led away as a prisoner.

At 8 P.M., when an outpost reported that it could hear engines idling, Captain Willoughby called the combat base and asked the big guns to test fire the defensive patterns one more time. Just to be sure.

Lang Vei was the northernmost of sixty-four Special Forces camps along the Cambodian and Laotian borders. The next two camps to the south, A Shau and A Loui, had been overrun and abandoned in 1966. Panic had added to the hard losses of that battle; one marine rescue pilot shot South Vietnamese and Montagnard soldiers off his skids so he could get his helicopter airborne. Since then, the heavily jungled A Shau Valley had become a major transshipment point for North Vietnamese weapons and supplies.

Captain Willoughby could call on considerably more support than his counterparts had enjoyed at A Shau—including American reinforcements. The First Battalion of the 26th Marines had been assigned eight combat missions at Khe Sanh, one of which was: "Be prepared to execute the contingency plans for the relief/reinforcement of Lang Vei. . . ." Colonel Lownds had rehearsed the plans two months earlier, ordering a rifle company to cover the five miles to Lang Vei without using Route 9 or obvious trails. The relief column had taken nineteen hours to reach the camp.

General Westmoreland had a special affection for the U.S. Army paratroopers who wore green berets. On January 14 he ordered General Cushman, the Marine commander in I Corps, and Colonel Jonathan F. Ladd, commander of U.S. Army Special Forces in Vietnam, to review together the plans for fire support and reinforcement at Lang Vei. The Marines, it was agreed, would keep two rifle companies ready to move by foot or helicopter to Lang Vei, and the Special

Forces would keep a Mobile Strike Force in reserve at Da Nang, ninety-five miles away.

Captain Willoughby usually had twelve Americans in his camp, and about 300 indigenous troops—"Sidge," they were sometimes called, after the acronym for Civilian Irregular Defense Group, Cee Aye Dee Gee, CIDG. The captain had asked for six more Green Beret medics after 2,700 sick and wounded Laotians settled in at old Lang Vei, a little more than a half mile east on Route 9, toward Khe Sanh. Some 8,000 civilians and demoralized stragglers, hoping to find a bomb-free zone, had set up housekeeping within a mile of the Special Forces camp; a typhus outbreak would be disastrous.

As the enemy pressure increased, Da Nang dispatched a 161-man Mobile Strike Force of Hré Montagnards to Lang Vei, with six more Green Beret advisers. Willoughby sent forty of these diminutive soldiers and two American sergeants to a fortified listening post eight hundred meters west on Route 9 to provide early warning of an attack from Laos.

The captain counted heads at dark. He had very close to 500 defenders, organized in four small companies of Vietnamese, one company of Bru Montagnards, three combat reconnaissance platoons—hardened veterans of the Ho Chi Minh Trail watch—and the Mobile Strike Force from Da Nang. More than 500 Laotian soldiers, disorganized but still armed, were camped a half mile away. Six Americans were with the Laotians, two at the outpost and the rest inside the camp—including a distinguished overnight visitor, Lieutenant Colonel Daniel F. Schungel, commander of U.S. Army Special Forces in I Corps. As "a gesture of diplomacy," he had helicoptered in during the day to greet the discouraged Laotian lieutenant colonel who had been forced to flee from his own country.

Lang Vei, built in a dog-bone shape atop a long, gentle rise that provided unusually good fields of fire for the defenders, was packed with weapons—many more than the garrison could possibly use at one time. The catalogue of arms included two 4.2-inch mortars with 800 rounds of ammunition; seven 81mm mortars with 2,000 rounds of ammunition; nineteen 60mm mortars with 30,000 rounds of high explosive shells; two 106mm recoilless rifles with 40 high explosive rounds; four 57mm recoilless rifles with 3,000 rounds—most of which were anti-personnel canister shot; one hundred Light Anti-tank Weapons (LAWs); two 50-caliber machine guns with 17,000 rounds of ammunition; thirty-nine Browning Automatic Rifles (BARs) with 200,000 rounds of ammunition; and two new M60 machine guns with 5,000 rounds. Most of the CIDG troops carried M-1 and M-2 rifles, for which the camp had stores of 250,000 rounds.

Willoughby also had one thousand fragmentation grenades, 390 Claymore mines—and a matched pair of 12-guage shotguns. All he had to do was speak numbers into the radio and the combat base would ring his camp with pre-arranged defensive fires.

He felt pretty good about his preparations, and he told a visitor that Lang Vei had been "built to take a regiment."

• • •

FEBRUARY 7 WAS forty-two minutes old when the radio in the command bunker crackled to life with the shocked cry:

"We have tanks in the wire!"

Schungel raced up the steps, looked out—and saw a fifteen-ton tank parked in a shredded tangle of wire and cyclone fence firing pointblank at the sandbagged bunkers of Company 104 in the southeast corner of the camp. Two platoons of steel-helmeted North Vietnamese soldiers were moving through the gap in the wire.

The colonel raced back down the steps, and shouted at Willoughby to mass artillery fire in front of Company 104 immediately, to get a Spooky on station with million-candle power flares and miniguns, to get air support, to get everything it was possible

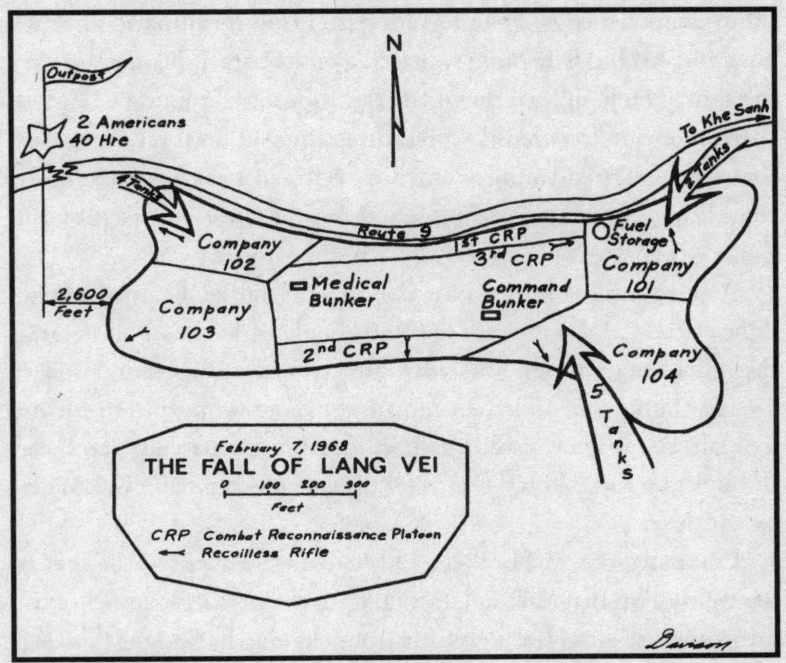

to get—and to ask for it from both the combat base and the Special Forces headquarters in Da Nang. These were *tanks!* The colonel ran up the stairs and outside to organize tank killer teams.

The first two enemy tanks had driven up a little-used road from the south, stopped at the defensive wire with the commanders perched almost casually in the cupolas, and waited while soldiers stepped forward to cut the chain-link fence. The fifty South Vietnamese of Company 104, civilian irregulars in fact as well as in name, froze in shock—and then mowed down the wire cutters. The two tanks buttoned up and bulled their way through the fencing, foot traps, mine fields, and barbed wire, then rolled right over the defenders, crushing bunker roofs with their great weight.

Sergeant First Class James W. Holt raced to one of the camp's two 106mm recoilless rifles as soon as he saw the tanks. He was the camp's senior medic. The mortars were firing illumination rounds now, and one big flare hung sputtering on its parachute directly over the tanks. Holt sighted down the big tube and, at a range of more than three hundred yards, scored direct hits on both tanks, setting them afire. Three young women carrying American-made M-16 rifles leaped from the lead tank and ran for cover—chased by the singing flechettes of Sergeant Holt's beehive rounds.

A third tank rumbled past the burning hulks, beamed a spotlight at the CIDG bunkers to blind the defenders, and obliterated the remaining strongpoints with direct fire from its cannon. Holt hit this tank, too, and then ran to get more ammunition for his weapon. He was never seen again. A fourth tank roared at top speed through the gap, blasted the recoilless rifle position, and was joined by a fifth tank.

Company 104 was broken, and its collapse exposed the rear of the eighty-two Bru Montagnards holding the northeast corner of the camp against a two-tank assault from the north. Caught between two murderous fires, the Bru died quickly.

Willoughby's urgent call for help—and a heavy enemy rocket / artillery barrage—arrived at the combat base at the same instant. The Marines dived for cover, and the first volley didn't get off until almost 1 A.M. Aimed at the southern approaches to Company 104, it landed squarely in the middle of the camp, stunning the defenders. The defensive fires were quickly adjusted, but the eastern end of the camp was in enemy hands.

Colonel Schungel knelt in the middle of the camp, with green tracers from enemy machine guns criss-crossing the ground in front of him, and wildly-swinging parachute flares overhead, and fired a LAW at the lead tank. The shell hit in a great shower of orange sparks, but the tank kept rolling. He moved closer with another LAW, but this time the disposable launcher refused to fire. Now he was close enough to roll hand grenades into the tank's treads, and to fire his rifle into the eyeslits. The tank kept rolling. Another team hit one North Vietnamese tank nine times with the shoulder-fired LAW rockets, and the tank kept rolling.

The ammunition dump exploded, and huge billows of black smoke from a fuel fire rolled thickly across the camp. Dust, churned up by the tanks and blasted into the air by shells and bombs, swirled in blinding clouds. The pilot in a small, circling plane—the spotter and guide for jet bombers—reported that NVA soldiers were using short bursts from flamethrowers to eliminate pockets of resistance.

Sergeant First Class Charles W. Lindewold radioed for help when two tanks and a North Vietnamese assault company hit his tiny outpost to the west. Wounded severely, he died with the Hré platoon. Sergeant First Class Kenneth Hanna was captured and led away.

Schungel's little force, frustrated by misfires, fell back toward the command bunker, pursued by tanks. One shellblast blinded a Green Beret soldier and knocked Schungel half unconscious; North Vietnamese infantrymen rushed forward to finish them off. First Lieutenant Le Van Quoc, deputy commander of the South Vietnamese Special Forces at Lang Vei, cut down the attackers with his M-16 and helped the dazed Americans around to the west side of the bunker.

Now, Schungel could see, tanks had broken through the west end of the camp, too. He was preparing to duel with one of them when a rocket hit it from behind, setting it afire. He killed the crew as they fled the flames.

It was impossible to return to the command bunker; enemy tanks were firing at both doors at a range of not more than fifteen yards. Schungel and a Green Beret lieutenant ran to the team house; they were driven out when North Vietnamese sappers threw satchel charges down the vents. The two men hid in the dispensary, so close to the battle they could hear runners carrying messages between the enemy commander and his assault leaders. Four Americans and forty CIDG made a break to the north, only to be caught in the flail of a Cluster Bomb Unit. Schungel and the lieutenant took the same route out of the camp minutes later.

The command bunker was in chaos.

Five Vietnamese interpreters and officers, twenty-five terrified CIDG soldiers, and eight Americans—six of them wounded—had taken shelter here. The pointblank cannon fire of the tanks slammed at their eardrums, and the enemy was dropping hand grenades and explosive charges down the vents and stairwells. One tank clambered up on the roof, crushing equipment and snapping off radio antennas—but the thick concrete held firm.

Captain Willoughby called heavy artillery fire directly on his position now, and he asked the Marines to execute the relief plan.

The Marines said no.

A relief company would almost certainly be ambushed if it took the fastest overland route to Lang Vei, Colonel Lownds felt, and the alternative plan—to lift the force in with helicopters—was no longer considered feasible now that the enemy had put tanks on the field.

Besides, Lownds believed the combat base was next.

The mood in the Khe Sanh command bunker was solemn. The pleas for help and the sounds of battle crackled from the radio speakers. "By tomorrow morning," one pessimistic staff officer said, "we'll all probably be eating rice, or we'll be dead." David Douglas Duncan, a *Life* photographer who became the only journalist to enter Lownds' command post (Duncan was an officer in the Marine reserves, a veteran of World War II and Korea, and a contemporary of the colonel), emerged from the bunker after listening to the radio exchanges between Lang Vei and Lownds. A *Time* reporter, and John Wheeler of the Associated Press, came over to ask him what he had learned.

"They told me to get out," Duncan said. "If any planes come in today, they told me to get on one."

• • •

WILLOUGHBY'S LAST DESPAIRING message, broadcast just before his antennas were shot away at 0310, went all the way to

Westmoreland. When he learned the Marines would not carry out the relief plan, the Special Forces commander in Vietnam, Colonel Ladd, called Saigon and demanded to be put through to COMMMUSMACV. Westmoreland was wakened, but he said he would not second-guess a commander at the scene. He rang off.

The general did authorize the Marines to use for the first time in the Vietnam war a secret new artillery shell code-named Firecracker. The shell popped like a dud when it hit, but it cast hundreds of golfball-sized bomblets over a wide area; an instant later they exploded like so many small grenades.

At four o'clock in the morning, the acting commander of Special Forces in I Corps—Schungel was presumed lost—asked the Marines to send a relief force at dawn. An officer in the Marine communications center noted the request and response:

0400—Conference call with Col Smith III MAF and Capt Edwards USSF—Wants relief force at first light
0405—Gen Cushman and Gen Tompkins confer
0406—Gen Tompkins passes word Negative on relief force

Willoughby could hear North Vietnamese soldiers chatting as they began to dig a large hole beside the wall of his underground concrete fortress. At 6 A.M., a thermite grenade exploded with a blinding flash that ignited maps and piles of paper and filled the bunker with acrid smoke. Fragmentation grenades and gas grenades bounced down the steps. The Americans shared the few available gas masks with one another, but everyone was vomiting from the chemical fumes and the dwindling oxygen in the bunker.

A few minutes after six, a North Vietnamese officer invited Willoughby to surrender—or be entombed when the bunker was demolished. The South Vietnamese officers and the CIDG troops went up the stairs; soon after the Americans heard frightened shouts and prolonged shooting.

At 0630, a tremendous explosion blasted a hole six feet wide and four feet high in the bunker's north wall and filled the interior with concrete shrapnel. Dazed and wounded, the Green Berets awaited the final rush.

The North Vietnamese never came—apparently diverted from finishing off Willoughby by a tiny counterattack.

Three of the Special Forces medics at old Lang Vei had rallied a hundred or so Laotians to try to rescue their comrades in the fallen camp. At dawn, with an American on each end of the line and one in the middle to stiffen the timorous Laotians' assault, they actually fought their way into the northeast corner of the camp where they found wounded Bru soldiers and others who had escaped the enemy's mopping-up efforts. As the small force pushed toward the center of the camp, two Vietnamese stood and waved from the top of the command bunker. The three Americans cried for everyone to fall flat—then dove to the ground just ahead of fire from hidden enemy machine guns. When one of the Green Berets was lifted from the ground and hurled sixty feet by a mortar blast, the Laotians broke and ran.

Four times that morning, the medics at old Lang Vei led counterattacks toward the fallen camp. In the final assault, with just two Green Berets and fifty nervous Laotians, one of the Americans was hit hard in the chest. The other medic lifted him, placed him in the back of a jeep, and raced back to old Lang Vei. He was almost there when an artillery shell hit the jeep—throwing him clear but killing his comrade in the back seat.

The command bunker was like a charnel house. One American had suffered serious head wounds and was raving deliriously. The survivors of the tank assault had been without water for hours. Almost everyone was sick or wounded.

Still, by timing U.S. Air Force strafing runs on the camp in the late afternoon, Willoughby and the other survivors were able to flee the bunker and escape to the north. They were met on Route 9 by a jeep driven by First Lieutenant Le Van Quoc, the same young officer who had saved Colonel Schungel's life.

Forty CIDG troopers and ten Green Berets flew in Marine helicopters to old Lang Vei in the last hour of light to move the surviving Americans to the combat base. Of nearly 500 CIDG defenders at Lang Vei, 316 were dead or missing. Ten of the twenty-four Americans had been lost, and eleven of the survivors were wounded. Among those who could not find a ride to Khe Sanh on the helicopters was First Lieutenant Le Van Quoc.

• • •

THE LOGBOOK OF the First Battalion/26th Marines for February 1968 does not mention the fall of Lang Vei. The *Summary* of 1968 actions published in Saigon by the United States Military Assistance Command's office of information described the battle this way:

". . . the defenders were compelled to withdraw from the camp under pressure. The North Vietnamese forces used several tanks in the attack. . . . This was the first enemy employment of armor in the war and was a failure."

Two months later, a heavily armed column of Army air cavalrymen pushed from old Lang Vei toward the abandoned camp. A short distance down the road, they came on an American jeep. In the back seat lay a weathered, blackened corpse in a Special Forces camouflage uniform. The skin on the face had been pulled back by the sun to show all of the teeth, and the soldiers were horrorstruck by the ghastly grin.

The long-dead medic was placed in a green body bag and helicoptered back to Graves Registration. Two morgue attendants unzipped the bag—and reeled back.

"Shit, this is a *gook!* What'd they bring him *here* for?"

"Look, Jesus, he's got on our uniform."

"I don't give a fuck, that ain't no American, that's a fucking *gook!*"

"Wait a minute," the other one said. "Maybe it's a spade. . . ."

• • •

GENERAL WESTMORELAND, WHO had been wakened a second time by Colonel Ladd when the Marines decided not to send a rescue force at all, flew to Da Nang early in the morning of February 7. He was profoundly disturbed by the developments in I Corps.

Westmoreland called together all the Marine and Army commanders in the northern region and listened to their reports. He gave terse orders to reopen roads, to establish new logistics lines, to reinforce at Hue, and to move troops to meet an enemy thrust toward Da Nang. It was Westmoreland who ordered the Marines to provide helicopters and the Special Forces to provide troops to go in and extract the survivors.

"One of Westy's best days," General Chaisson wrote in his pocket diary.

But Westmoreland was steaming. His intelligence people put the North Vietnamese Army's 325C and 304 Divisions at Khe Sanh and the 320 Division near the Rockpile, one enemy division fighting in Hue and two other NVA divisions loose in I Corps—one of them driving toward the vital Da Nang airport/seaport facilities. Radio Hanoi was boasting that "the U.S. defense line along Highway 9 has been breached," and that President Johnson was "very afraid of another Dienbienphu." Westmoreland had shifted the U.S. Army's America Division, a South Korean Marine division, the 1st Air Cavalry Division and a brigade of 101st Airborne Division to I Corps—and yet the problems seemed to be getting worse, not better.

"General Cushman and his staff appeared complacent, seemingly reluctant to use the Army forces I had put at their disposal," he said. "I grew more and more shocked."

The fall of Lang Vei evaporated Westmoreland's last reserves of confidence in the Marines. Two days later he sent his deputy, Army General Creighton W. Abrams Jr., to oversee the deployment of troops in northern I Corps. And he jammed the tactical aircraft issue. Westmoreland was deeply offended that the Marines had taken the argument over his head and now he demanded that he be given full authority to dispose of Marine aircraft as *he* saw fit—not as General Cushman saw fit.

• • •

THE APPEARANCE OF enemy armor on the battlefield in South Vietnam had shocked American military leaders, although the six tanks at the combat base were happily looking forward to a duck shoot. The hulks at Lang Vei had been identified as old models of a thin-skinned Russian amphibious tank that was absolutely no match for the Marine behemoths. Still, some fighter-bombers over Khe Sanh changed ordnance from Cluster Bomb Units to tank-destroying rockets, and Marines re-read the instructions printed on the side of the LAW tubes—and recoilless riflemen stacked high-explosive rounds beside their stores of flechette shells.

The Marines were unusually alert, therefore, when enemy mortars threw hundreds of shells into the combat base beginning at 4 A.M. the next morning, February 8.

The shelling was heaviest on A Company, stationed with the 1st Battalion/9th Marines at the Rock Quarry. One of A Company's platoons (about fifty men) was holding a little pimple of ground—Hill 64 on the maps—five hundred yards west of the quarry. Second Lieutenant Terence R. Roach Jr. radioed at 0420 that he had enemy soldiers in the wire.

North Vietnamese assault units hit the platoon outpost from the northwest and southwest, threw canvas over the barbed wire—and rolled into the forward trenches.

The Marines were nineteen-year-old short-timers, who counted their remaining time in Vietnam in weeks instead of months, and they fought like veterans. North Vietnamese soldiers knocked out the Marine bunkers one at a time with satchel charges and rocket-propelled grenades. Lieutenant Roach was killed trying to rally the defenders, and finally the platoon's fire fell off. Enemy soldiers collected souvenirs in the captured trenches, one taking a family Christmas photograph from the wallet of a Marine who lay shell-shocked and paralyzed, but fully conscious behind the fixed stare of his open eyes.

Reinforcements reached the hill at 9 A.M. The rescue force found twenty-one dead, twenty-six badly wounded, and four missing in action. One Marine emerged unscathed.

The commander of A Company reported 150 enemy dead, and several years later Colonel Lownds, in testimony before a Congressional committee, named this bitter little battle as one of the Marines' victories at Khe Sanh. He described Marine losses on Hill 64 as "light."

The Marines were watching body bags being loaded when the first of more than six thousand refugees streamed to the front gate of the combat base. The carefully cleared fields of fire became a parade ground of Babel.

Here were the thrice-beaten soldiers of the 33rd Laotian Elephant Battalion and their wives and children and mothers; a clump of Ca Montagnards who had also been driven out of Laos; some two hundred scattered survivors from Lang Vei, including Hré Montagnards of the Mobile Strike Force, South Vietnamese CIDG troops and ARVN Special Forces cadre, Bru Montagnards in CIDG camouflage—and thousands of Bru civilians, many of them mourning for husbands and sons lost at Lang Vei. There were six different kinds of uniforms in this mob, hundreds of rifles and machine guns and, for all Colonel Lownds knew, ten North Vietnamese Army sapper squads in disguise.

The great crowd of military and civilian refugees outnumbered the combat base defenders, and Lownds had no intention of letting this weapons-bearing mélange inside his fortress. Neither did he want them standing in a sullen, armed mass outside his main gate where they could shield an enemy attack—or join one.

Colonel Lownds ordered the weapons seized, and then he warned the crowd of 6,000 to disperse—or risk being caught in a terrible crossfire.

Two thousand five hundred demoralized Laotians had nowhere to go except back through enemy lines to their country. They trudged west on Route 9. American jet bombers, looking for the North Vietnamese who overwhelmed Hill 64 that morning, started Cluster-Bomb Unit runs on one column but were called off when a spotter pilot flew low enough to see it was "mostly old men, women, and children." Thousands of Bru, and some of the CIDG soldiers, walked east on Route 9—hoping to reach Quang Tri City.

One of the most forlorn was First Lieutenant Le Van Quoc. The South Vietnamese Special Forces officer expected harsh treatment if captured by the North Vietnamese. He had fought until it was impossible to fight any more inside Lang Vei, then escaped to the north. He returned to the camp several times, and helped Willoughby and other wounded Americans reach old Lang Vei. The Green Berets at old Lang Vei, sorry they could not take him in the last helicopters to safety, had told him to try to get to the combat base on his own. Le Van Quoc had crawled past enemy patrols on the night of the seventh and, still in uniform and still carrying his weapon, he reported for duty at the combat base on the morning of the eighth. He was disarmed at the gate.

"I don't know why they take our weapons," Le Van Quoc cried in the afternoon. "I don't know what we'll do."

• • •

WESTMORELAND FLEW BACK to Saigon from Da Nang feeling very much in charge. He'd finally blasted the logjam free in I Corps, and he could hope the problems were on the way toward solution. The situation had required a take-charge officer, and Westmoreland had shone.

Now there were other problems to be dealt with, and Westmoreland called his staff together in the Saigon headquarters. One item on the agenda was the new report on comparisons between Khe Sanh and Dienbienphu.

Colonel Argo could hardly have been more gloomy. The Marines were cooped up inside their barbed wire while the enemy could move and probe and concentrate his forces for specific attacks, Argo said. The fatal fault at Dienbienphu and at every famous siege in history was the defenders' loss of initiative. He could see the same fate for the combat base.

The room froze in stunned silence. The unthinkable had just been spoken. Every officer in the room kept his eyes fixed intently on Colonel Argo—never once glancing toward COMMUSMACV.

Westmoreland stood, assumed the Command Presence, and demanded the attention of all.

"It's good that we have heard the worst," he said, pronouncing his words precisely, firmly. Then he put steel in his voice:

"But we are not, repeat, not, going to be defeated at Khe Sanh. I will tolerate no talking, or even thinking, to the contrary."

Westmoreland's eyes strobed the officers, and then he performed an about face with a First Captain's sharpness—and strode from the room.

9.

Life in the V-Ring

The Khe Sanh combat base was a reeking trash heap by the first week of February.

Torn ponchos, half-empty cans of beans with ham, soggy crumples of paper, shell casings, soleless boots, duds from the ammunition dump explosion, moldy bits of canvas, splintered fiberglass plates from ripped flak jackets, shrapnel chunks, and broken timber littered the dugouts and shallow fighting trenches.

Not far from the Tactical Operations Center—the old French bunker that served as the Marine command post—a terrible heap of stained fatigues smoldered fitfully in the fog. It was the burn pile from Charlie Med: sweat-soaked shirts and baggy pants, underwear and socks almost purple with blood, mangled boots, and holed camouflage covers. Doctors and corpsmen in the tough little tent hospital by the airstrip tied off spurting vessels and tidied up traumatic amputations for the one-hour helicopter ride to excellent surgical facilities at Phu Bai.

Round-the-clock bombing and shelling and digging and bulldozing and piling had filled the air with the red dust of the plateau.

Smoke and the smell of things burning lifted the back of the tongue almost to gagging. Dark blue exhaust fumes pumped from generator housings; neat, white clouds drifted from close-in air bursts; dirty, grey gouts leaped from mortar hits.

Smoke rose from trash fires and garbage fires and petroleum

fires, and it rolled in black, choking billows from the fifty-five gallon drums in which shit and diesel fuel had been mixed. The gruesome brew was stirred constantly to keep the flames alive. "It hangs, hangs," groaned a visitor, "taking you full in the throat. . . ."

Water was scarce, and most of the Marines wore scraggly beards. Few washed regularly. The sleeping bunkers were dank stench chambers, redolent of sweat and urine, diarrhea and fear, C-ration garbage, vomit, farts, feet, and fungus.

Rats ran across the dirt floors, gnawing at shelves and boots and fingers, chittering in fear when the big guns fired and sometimes scratching faces as they raced across sleeping Marines in the dark bunkers.

The camp looked wrecked, "like a shanty slum on the outskirts of Manila." Enemy rockets and shells had flattened the officers' club, broken the "hardback" huts, deroofed the beer hall, and toppled antennas. Fragments of helicopter blade, hingeless truck doors, hopeless tangles of communications wire, blowing cardboard cartons, shattered windshields, and rotting sandbags were scattered everywhere.

The sounds of war were unceasing. Fighter-bombers roared in very low to hit North Vietnamese positions, enemy shells whapped on the steel plates of the runway, truck horns blared warnings of inbound artillery, machine gunners fired clearing bursts along the perimeter, B-52 strikes rumbled like heavy thunder in the mountains, sniper rifles cracked, and helicopters thudded overhead to carry ammunition and replacements to the hilltops—and casualties to Charlie Med.

Almost every day the heavy popping of North Vietnamese .50 caliber machine guns could be heard to the east, followed immediately by the full-throated roar of a four-engined cargo plane lowering through the fog on instruments.

Getting supplies to the combat base was proving to be more difficult than expected.

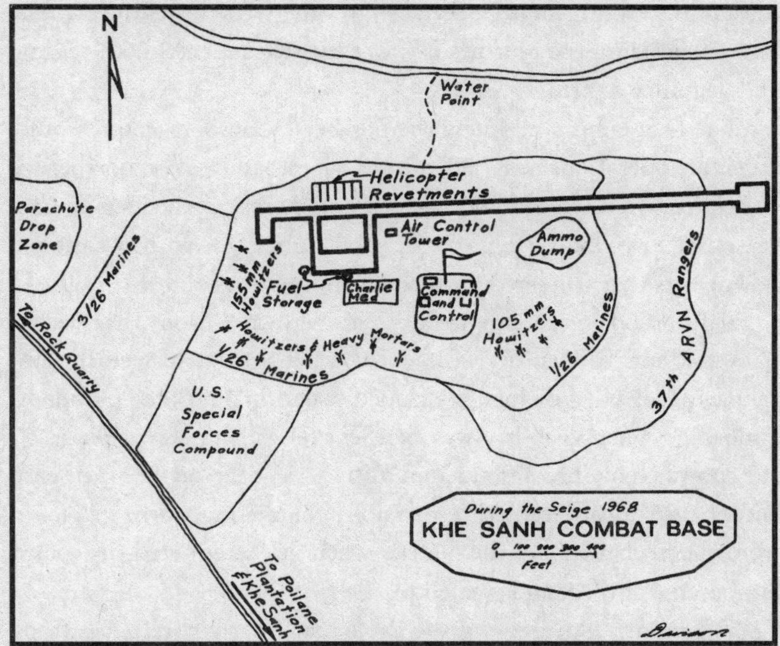

The U.S. Air Force was confident it could deliver sufficient bullets and beans to Khe Sanh; it had resources that beggared the French effort at Dienbienphu—and only half as many people to feed. The French, for example, had to operate from an airfield seventy-five minutes from Dienbienphu, with airplanes that could carry only a ton or two of supplies. The Americans would fly from the sprawling supply complex at Da Nang, just thirty minutes from Khe Sanh, with huge C-130 Hercules cargo planes capable of carrying fifteen to eighteen tons each.

The Air Force could count on unparalleled fire support to suppress enemy ground fire, and could land on a recently-rebuilt airstrip that was thirty-nine hundred feet long; the French should have been so lucky.

But starting on the first day of February and continuing through most of the month, an impenetrable grey fog settled over the combat base—enclosing the Marines in a wet fist that reduced both ceiling and visibility to zero.

The U.S. command knew the northern monsoon season would affect air operations at Khe Sanh. Marines had worked northern I Corps for several years, and had learned to resign themselves to a season of low clouds, fog, drizzle, and light rain, with occasional downpours that triggered flash floods in the rivers and streams.

Still, no one was ready for the zero-zero conditions that nearly paralyzed airlift operations in February. "The airstrip seemed particularly bedeviled by fog," concluded one formal report. "On many a morning when visibility was excellent [elsewhere on the plateau], the runway remained shrouded in mist. . . . A deep ravine at the east end of the runway seemed responsible, channeling warm moist air from the lowlands onto the plateau where it encountered the cooler air, became chilled, and created fog."

The French families and the Bible teachers, now refugees from the rubble of what had been Khe Sanh Village, could have told the Marines about the unique weather at the combat base. Carolyn Miller found after she moved a mile from Lang Bu to Khe Sanh Village that she could no longer dry diapers on the line. Madeleine Poilane hung wet clothing in one of her husband's coffee-drying sheds during the monsoon season.

"I remember looking wistfully out of the west during those long, cold, misty months and seeing the sun shining brightly," Carolyn Miller recalled. "One of our colleagues who lived with us for awhile threatened to write a book entitled 'The Sun Always Shines in Laos, or Why I Defected to the Viet Cong.' "

It was the worst flying weather the Air Force encountered in Vietnam—"a severe obstacle to aerial operations"—and it threatened the Marines' lifeline.

"February 1968 made an old man out of me," said General

Tompkins, the Marine commander responsible for the combat base. "Zero, zero, day after day."

But the airlift was Khe Sanh's aorta; it *had* to work.

The Air Force had sophisticated radar and guidance systems, of course, but as the Marines dug deeper into the plateau (the communications center finally buried itself in room-sized steel boxes sixteen feet underground), the profile of the base vanished from instrument screens. Ground radar crews provided an electronic beam for the final approach, and then talked the big planes down through the fog.

It was risky business in a landscape featuring three-thousand-foot mountains, and it got worse when the North Vietnamese set up anti-aircraft weapons along the approach route. The prevailing winds and the east-west axis of the runway fixed the line of approach as surely as berms. Enemy gunners fired straight up—blindly—and scored hits on heavily burdened planes locked in a final instrument approach in zero-zero weather.

The air crews on these dangerous missions were not supposed to be in Vietnam. Westmoreland had already reached the troop limit established by the Commander in Chief and the Congress, so planes and crews were sent to Vietnam on "temporary duty" assignments of thirty days—then rotated out before they were counted in the monthly troop totals.

Seventy-two of the C-130s were on temporary duty assignments from bases in Japan on the first day of February. The number rose to eighty-eight during the month, then ninety-six, as Westmoreland reached out to the Philippines, Okinawa, and Taiwan for more planes to fill the logistical maw of a quarter million fighting men in I Corps.

On February 10, a Hercules carrying flexible bladders of high-octane fuel was ripped by enemy bullets in the final seconds of its blind approach. Fire was licking at the plane when it touched down.

It rolled almost three thousand feet, then was rocked by muffled explosions, careened off the edge of the metal strip and began to burn furiously. Fire fighters in hooded heat suits waded into the furnace to pull out the passengers. Six escaped and six died.

Later that day, another C-130 was hit by enemy fire and then crippled by mortar shells as it unloaded. After two days of repair work, the plane was able to take off for Da Nang where awed mechanics counted 242 holes in the fuselage and wings. Almost every plane suffered battle damage in early February, or blew tires on jagged holes on the airstrip.

On February 13, Westmoreland's deputy for air operations, General Momyer, banned C-130s from landing at Khe Sanh: The big cargo planes were "a make-or-break resource . . . too valuable to be risked needlessly."

Instead, the most urgently needed supplies—wooden beams for bunkers, pallets of pierced steel plate for the airstrip and bunker roofs, and artillery shells—would be delivered by the Low Altitude Parachute Extraction System.

On a LAPES mission, the C-130 came in exactly as though it was going to land—but stayed five feet off the runway. On a timed signal, a large, trailing, wrapped parachute was popped open with a special explosive charge, and the jolt jerked the cargo bundle out of the open tailgate. Because a tilted wing could cartwheel forty tons of aviation fuel, ammunition, and timber into the heart of the combat base, the pilot had to ignore the countdown and the enemy shelling during the critical seconds over the runway—and then climb sharply under full power to avoid flying over North Vietnamese guns to the west.

When the pilot held his aircraft exactly sixty inches off the runway at a perfect 130 knots, and when the cargomaster and ground control achieved a perfect countdown and the parachute deployed exactly on schedule, and when the winds and the gods were neutral, the Low Altitude Parachute Extraction System could set enormous bundles on the airstrip the way a mother lays her baby down.

On February 13, on the first LAPES mission of the siege, the parachute didn't open properly. An eight-ton pallet of lumber on a steel sled skidded like a berserk missile down the runway—and through the side of a mess hall, crushing three Marines to death as they sat eating lunch.

It was clear in the first few days that LAPES could never deliver the tonnages needed at Khe Sanh. The risks to the C-130s were nearly as great as landing, and the specially constructed steel pallet/sleds were difficult to recover and return to Da Nang. And the explosive cartridges essential to the timely opening of the parachute soon ran out.

Over the next six weeks the Air Force managed to deliver less than five days' worth of supplies via LAPES.

Late in the siege, the Air Force tried a system in which the C-130 made a LAPES-like approach, but tried to snag an arresting cable with a trailing hook—quite similar to the system used on aircraft carriers, but with the hook attached to cargo bundles instead of the plane.

On the very first mission, a C-130 successfully hooked the ground cable—but jerked the entire system from its moorings and flew off into the fog trailing cables and stakes. One plane eventually managed to drop a multi-ton bundle on the runway so carefully that not one shell was broken on the thirty dozen fresh eggs added to the cargo for showmanship. Still, only fifteen of these hook and cable deliveries were tried at Khe Sanh.

The real work would have to be done by parachute, just as at Dienbienphu.

And it would have to be done quickly.

The extraordinary persistence of the fog and the banning of the C-130s had put the combat base on the brink of a logistics crisis. On

February 15, a chipper Marine told a CBS television correspondent that he was worried his mother might be worried.

"We've had no mail or resupplies," explained Corporal Charles Martin, who then turned to the camera:

"So to Momma back there in Greenfield, Tennessee, hello Momma."

Firsthand testimony like this, appearing on the evening news shows in the United States, had immediate impact on both mommas and Presidents. On February 17 and 18, in weather so dismal that no other planes were in the sky, eighteen C-130s bored into the mists over Khe Sanh and parachuted 279 tons of supplies—including the first mail delivery in more than a week.

Deliveries dropped to zero the next day when enemy artillery knocked out the ground control radar system.

Marine replacements, delicate equipment, medical supplies, and sensitive ammunition could not be delivered by parachuting them into the fog or jerking them out of the back of a plane. They flew to Khe Sanh in a sturdy cargo plane named the Provider, whose two engines had been fitted with auxiliary jet power boosters.

The C-123 Provider came down the same flak alley that the C-130 Hercules did, but it could make a much steeper approach and it needed only half the runway.

Providers rarely stopped on the ground. The pilot drove his plane like a truck through the unloading area, the cargo master rolled one-ton pallets off the open tail gate, and the plane turned for takeoff.

In the final seconds, Marines whose thirteen-month tour of duty was over, sons going home on emergency leave to visit a dying parent, and news reporters with filled notebooks leaped from nearby trenches and ran through enemy shellfire toward the moving plane. It was a sprint of terror, with cries and shouts and the mad jouncing of equipment—and a final desperate leap for the Provider's gaping jaw. The adrenalin rush soaked some of the passengers in sweat;

others lay face down on the floor, crying, "Thank God, Jesus Christ, thank God."

With the roar of the power-boosted engines filling the fog, with enemy mortar shrapnel hitting the fuselage and Marine guns firing counterbattery missions, the C-123s lifted from the runway—and vanished instantly in the mists. Green tracer rounds from North Vietnamese guns tracked them into the fog.

Three minutes from touchdown to wheels-up was about average for the Providers, but some pilots had done it in a minute flat. Still, during the worst weeks of late February, only fifty-eight planes managed to land at the combat base—with a meager three hundred tons of supplies.

The airlift ran into unexpected problems. The pallets that made speed-offloading possible were stout, aluminum-reinforced plywood platforms custom made (at $350 each) to carry one-ton packages in the holds of cargo planes. The Marines, unable to find roofing material that could stop an enemy shell, started stealing the pallets to strengthen their bunkers. The best efforts of Air Force and Marine guards could not keep the vital pallets from disappearing before they could be returned for repackaging.

And the logistics crush at Da Nang, the main transshipment point for the quarter million Allied troops in I Corps, was so great that it was easier to fly from other bases—like Can Ranh Bay, seventy-five minutes away; and Tan Son Nhut, ninety-five minutes to the south.

Marines at the Rock Quarry, who had to sweep the drop zone every morning for mines and booby traps, found it impossible to recover all the parachuted supplies before the 4 P.M. deadline for being back in their bunkers. Some cargos had to be destroyed by Marine artillery to keep them out of enemy hands.

The quite confident comparisons with the airlift at Dienbienphu no longer held. "Theoretically, [the Air Force] could deliver six times as much as the French had been able to, but maintenance requirements, the time needed to rig loads, and other considerations cut this tonnage in half."

Zero-zero weather, enemy fire, and equipment failures caused further constrictions in the supply line. On many days, the Air Force delivered fewer tons than the French had delivered to Dienbienphu.

Luxuries that were commonplace for American fighting men in South Vietnam were not available at Khe Sanh. Even food was more likely to be en route than on the table.

At the end of February, a magazine writer reached into his pack and pulled out some heat tabs—little chemical pills that burn so intensely they can boil a canteen cup of water or heat a can of C-rations. Every Marine in the darkened bunker showed white teeth in a dirty face; it would be the first hot meal in "days, weeks." They sighed at the mention of peaches in syrup.

Lieutenant Colonel John F. Masters Jr., commander of the small Air Force ground team that coordinated parachute and LAPES deliveries, had no more success than the Marines in obtaining necessary supplies. Six of his people had been wounded by enemy shelling, and one evacuated with rat bites. Masters asked repeatedly for fire extinguishers, toilet paper, and rat poison, but he never got his package.

• • •

ONE OF EVERY ten Marines at Khe Sanh had been wounded or killed by the end of the first week in February, and the highest priority item in the airlift changed from ammunition to bunker material. None of the trees in the area could be used; the wood was too filled with shrapnel to be cut, or too green to support tons of sandbags.

Most bunkers started as eight-by-eight-foot dugouts, with upright beams in each corner and one in the middle for support. With a roof of pierced steel plates or pilfered pallets, then two or three layers of sandbags, the bunker was considered sufficient to stop an 82mm mortar shell. Some Marines heaped several feet of loose earth on the roof, then pounded old 105mm shell casings into the dirt like huge nails hoping the forged brass shell base would predetonate an enemy rocket or artillery shell before it entered the bunker.

The best bunker at the combat base was the spacious, well-lighted fortress constructed underground by the U.S. Navy Seabees. The sign on the door said "The Alamo Hilton." Visiting news reporters made the Hilton their headquarters at the combat base, and paid the innkeepers in whisky and beer—rare treats in an outpost where even combat rations were sometimes rationed.

Envious Marines asked the Seabees to share, but the engineers ignored them. "Fuck 'em," said one Navy man after a shouting incident at the door. "Before the siege began, Marines sat on their tails when they should have been digging. They worked nine to four, knocked off, and went to their beer hall."

Some Marines mocked the Seabees for their prowess underground, calling it candyass. Fighting from holes was somehow sissy—contrary to the aggressive ethic of the U.S. Marine Corps. Digging was demeaning. Even the hospital at the combat base was above ground, with leaning walls of sandbags to provide blast protection. The roof of Charlie Med was canvas; doctors and corpsmen wore flak jackets and steel helmets in the operating theater.

"It gives you the feeling you're digging your own grave when you go too deep," explained a senior officer at Khe Sanh.

Besides, it hardly seemed to make any difference.

Nothing at the combat base could stop the long-range artillery shells from Laos, or the big 122mm rockets from Hill 881 North. The guns on the face of Co Roc Mountain, which were wheeled back into tunnel mouths after they were fired, were so close that even duds went four feet into the ground.

Colonel Lownds, cramped in the old French bunker, had ordered a new command post to be built. The engineers supplied the specifications for a roof that would stop a 122mm rocket, but Lownds decided to double the thickness. One day before the regimental staff was scheduled to move from the old bunker, a 152mm artillery shell shrieked in from Laos and ripped through both thicknesses to explode inside the new bunker.

Two thirds of the enemy's artillery shells came from hidden guns twelve to fourteen miles northwest of the combat base, in Laos, on a compass reading of 305 degrees from India Company's hilltop. Dabney's men tried to locate the guns, but were frustrated by the extreme range, an omnipresent bomb-induced dust haze, and the enemy's rigid camouflage procedures.

The heart of the combat base, and the enemy's prime target, was the tight cluster of bunkers and tents next to the cargo offloading area, including Colonel Lownds' command post, Charlie Med, the ground control radar facilities, the radio relay center, and trenches for outbound air passengers.

Here, too, was Khe Sanh's emergency reserve—a demoralized reconnaissance company whose only duty was to sit and be pounded until called to repel an enemy breakthrough.

Many rifles have an etched steel V for a rear sight and a perfect round bead for a front sight. A marksman sets the bead on the shoulder of a deer, or the neck of a squirrel, snugs the bead in the apex of the V, and smoothly squeezes the trigger. To be in the V-ring is to be dead.

The 3rd Marine Division's reconnaissance company was camped in the V ring.

This proud outfit boasted it was "The Eyes of the 26th Marines"—point man for the whole division. Its men usually operated in small teams far from friendly lines, and its banner was a grinning skull and crossed bones, with the motto: "Swift, Deadly, Silent."

The recon teams had taken heavy casualties in January, and since January 20 all patrols had been limited to a few hundred yards, or line of sight—whichever was less. Now the elite recon Marines huddled in bunkers, "in reserve." More than half the men in the company had been wounded or killed by mid-February—or evacuated when their eyes locked in "the thousand-yard stare."

One Marine veteran of World War II and Korea looked at the strained faces of the Marines at Khe Sanh in February and compared it to the look in the eyes of tethered bullocks waiting for the tiger. Another visitor to the combat base said:

"It was never easy to guess the ages of the Marines at Khe Sanh since nothing like youth ever lasted in their faces for very long. It was the eyes. Because they were always either strained or blazed-out or simply blank, they never had anything to do with what the rest of the face was doing."

Colonel Lownds didn't like waiting either, but he was operating under unique pressures and he chose to keep a low profile. He was a slight man, forty-seven years old, with Purple Hearts from Saipan and Iwo Jima. Two months earlier he had worked with a single battalion at Khe Sanh, isolated and almost-forgotten out at the end of the line. Now nearly 7,000 men looked to him for leadership, and millions of Americans—including especially the President of the United States—looked over his shoulder to examine every tiny decision.

"Thanks to a small army of war correspondents and reporters, millions of people followed the battle day by day," noted the formal Marine history of the siege. "The well-publicized struggle had long since become more than just another battle; it was a symbol of Allied determination to hold the line in Vietnam."

Colonel Lownds had very nearly been sacrificed to appease General Westmoreland, and he appeared to some to be a "meek, low-keyed, distracted, and even stupid man . . . utterly insensible to the gravity of his position."

Certainly no colonel in the world had to justify himself more perfectly to more people—to General Tompkins, who had interceded to save him and who helicoptered to the base every day to make sure Lownds was doing things right; to General Cushman, the

Marine commander in I Corps who thought a more dynamic leader might ease the strains with Saigon; to General Westmoreland, who was increasingly worried about the Marines' abilities, and of whom *Time* said on February 16: "The blade is . . . poised above Westmoreland. His reputation—and much more—is riding on the ability of that barren, hill-girt outpost to stand."

Lownds cultivated a luxurious regimental moustache with upswept waxed tips—and an air of quiet confidence:

"Can we hold this place?" he said, echoing a reporter's question in the first week of February. "Hell, yes. The morale and discipline of my men are high."

Lownds said he was not surprised when the North Vietnamese failed to follow up their January 20 attacks. "I expect a thoroughly Oriental kind of battle. The enemy takes his time. He's going to bang us when he's ready."

And what if the North Vietnamese really did hurl tens of thousands of soldiers at the combat base, as they had at Dienbienphu?

"I should like to hope they don't have enough," Lownds answered. "Anyway, we're here to stay."

General Tompkins' decision to restrict Marine patrols to line of sight from the base perimeter was endorsed by the majority of officers—and not just because it permitted Niagara to rain bombs on the plateau without fear of hitting friendly troops.

"If you go out after the North Vietnamese with a platoon, they hit you with a company," explained Lt. Col. Edward Castagna, who directed operations for the 26th Marines at Khe Sanh. "And if you go out with a company, they slam you with a battalion.

"That's the way it is."

"Inevitably," said another Marine officer, "they pick just the right piece of terrain and they dig in and wait for us in the bottleneck."

Even Army officers preferred not to engage the North Vietnamese on terrain of their choosing. "You don't fight this fellow rifle to rifle," said Brig. Gen. Glenn D. Walker. "You locate him and back away, blow the hell out of him, and then police up."

The deluge of bombs, unprecedented even in a war that had already surpassed the tonnages of World War II, was changing the geography of the northern border region—erasing ridgelines, diverting streams and rivers, reducing hills, cratering the plateau, and starting fires that burned for days.

Twenty-five years earlier, American bombers dropped 478 tons of bombs on the Schweinfurt ball bearing factories that kept the Nazi war machine on wheels; 650 American servicemen lost their lives in the one-day raid. The B-52 Stratofortresses over Khe Sanh routinely tripled the tonnage of the Schweinfurt raid every day—without the loss of a single plane.

The big bombers came from Andersen Air Force Base in Guam, U Tapao Airbase in Thailand, and, after the first week of February, from Kadena Air Base in Okinawa. The additional planes made it possible to put two cells of three B-52s over Khe Sanh every three hours around the clock.

Clods of dirt vibrated from the bunker ceilings and the earth itself trembled rhythmically as the B-52s bombed suspected enemy road systems, troop bivouacs, supply depots, bunker complexes, and gun positions.

For every B-52 visit, ten fighter bombers arrived over the combat base—Phantoms and Intruders, Crusaders, Skyhawks, Thunderchiefs, and even rugged old Skyraiders, prop-driven planes that looked like they'd come from the museum. They came from the 1st Marine Air Wing, the 7th Air Force, the Strategic Air Command, U.S. Navy Task Force 77, the Vietnamese Air Force, varied U.S. Army aviation units, and once from an air wing in North Carolina that flew halfway around the world just to show it could be done.

Many of the fighter bombers had been diverted from missions against North Vietnam. The weather over the enemy homeland in

February and March was so terrible that 5,900 of the 8,383 bombers that set out for North Vietnam diverted to targets near Khe Sanh.

An airbone computer control module named Sky Spot kept as many as eight hundred aircraft a day at appropriate altitudes and speeds until they could augur down through the swarm and strike at an enemy target.

Side-looking airborne radar systems, infrared and chlorophyll-loss detectors, seismic and acoustic sensors, and aerial photographs provided up to 150 targets a day—and the bombing did not slow because of darkness or fog: two thirds of all bombing missions at Khe Sanh in February were instrument controlled; the pilot never saw the target. A computer in a heavily sandbagged van at the combat base juggled radar readings, map coordinates, the ballistic characteristics of various bombs, compass headings and wind speeds, and guided the planes through the gloom to precision bombing runs.

The most instantly responsive fire support at Khe Sanh was the Marines' own artillery, some forty-six tubes in all. Colonel Lownds liked to walk into the fire support control center from time to time, point at a spot on a giant wall map, and order it destroyed. Using a Field Artillery Digital Automatic Computer to digest the information beneath Lownds' finger, the fire support control center could have shells on the way within forty seconds.

By mid-February, Niagara was the great thundering waterfall of explosives that General Westmoreland had envisioned. Every day B-52s dropped more than one thousand tons of bombs on the plateau, fighter bombers roared in at five or ten minute intervals, and hundreds of artillery missions churned and rechurned the red soil.

But it did not silence the North Vietnamese guns.

Every day, 100 enemy shells—or 350 or 500—hammered the combat base. Every day, one Marine would be caught in the open and flailed by shrapnel or another mangled when a rocket ripped through a bunker roof.

This was hardly shelling of historic proportions, and many experienced military leaders pooh-poohed the North Vietnamese effort. On their very best day, enemy gunners fired 1,307 shells and rockets at the Marines—hardly more than Dabney's mortar crews had pumped out in a few hours during the battle for Hill 861 Alpha. Furthermore, the impact of the enemy shelling was dissipated over the two square miles of the combat base and a half dozen scattered hilltop positions.

Dienbienphu had absorbed up to forty-five thousand shells a week, and during the Korean War a tiny Allied outpost just 275 yards square had taken fourteen thousand rounds in twenty-four hours.

S.L.A. Marshall, the military historian and analyst, scoffed in print at the use of the word "barrage" to describe enemy shelling at Khe Sanh. The North Vietnamese shells falling on the Marines, he argued, were a mild sprinkle compared to the thunderstorms of explosives in previous battles.

In the opening days of World War II, the Japanese battered Americans on Corregidor with 3,600 five-hundred-pound shells, then 16,000 shells in just twenty-four hours, and then "an artillery barrage so heavy that the flashes and sounds of the explosions ran together in a continuous sheet-lightning, a continuous roll of thunder."

Mocking the North Vietnamese artillery was easier in New York, or Washington, than it was at the combat base where a kind of knee-hugging, ground-huddling helplessness gripped the Marines every time the klaxons blared.

It wasn't the weight or the accuracy, but the *persistence* of enemy shelling that slowly eroded the Marines' cocky readiness for battle. Every hour of every day, in clear weather and foul, fighter bombers and B-52s burned the jungle scrub with high explosives and jellied gasoline and white phosphorus—and still the enemy lobbed a few hundred mortar shells at the Marines every day.

The shelling slowly wore them down.

Marines spent the nighttime hours staring into the swirling fog, waiting for battalions of North Vietnamese assault troops to charge the wire. In the daylight hours, they filled sandbags until the fog lifted enough for enemy spotters on the surrounding hills to direct artillery fire at the combat base. Then the Marines went underground again.

"We went into some tough places [in World War II] . . . Tarawa or Peleliu, parts of the 'canal, Tinian," said a Marine general who had fought in the Pacific island campaigns, "[but] I don't think we were ever asked to carry out—day in, day out, no Sundays, thirty-one days a month, twenty-four hours around the clock, 360 degrees of direction—a fight that you were involved in during your whole twelve-to-thirteen-month tour.

"It's a pretty dreary, dirty, miserable war."

Marine Lieutenant C.J. Stack counted his losses from enemy shelling and told a news report:

"When I get back, I'm going to open a bar especially for the survivors of Khe Sanh. And any time it gets two deep at that bar, I'll know someone is lying."

In one of the open trenches, Lance Corporal Richard Morris strummed his guitar and sang the mournful song that had reached the Top Twenty list in early 1968: "Where have all the soldiers gone? To the graveyard, every one. When will they ever learn? When will they ever learn?"

"All they ever do is peck, peck, peck," an impatient battalion commander complained toward the end of February. "There's no sweeping battle. They just keep pecking away."

One Marine was evacuated from the base because he masturbated every day in the bunker, the trench—and in the tent where he was sent to be examined. Others were sent to the rear when they shook helplessly every time the big 122mm rockets walked the length of the combat base.

"This ain't the Marine Corps I know," complained one senior sergeant.

The waiting and the shelling and the weariness were worse on the hilltop outposts—and worst on 881 South.

For India Company alone, the North Vietnamese installed two 120mm mortars—the biggest such weapon in their arsenal. The extremely large fragmentation pattern of the giant mortar's shells virtually guaranteed that any Marine caught above ground would be wounded or killed. And the 120s, hidden in a U-shaped fold of ground called the Horseshoe about a mile and a half from the hilltop, punched through the thickest overhead covering the Marines could devise.

U.S. fighter bombers filled the Horseshoe with canisters of napalm, thousand-pound bombs, tear-gas crystals, chemical smoke, and hundreds of tons of high explosives, but they never silenced the big mortars.

Twenty-four hours of tension robbed the Marines of sleep, just as foul weather robbed them of food, ammunition, water, and the hope of speedy medical care. The North Vietnamese attacks on Hills 861 and 861 A, and the overrunning of Lang Vei and Hill 64, wound the spring tighter. Individual enemy soldiers crept close to the Marines' positions. One sniper drilled a veteran gunnery sergeant through the head on Hill 861; another particularly fine marksman dropped ten of Dabney's men in a single week.

India Company was often able to warn the combat base of incoming shells. The Marines on 881 South could see muzzle flashes on the face of Co Roc, or hear the loud rustling of shells from Laos passing close overhead—"like a squirrel running through dry leaves," said Dabney—and radio a terse warning:

"Arty, arty, Co Roc" or "Arty, arty, 305."

A Marine monitoring the radio net at the combat base instantly pressed two wired beer can lids together—closing an electric circuit that honked a truck horn mounted in a tree. When India Company was on its toes, Marines at the combat base had five to eighteen seconds to find cover.

Once, a wedge-shaped bull of a Marine corporal named Molimao Niuatoa, a Samoan Islander known in India Company as Pineapple Chunk, actually spied an enemy gun more than six miles away. Becoming absolutely still behind his tripod-mounted twenty-power naval binoculars, never blinking the eyes that had helped him to a 241/250 score on the rifle range, Corporal Niuatoa guided a flight of bombers to the camouflaged gun. Spotters usually correct friendly fire by saying "Add five zero, left one hundred," which tells the gunners to fire the next shell fifty meters farther and one hundred meters left of the last shell. Because of the extreme range to the enemy gun on this day, Niuatoa corrected the first bombing run by saying, "Add two ridgelines, left a half mile." The jets finally closed on the gun and reported it destroyed.

Captain Dabney always used sick or wounded men to carry badly hurt Marines to the helicopter landing zone; they could climb on the ship and fly out, while healthy Marines would have to run back through 120mm mortar fire to the bunkers.

A Marine with a severely impacted wisdom tooth carried a wounded comrade to the landing zone one day, and was climbing into the open tail ramp of a double-rotored Sea Knight when mortar rounds bracketed the helicopter. The pilot hit the Git button, and the ship lurched into the air. The dental patient hung desperately by his fingertips for a few seconds, then fell twenty feet to the ground. He limped painfully away.

Later in the day a smaller ship swooped in to pick up a new casualty. The Marine with the aching tooth scrambled aboard and the chopper lifted quickly—only to have its tail rotor sawed off by enemy machine gun fire. It crashed on the crest of the hill, the first of five helicopters to die on 881 South. The Marine limped once more to his bunker.

Just before dark the swollen-jawed Marine had one more chance, but now the passenger list had grown to fourteen, including the crew of the downed helicopter and ten wounded Marines. The load-master turned him away; the ship was overloaded.

Sometimes, the helicopters wouldn't come at all.

One of India Company's corporals took a 120mm shell fragment in the head at ten minutes after ten in the morning; the Marine considered it a decent time to be wounded because the fog lifted about noon. The fog didn't lift. Thirty-mile-an-hour winds pushed "billowing soft mountains of white" out of the valleys to cloak the hilltop in clouds. The young medics on 881 South radioed the combat base's surgeons for advice that night, then called again the next day—after they ran out of glucose and the corporal slipped into a coma.

"It's now or never for this man," India Company radioed at the end of the second fogbound day. "He can't last the night."

One helicopter searched for the hill in the fog, but turned back when it ran low on fuel. As the ship returned to base, India Company announced the corporal's death: "Be advised that medical evacuation is now routine. Repeat: now routine."

"We just couldn't see you," the chopper pilot radioed.

"We understand," India closed. "Thank you for the try. Thank you very much."

Helicopter losses were quite serious in the early days of the siege. One Marine officer at Khe Sanh counted seventeen destroyed helicopters, but another—a chopper pilot who was named "Marine Aviator of the Year" in 1968—remembered that before the end of February "we'd lost more than half our aircraft to enemy fire." Lieutenant Colonel David L. Althoff, who was shot down four times, described aerial operations over Khe Sanh as "pure hell."

In late February, the Marines' air arm conceived Super Gaggle—a swirling mix of jets and choppers designed to disrupt enemy fire.

Four Skyhawk fighter bombers, small attack jets that were so maneuverable the pilots called them "Scooters," opened a Super Gaggle by hitting enemy positions with napalm and bombs. More Skyhawks then streaked in to saturate North Vietnamese gun sites with tear gas. With thirty seconds to go, still more jets laid down a heavy smoke screen on the facing slopes of enemy-held hills. Twelve big Sea Knight cargo helos, each carrying a two-ton load in a rope sling, rotored in through the smoke and fog and fire, followed closely by gunships prepared to engage individual enemy guns or to pick up the crews of downed choppers.

India Company welcomed the supply run by pitching smoke grenades down the hillside, but nothing could silence the 120mm mortars. The two-man helicopter support team that guided choppers in, unhooked cargos, collected heavy nets and reattached them to hovering helicopters, had to stand in the landing zone to do their work. India Company went through four teams in February.

Super Gaggle sharply reduced helicopter losses, and reopened the supply line to the hilltops. It was none too soon. Combat fatigue had become more common by late February. "We had trouble with psychological breakdowns," Dabney said. "There's an absolute limit to what someone can take." Some painted their toes with peanut butter to get rat bites that would put them between clean sheets in Phu Bai. "Accidental" rifle discharges were frequent. Some Marines just huddled on the floor of their bunker, refusing to emerge even for scheduled R and R trips.

"If it wasn't for the Gaggle," said Dabney, "most of us probably wouldn't be here."

As the weather cleared, and the counterfire measures began to take effect, the helicopters began to operate with more panache. Gunners in hovering helos would suddenly sling their weapon, pitch out a case of soda pop, and return immediately to firing at enemy positions. Once, working behind the code name Cool It, the chopper crews scrounged large quantities of dry ice—and delivered hundreds of Dixie cups of ice cream to the hilltops. India Company was under such heavy enemy fire that it could not recover the surprise until after it had melted to goo.

While the Marines on the hilltops were discouraged, even despairing on some days, they never really lost a cocky sureness that they could do the job. "One thing for certain: we would never have surrendered," said Dabney, quite firmly, as he discussed the differences he saw between the French at Dienbienphu and the Marines at Khe Sanh. "At the end, the colonel and the sergeant major would have gone down with their backs to the flagpole." The Marines grew weary of the waiting and shelling, but they did not fear a face-to-face fight with the North Vietnamese. Most of them went about their duties with a kind of tough, macabre humor.

Captain Breeding and E Company, who had thrown back the enemy attack on Hill 861 in early February, once went without water for days. When the supply helicopter finally arrived, it was panicked by enemy fire and cut loose its cargo from two hundred feet up. The plastic water containers burst apart in mid-air as the parched Marines watched.

"One of the prettiest waterfalls I've ever seen," said Breeding.

India Company pumped itself up for each day's trial with a brazen flag ceremony designed to thumb Marine noses at the North Vietnamese. "Attention to Colors!" Dabney shouted early each morning. Every man would stand straight—though dirty, unshaven, and often in rotting fatigues—while two Marines tied a shredded United States flag to a radio antenna and then raised the antenna. Second Lieutenant Owen S. Matthews lifted a bugle and played a truncated version of "To the Colors."

The first, heavy metallic "Thonk" sounded in the Horseshoe, then again, and again.

In exactly twenty-one seconds, the Marines knew, the first 120mm shells would hit the hilltop. The instant Matthews dropped the bugle, every man dived for cover as "huge explosions walked across the hilltop spewing black smoke, dirt, and debris into the air."

India liked to wave a pair of red silk panties on a long pole after the morning shelling. It was "Maggie's Drawers," the traditional signal on firing ranges for a miss. Some Marines just stood and jabbed stiff middle fingers in the air, shouting obscenities at the North Vietnamese.

The enemy was hurting, too.

Once the clouds suddenly parted, exposing a North Vietnamese platoon climbing a nearby hill. Artillerymen on 881 South quickly knocked aside the parapet, depressed the howitzer's barrel, and slammed a dozen rounds of direct fire fused shells into the unit—killing them all.

After one unusually heavy bombing on 881's slopes, a six-foot tall, beautifully-muscled, dark-haired North Vietnamese soldier—nude, without a mark on his body—walked into the perimeter and stood trembling as the Marines gathered around. When a shell hit nearby, he squatted reflexively and began to defecate and urinate uncontrollably.

The Marines on 881 South hunted down North Vietnamese snipers with a 106mm recoilless rifle—blasting the sniper and the tree he sat in into bloodied splinters. When the North Vietnamese installed a rifleman who failed to hit a single Marine even with thirty shots a day, India Company let him live.

The combat base also had a pet sniper.

A North Vietnamese soldier had lugged a .50 caliber machine gun to a spider hole not much more than two hundred yards from the perimeter. Every day and night he fired at the Marines or at arriving and departing aircraft. The Marines actually caught glimpses of his face through the scopes on sniper rifles, but neither marksmen nor mortars nor recoilless rifles could knock him out. Finally, napalm was called in. For ten minutes the ground around the sniper's position boiled in orange flame and black smoke, the vegetation crisping and the soil itself seeming to burn. When the last oily flames flickered out, he popped out of his hole and fired a single round.

The Marines in the perimeter trenches cheered. They named him Luke the Gook, "and after that no one wanted anything to happen to him."

Some of the Marines, dirty and unshaven, lounged in trash-filled bunkers and laughed out loud when asked how their officers might react to their slovenliness.

"What's he gonna do to me? Send me to Vietnam?" said one, turning back to the war comic he was reading.

"I think those North Vietnamese are nervous," a squad leader said, wondering why the enemy had not attacked. Nearby, a six-foot-high speaker boomed Smokey and the Miracles' "I Love You, Baby" toward the enemy hills.

One Marine grumbled aloud in a bunker as the combat base braced for another shelling: "There's six thousand of us, forty thousand of them. Let's kill our seven each, and go back to bed."

• • •

IT WAS FALSE confidence.

The combat base hung by a single thread; not all the B-52s in the Strategic Air Command, and not all the bravado and bravery of young Marines could have prevented the North Vietnamese from turning off the water.

The Khe Sanh plateau was scored by dozens of creeks and streams, but nearly all the Marine positions were on high ground—militarily sensible, but dry. On the hilltops, where water shared first priority status with ammunition, Marines rigged ponchos to capture moisture droplets in the monsoon mists.

The combat base drew its water from a small stream about one hundred yards north of the perimeter. This stream fell in sharp waterfalls to the Rao Quang River, frothed down and across the province, and flowed beneath the walls of the citadel in Quang Tri City, where the helicopter pilots ate hot meals and drank cold beer—but the stream rose in the enemy-held hills to the north.

If the North Vietnamese had poisoned the stream, a fairly basic tactic in siege warfare, the 26th Marine Regiment would have been forced to attempt a breakout.

"Had we had to fly water into that place in addition to everything else," said General Tompkins, "we would never, never, have reached the fifty pounds per man per day necessary.

"Never."

General Westmoreland said later he was surprised the enemy didn't contaminate the combat base water supply.

• • •

ON FEBRUARY 21, a little before one in the afternoon, North Vietnamese mortars pounded the 37th ARVN Ranger Battalion, and then eighty enemy soldiers made a desultory probe on the Ranger lines. No casualties were noted.

On February 23, enemy guns fired the most shells of any one day of the siege: 1,307. American intelligence officers had expected much heavier rocket artillery from two first-line enemy divisions. Still, the shelling triggered two spectacular explosions in the ammunition dump, killed ten Marines and put thirty in Charlie Med.

On February 25, twenty-nine men from Bravo Company set out from the combat base to look for a small mortar that had been hammering their position with uncanny accuracy. For this first foray beyond line of sight, each man carried five hundred rounds of ammunition and six fragmentation grenades. Two machine gun crews took along eighteen hundred rounds apiece. The patrol was to follow a precise route so that combat base artillery could provide instant supportive fire.

Minutes after his first radio check, Second Lieutenant Don Jacques, the patrol leader, spotted three North Vietnamese soldiers, without rifles, walking casually up the road from Felix Poilane's plantation, "trolling along, without a care in the world." An enemy soldier who had defected to the Americans, one of dozens who worked with the Marines in a program called Kit Carson Scouts, raised his hand in warning, but the sight of live North Vietnamese soldiers after thirty-six days of phantoms was too great a lure. With Lieutenant Jacques leading, the Marines galloped off to capture some prisoners.

They charged across the plantation road—and into the mouth of a crescent-shaped bunker line. A sheet of rifle fire drove them to the ground.

"I was up with the radio when I heard a cry behind us," said John A. Cicala Jr., a corpsman from Detroit who had "Motown Doc" written across his helmet. "It was a guy I once evacuated with infected leech bites. He'd taken a bullet through the left eye and it made a terrible hole in the side of his head.

"He was gone. I knew he was gone; there was no way we could get a chopper in there.

"I put a dressing on his head. When I got ready to leave, he asked for his weapon back. I will never forget him saying that."

Cicala heard someone else shout "Corpsman!" but when he tried to run forward he was hit in the chest, then spun by a bullet in the kneecap. A grenade went off only a few feet away, and he blacked out.

One squad tried to work its way around the flank of the enemy position, but bumped into the crescent's hook: every man was killed.

A fifty-man relief force sprinted toward the trapped patrol, but ran into "extremely heavy small arms, rocket-propelled grenades, mortar and machine gun fire" as it reached the road. The North Vietnamese had established a blocking force to delay reinforcements.

With the relief force pinned down and Lieutenant Jacques pleading for help on an open radio channel, Bravo Company prepared to leave the perimeter to go break the ambush.

Colonel Lownds said no. He had no appetite for feeding troops piecemeal into a battle on the enemy's ground. The North Vietnamese grip would have to be broken by firepower, he said.

Fighter bombers and heavy artillery pounded the enemy positions while the surviving Americans pulled back from the ambush site.

"Are there any more out there?" an officer asked as the last men in the relief force stumbled back. "Is anyone else alive?"

"I don't think so," answered a Marine, "not after the jets got through with the bombs and napalm."

Corporal Roland R. Ball, a full-blooded Sioux Indian, came back carrying Lieutenant Jacques' body and the patrol radio. The Motown Doc made it out by crawling for three hours to reach the base.

Twenty-five other Marines lay sprawled in death eight hundred yards from the combat base perimeter. They would lie there for more than a month—a canker on the Marines' cocksureness.

• • •

BRAVO COMPANY'S GRIEVOUS loss was not as shocking to commanders at Khe Sanh as the patrol's discovery of a dozen long trenches that reached like greedy fingers toward the combat base.

Under cover of fog, the North Vietnamese had been digging zigzag trenchlines from positions near the Poilane plantation toward the combat base. Some were already a mile long. They wound through the groves of coffee trees, beside the Bru trails, between the bomb craters and creekbeds, and across the access road from Route 9. Some survivors of the double ambush had escaped the killing ground by hiding in the trenches during their return to the base.

General Westmoreland declared an "immediate emergency." His scientific advisers hurried to Khe Sanh with seismographic equipment. They ran slender probes into the soil of the plateau to listen for the sounds of digging; the French had lost critically important positions at Dienbienphu when the Vietnamese tunneled beneath them—and dynamited them off the face of the earth. Westmoreland also ordered the Air Force and Marine air staffs to increase the bombing.

Westmoreland in mid-February had told General Momyer that he was unhappy with the B-52 results. He suggested the big bombers start working inside the two-mile limit established to protect friendly troops. The Air Force was nervous about using strategic bombers for close support of ground troops, but prepared to go ahead after the discovery of the trenches.

The B-52s made their first close-in runs on the plateau on February 27—and the Marines loved it. They came out of their bunkers, and stood atop the sandbagged trench lines and cheered as hundreds and hundreds of almost simultaneous explosions hurled trees and brush and fountains of red earth into the sky. The big planes flew 589 close-in bombing missions over Khe Sanh during the siege. "One hiccup," said an Air Force commander who flew Sky Spot, "and we would have decimated the base."

Yet the bombing had little effect on the trenchlines. They advanced as much as one-hundred yards a night, and some began to branch into headers and T's—the final stages before assault ramps were built. Navy jets put one-thousand-pound delayed-fuse bombs into the enemy positions to erupt "like a string of volcanos." Other planes spilled drums of jellied gasoline into the trenches until the petroleum was puddled everywhere—then touched off a napalm tornado with a white phosphorus rocket.

At night, Marines on the southern perimeter could see red and white lights bobbing down the trenches as the North Vietnamese pushed their lines forward. "God," marveled a sentry on the line, "they don't even care about being seen."

To save his soldiers from the firestorm at Dienbienphu, General

Vo Nguyen Giap had put laborers into the front line to dig trenches to the very face of the French defenses. Now, with exactly fourteen days to go to the anniversary of the Vietnamese attack on Dienbienphu, the Marines watched in fascination as the trenches moved toward them "like long, thin arms, with fingers on the end." *Dac cong* rattled the wire in some sections of the perimeter—and removed mines and flares from other sectors without a sound.

On the last day of February, the fortieth day of the siege, the trenches reached to within 350 feet of the combat base.

The Marines braced for the terrible rush that would finally bring them face to face with their enemy.

10.

THE FALSE FINISH

The whole world was watching.

During February and March, the siege at Khe Sanh was a cover story in *Newsweek* and *Life,* the lead story in half the reports from Vietnam by the "CBS Evening News," and the top story in dozens of page one accounts in the *New York Times*, the *Washington Post*, the *Baltimore Sun*, the *Boston Globe*, the *Kansas City Star*, the *Rocky Mountain News*—and hundreds and hundreds of other newspapers across America. Walter Cronkite described it as a "microcosm" of the Vietnam war, and Senator Robert F. Kennedy called it an example of the folly of U.S. involvement.

"The forthcoming battle at Khe Sanh, all neatly being arranged under the eyes of television cameras, [has] swelled to near-Gettysburg proportions," the *New York Daily News*, the nation's largest newspaper, reported in early February. "Gettysburg . . . is the way the fight at Khe Sanh is developing in the public mind. A major victory would ease a lot of frustration around the countryside at home."

It was already a battle of firsts—the first time a field commander had begun preparations for the tactical use of nuclear weapons, the first sustained use of B-52 strategic bombers for close-in support of ground troops, the first deployment in combat of the seismic / acoustic sensors, the first use of the secret "Firecracker" artillery shell, and the first time a Commander in Chief had insisted on written assurances from his generals that a battle would be won.

"No single battle of the Vietnam War has held Washington—and the nation—in such complete thrall as has the impending struggle for Khe Sanh," said *Time* in mid-February.

President Johnson focused the country's attention even more intently on the combat base when he flew to California February 19 to personally wish "Godspeed" to a Marine regimental landing team being rushed to I Corps.

"This is a decisive time in Vietnam," the President told the Marines. "The eyes of the nation and the eyes of the entire world—the eyes of all of history itself—are on that little brave band of defenders who hold the pass at Khe Sanh. We do not doubt the outcome."

Colonel Lownds accepted the challenge with firm, blunt optimism. "My mission is to stay here, damn it, and we're going to stay here. What's there to panic about? That's our job. That's what we get paid for.

"It's only a question of how much Giap is willing to lose. I would hope it would cost him 40,000 or 50,000 men, maybe more."

Yet at the back of every military mind, and lodged irretrievably in the American consciousness, was the unspoken, unspeakable, possibility that Khe Sanh could fall. No one ever put it more starkly than the wide-eyed, war-awed correspondent for *Esquire* magazine:

> What if those gooks that you think are out there are *really* out there? What if they really want Khe Sanh, want it so badly that they are willing to maneuver over the triple lines of barbed wire, the German razor wire too; over barricades formed by their own dead (a tactic, Colonel, favored by your gook in Korea), coming in waves, *human* waves, and in such numbers that the barrels of our .50 calibers overheat and melt and all the M-16s are jammed, until all of the death

in all of the Claymore mines on our defenses has been spent and absorbed? What if they are still coming, moving toward the center of a base so smashed by their artillery that those pissy little trenches and bunkers that *your* Marines half got up are useless, coming . . . coming at you 20,000 to 40,000 strong? And what if they pass over every barricade we can put in their way . . . and kill every living thing, defending or retreating . . . and take Khe Sanh?

In the afternoon of the last day of February, the sensors along Route 9 began to broadcast alerts in sequential order from Lang Vei toward Khe Sanh Village and then on to the combat base. To the earphoned analysts deep underground in the Fire Support Control Center, it sounded like a regiment on the march. At any instant, they warned, 1,500 North Vietnamese soldiers might burst from the fog.

Colonel Lownds put the base on Red Alert; for only the second time in the siege, every able man took a place in the fighting trenches.

For DEROS counters, February 29 was a bitter extra, a Leap Year "gift" that meant they would serve thirteen months and one day in Vietnam while most Marines would serve thirteen months. Army soldiers served 365 days, so the extra day had no effect on their tour of duty. It was one more bit of evidence that Marines always got the dirty end of the stick, one more confirmation that they were truly grunts, that they might have to fight and die on a day that wasn't even supposed to be on the calendar.

Every mortar and artillery battery fired continuous volleys along the enemy's presumed approach route. Radar-guided fighter bombers lowered through the fog every few minutes, and two flights of B-52s were diverted from other targets to bring their strings of bombs to within eight hundred yards of the Marine perimeter.

More than 6,000 U.S. Marines were staring into the fog when 78 North Vietnamese suddenly jumped from a concealed trenchline and charged the ARVN Rangers. Massed rifle fire from the South Vietnamese troopers dropped the attackers before they had penetrated even the outermost barbed wire barrier. Two dozen enemy soldiers tried the Rangers again a half hour before midnight, and a dozen weakly probed the ARVN position at 3:15 A.M. The South Vietnamese reported 78 enemy dead.

"This was not their best effort," Lownds declared, lifting the Red Alert. "It was just another probe."

• • •

ON MARCH 6, a C-123 Provider took a hit in the left engine as it approached the airstrip. Straining on a single engine, the plane turned away and tried to return to Da Nang. Four miles east of the combat base, the over-stressed engine quit, and the aircraft—with four U.S. Air Force crew members, forty-three Marines, a Navy corpsman, and a civilian photographer named Robert Ellison, slammed into a hillside and burned.

That same week, one of the Marines' big choppers suddenly plummeted out of a Super Gaggle, carrying twenty-two men to their deaths.

• • •

STILL, IT SEEMED too quiet.

Every night during the first week of March, one or more of the enemy trenches moved inexorably forward another hundred yards, yet there were fewer than a dozen trenches—nothing like the maze of diggings that had strangled Dienbienphu.

All of the infantry attacks so far had been quite small, with the enemy committing only a few hundred men at a time.

The North Vietnamese artillery had fallen far short of the pulverizing barrages that U.S. intelligence had expected, and the antiaircraft fire was, frankly, "unsophisticated."

Where were the tens of thousands of North Vietnamese? Why had they not struck when the Marines were stunned by the titanic blast that destroyed the American ammunition stores, or when dense fog paralyzed U.S. air support?

Some of the highest-ranking military officers in Vietnam believed that Khe Sanh had never been the enemy's prime target, despite Westmoreland's assertion that it was "a vital link in the northern defenses."

"Khe Sanh was a trap that the enemy could use whenever he wanted to force you into the expenditure of absolutely unreasonable amounts of men and material to defend a piece of terrain that wasn't worth a damn," said Major General Lowell R. English, deputy commander of the 3rd Marine Division, which defended Khe Sanh. "There was no reason why the enemy had to pass through there; the reason it became an outpost was because Westmoreland wanted it."

When Congressional investigators asked retired Marine General David M. Shoup—a Medal of Honor hero, a former commandant of the Corps, he'd even been born in Battle Ground, Indiana—why the Marines were at Khe Sanh, he said:

"Somewhere along the line there is some strategy with respect to Khe Sanh that we don't know, and this is one thing I don't think we should know, else the enemy might find it out, too. I have to feel that there is some strategy in which it is expected that eventually we will gain a great deal by maintaining Khe Sanh. And I don't think they are going to take Khe Sanh.

"I continue to believe that there is, there must be, some good sound reason for being there."

But critics argued that Khe Sanh had been a feint, a gesture with the left hand to catch the eagle's eye while the enemy's right hand struck like a mailed fist at South Vietnam's cities. General

Westmoreland had dismissed the idea on the first morning after the Tet Offensive, but on February 5, Joseph C. Harsch, a commentator for ABC News, wondered aloud if the North Vietnamese had conducted "minor jabs at Khe Sanh . . . to keep our troops concentrated where they can have the least influence on the outcome of the [Tet] campaign.

"Perhaps our generals prepared for the wrong battle," he said.

A few days later the U.S. Army's respected chronicler, retired Brigadier General S. L. A. Marshall, told *Newsweek*:

"I am inclined to doubt that Khe Sanh is really going to come off. I am very suspicious of all this publicity. They simply don't telegraph punches this way. Maybe Khe Sanh is just a feint to cover the Viet Cong attacks of last week."

In mid-February, General Westmoreland's chief information officer, Brigadier General Winant K. Sidle, told senior news reporters in Saigon that it was "illogical" the North Vietnamese had not already attacked Khe Sanh. It was possible the enemy forces had not yet completed preparations for the attack, he said, or that they had been badly hurt by the bombing, but it was also possible that they had never planned to attack at all.

General Westmoreland looked over the latest radio intercepts, aerial photographs, and intelligence summaries and came to the conclusion on March 6 that the enemy had turned his attention from the combat base.

Within hours, the vast enemy force believed to be in the siege ring around Khe Sanh, still unseen, melted away. The Marines at the combat base wouldn't learn about the enemy's departure for nearly a week, but Westmoreland told President Johnson on March 9 that the enemy at Khe Sanh had dropped to "between 6,000 and 8,000 men." On March 10 the general reported to Washington that the North Vietnamese had stopped repairing their trench systems.

The siege, it appeared, might be over.

• • •

It was on March 10 that the *New York Times* printed on page one a detailed story about Westmoreland's "urgent" request for 206,000 additional American soldiers. The news, coming at the moment the U.S. Command proclaimed victory in the Tet Offensive, jolted the American public almost as much as the enemy's surprise attacks.

Westmoreland was still fitting newly arrived reinforcements—the U.S. Marines' Regimental Landing Team 27, a brigade of the 82nd Airborne Division from North Carolina, and the last units of the 101st Airborne Division—into key positions in I Corps. He now had fifty-two U.S. infantry battalions, more than half the American infantry units in Vietnam, prepared for battle in the northern provinces, and he had announced a triumph of sweeping proportions in the Tet battles.

Why did he need more?

The general explained on March 11, amid rising political clamor in the United States, that he expected "very, very heavy fighting" in the two northern provinces—nothing less than a full scale invasion across the DMZ, with both Khe Sanh and Hue as potential prizes. None of the powerful enemy divisions that had materialized in the DMZ in the weeks before Tet had yet entered the battle, he said.

Westmoreland believed he had been presented with a tremendous opportunity to hasten an end to the war. He thought Vo Nguyen Giap had "lost the cream of his army" in the foolish Tet attacks. The Communist forces were on the brink of defeat; another 200,000 American troops might push them over the edge.

A growing number of Americans in the military and political and diplomatic worlds of Washington, D.C., and in the cities and towns of the rest of the country, did not interpret the numbers of Tet with the same ebullient enthusiasm they induced in Westmoreland.

To America, the enemy had never seemed stronger. On March 7 the U.S. Command announced that 542 Americans had died in battle the previous week—just one less than the record toll in the third week of February. The shocking television film of house-to-house fighting in Hue and Saigon, the haunted faces of the Marines at Khe Sanh, and the looming threat of a massive north Vietnamese offensive in I Corps cracked Westmoreland's credibility.

"We think the American people should be getting ready to accept, if they haven't already, the prospect that the whole Vietnam effort may be doomed," the *Wall Street Journal* editorialized on February 23. The war was costing the United States too much, the *Journal* said, and American firepower seemed to be destroying the country it was supposed to save.

On February 27, Walter Cronkite told nine million CBS viewers:

"To say that we are closer to victory today is to believe, in the face of evidence, the optimists who have been wrong in the past. It seems now more certain than ever that the bloody experience of Vietnam is to end in a stalemate."

During February and March, a majority of the American people began to rethink U.S. involvement in Vietnam.

"Nobody in Saigon, to my knowledge, anticipated even remotely the psychological impact the offensive would have in the United States," said Westmoreland. He blamed the news media for creating a national mood of gloom in the midst of victory.

"They got so damn hysterical back in Washington over the Tet Offensive," fumed Admiral Sharp, the commander of all Americans in the Pacific, "that they sort of went off the deep end and decided to get the war over with—even if we weren't going to win it."

• • •

MILITARY ASSESSMENTS OF the Tet Offensive were more sober than the public proclamations of triumph. The chairman of the

Joint Chiefs of Staff told President Johnson that only the surprising performance of ARVN had held the fragile government of South Vietnam together in the first confused days of the enemy offensive. "If they hadn't performed well, we'd have had a catastrophe," General Wheeler said.

The earlier criticism of Westmoreland's border fighting now sharpened.

"The search-and-destroy strategy, combined with a fixation on the infiltration routes, dispersed American forces all over the . . . Vietnamese map," wrote the British military analyst Sir Robert Thompson. "The doors were left wide open for the Tet Offensive."

An Australian military writer said Westmoreland could not guarantee the security of both the combat base and the cities of South Vietnam, "and the point was made to the whole world that even 525,000 American troops were not enough to deprive Giap of the strategic initiative."

General Westmoreland knew he could not guarantee freedom from terror for the South Vietnamese people, even with 206,000 more American troops. "To maintain an American, Allied or ARVN presence everywhere all the time," he said, "would have required literally millions of men—and I still would have had to maintain a reserve to counter big unit threats."

The United States Army had known these numbers for years, but they had been lost in the institutional memory. In the early 1950s, General Matthew B. Ridgeway had studied the prerequisites for an American military campaign in Indochina—and found them "chilling": up to a million men, enormous construction costs, and a national mobilization that he predicted might become "politically very messy." Because the land was particularly suited to guerrilla operations, Ridgeway said, "every little detachment, every individual that tries to move about the country, will have to be protected by riflemen. Every telephone lineman, road repair party, every ambulance, and every rear area aid station will have to be under armed guard. . . ."

Ridgeway's worst fears had been realized, and now the war strained the United States' strategic responsibilities.

The little counterinsurgency in South Vietnam had grown into a major war that consumed U.S. military resources so rapidly that the Joint Chiefs no longer felt confident they could defend more critical American interests elsewhere in the world. The United States was spending more than $30 billion a year in Vietnam while its strategic foes, Russia and Red China, were spending hardly a billion. Americans had shed tears on more than twenty thousand coffins, but no Russian or Chinese mother mourned lost sons in Vietnam.

If some unexpected flashpoint suddenly escalated into war with the Soviet Union, a high percentage of the United States' best strategic bombing crews would already be busy—dropping five-hundred-pound bombs on Vietnamese jungles.

Simple, straightforward military logic—uncomplicated by political concerns about nuclear warfare or world war—called for the smashing of the enemy's capital city, the closing of his harbors, and the squeezing off of his supply lines—even if the supplies came in Russian or Polish or French ships.

The fear of Chinese intervention in the war, and the possibility of triggering World War III, kept American bombers from leveling Hanoi and Haiphong.

Denied permission to wage a war of annihilation, Westmoreland had chosen to fight a war of attrition, to try to kill enemy soldiers in South Vietnam faster than they could be replaced—"to kill the tree by plucking leaves faster than new ones could grow."

To kill in war means to risk being killed, and Westmoreland's way of war had grown more costly—from a monthly average of 114 dead Americans in 1965, to 417 dead Americans a month in 1966, to 782 dead Americans each month of 1967. Now, in the first months of 1968, the death tolls were surpassing 500 a week.

• • •

Some unmarked threshold of pain was crossed in March of 1968. One in five Americans switched from support of U.S. involvement to opposition.

The news on March 10 that Westmoreland had asked for 206,000 more Americans for Vietnam duty startled the nation into a reassessment of the war. Treasury Secretary Henry Fowler, deeply worried about a world monetary crisis, warned of severe jolts to the U.S. economy if the request was granted. A group of governors, fearing renewed rioting in the nation's big cities, pleaded with the President not to call the National Guard for duty in Vietnam; the Guard was needed at home.

On March 12, Senator Eugene McCarthy, who opposed the war, confirmed the collapse of Johnson's political consensus when he came within 330 votes of the President in the New Hampshire presidential primary.

On March 16, Senator Robert Kennedy announced he would oppose the President in the remaining Democratic primaries.

On March 18, 139 members of the U.S. House of Representatives called for a thorough Congressional review of American policy in southeast Asia.

It was almost over.

The President searched for some way to demonstrate his desire for peace. He had in his hands a detailed memorandum from U.N. Ambassador Arthur Goldberg that recommended a halt to the bombing of North Vietnam. President Johnson knew that pilots, Defense Department analysts, and America's friends abroad were sharply critical of the bombing, but he could not bring himself to issue the order—because of Khe Sanh.

"What would happen," he wondered, "if we stopped the bombing and the North Vietnamese then launched a major offensive, overran Khe Sanh, and killed thousands of Americans and South Vietnamese?

"The American people would never forgive me."

Dissent among his most trusted counselors, the polling evidence of a sea change in American attitudes, rising opposition inside the Congress and his own Democratic Party, and sleepless nights over the fate of the combat base had wrought a profound change in President Johnson. He decided to lay his burden down.

The President began to set the country on a new course by announcing on March 23 that General Westmoreland would be coming home.

The general was not quite ready. His plans for a capstone battle—a clean, crushing victory to highlight his Vietnam years—had not come off exactly as hoped. The Khe Sanh combat base was still being pounded by enemy shells: the North Vietnamese celebrated Westmoreland's transfer with 1,109 rounds on the base—the heaviest one-day shelling of the month.

General Westmoreland flew to Washington, D.C., a few days later to personally brief the Commander in Chief on the plan to relieve the siege.

He believed it was important to end the siege with a symbolic demonstration of American military might. Khe Sanh, after all, had become a symbol of American determination in Vietnam; it would be distinctly anti-climactic if the biggest battle of the war ended without taking place.

Now that he had the equivalent of a field army assembled in I Corps, and now that the logistics problems were solved, and especially now that the weather had begun to clear, General Westmoreland could once again wage war the American way, and he was thinking *big*.

More than 30,000 men would be involved in the relief operation, Westmoreland told the President, with the flying horses of the U.S. Army's 1st Air Cavalry Division leading the way. The Air Cav would custom-make its own landing zones with ten-thousand-pound parachute bombs to eliminate the risk of landing in ambushed jungle clearings. Operation Pegasus, two months in the planning, would be the perfect conclusion to the Marines' stand against the North Vietnamese—and it had been meticulously prepared.

Two U.S. Marine battalions had already secured the road from the Rockpile to Ca Lu, clearing the way for continuous truck convoys of supplies, fuel, ammunition and construction material. Three battalions of engineers—one each from the Army, Navy, and Marine Corps—were leveling ground for a new airfield, building parking ramps and logistical facilities, and digging artillery pits, trenchlines, and bunker complexes for a powerful forward base at Ca Lu.

From there, it was only twelve miles to Khe Sanh.

Nothing was being left to chance, the general assured President Johnson. Heavy bombing would soften up the enemy positions, then the Air Cav would leap forward like knights on a chessboard—surprising enemy defenders with vertical envelopment tactics. A Marine infantry regiment would thrust west on Route 9 to shepherd the engineers as they rebuilt the road to Khe Sanh. The 3rd ARVN Airborne Task Force would follow the U.S. juggernaut.

Using maps of the northern provinces to illustrate the plan, Westmoreland showed the President how Pegasus even included a regimental-sized diversion in eastern Quang Tri province.

These were unusually elaborate preparations, considering that Westmoreland had believed as early as March 6 that the North Vietnamese no longer prized Khe Sanh. By March 15, Westmoreland judged that the enemy had "given up, his attempted repeat of Dienbienphu an abject failure." But the general believed it was important to conclude this unfinished chapter of the war with a great show of force—for morale and for good public relations.

President Johnson was usually very attentive in his military briefings, prodding the generals with questions, nodding reluctantly at explanations, and asking to be shown aerial photographs or maps. But as Westmoreland spoke, on March 26, part of the President's mind was shaping the words that would end a lifetime in politics: he had decided not to seek reelection.

The President had been stunned on March 25 and 26 when his most trusted counselors—a group of distinguished former ambassadors and cabinet officers and retired generals whom Johnson called the Wise Old Men—recommended by a two to one margin that he move the country toward disengagement from Vietnam. The same group—sober, steady men who had been tested in earlier crises—had unanimously endorsed the President's escalation policies as recently as November.

It was now clear to the President that the American people did not want to pay the current high costs of the war, and that they were firmly opposed to higher costs when it was impossible to guarantee a successful conclusion

Troops already in the pipeline would swell American strength in Vietnam to 549,000, a new President would send B-52s to bomb Hanoi, the American death toll would rise past 55,000, and the war would continue for years—but these stressful days in February and March of 1968 were the turning point: America had reached the end of the line.

On March 31, President Johnson told the nation he was stopping the bombing of North Vietnam, and that he was ready to go "to any forum at any time to . . . bring this ugly war to an end."

And then the President added the words that shocked some of his closest friends and advisers:

"I shall not seek, and I will not accept, the nomination of my party for another term as your President. . . ."

Westmoreland felt betrayed.

"It was like two boxers in a ring, one having the other on the ropes, close to a knock-out," the general said, "when the apparent winner's second inexplicably throws in the towel." But Westmoreland wouldn't let it spoil Pegasus.

On April first, at exactly seven in the morning, the 1st Marine Regiment attacked west on Route 9, and the 1st Air Cavalry Division leapfrogged to new landing zones halfway to Khe Sanh. The relief force encountered no resistance, but this was a military operation for cameras and politicians—not for war.

The commander of the 1st Air Cav, Lieutenant General John J. Tolson, knew it was a charade. He had read the intelligence reports and he did not expect to find any North Vietnamese at Khe Sanh. Still, he understood the need to get the Marines moving again.

General Tolson had been horrified when he first flew into the Combat Base to discuss Operation Pegasus:

"It was the most depressing and demoralizing place I ever visited," he said. "It was a very distressing sight, completely unpoliced, strewn with rubble, duds and damaged equipment, and with the troops living a life more similar to rats than human beings."

Most U.S. Army officers were shocked by Marine tactics and leadership. The man that Westmoreland sent north to coordinate Army and Marine operations in northern I Corps, Lieutenant General William B. Rosson, was most diplomatic when he suggested the Marines had "not sufficiently prepared their troops for the kind of war . . . that has evolved along the DMZ."

In the first ten days of March, Westmoreland firmly established his ascendancy over the Marines, first by taking over their air assets and then by naming an Army general to direct military activities in the north. The Marines had fought all the way to the Joint Chiefs of Staff to hold on to their aircraft. Westmoreland was adamant, however, and for the first time in his years of frustration in Vietnam, he considered resigning. Here was an issue for which he would fall on his sword. The Joint Chiefs of Staff shied away.

The Marines had lost every political battle, and they could see the dirty end of the stick about to be pushed at them again. They had not wanted to defend Khe Sanh in the first place, and then they were criticized for not defending it well. Now, with the 1st Air Cavalry Division on the way, they were almost certainly going to be "rescued."

It would be the final humiliation. General Cushman was insistent at every planning meeting for Pegasus: "I want . . . no implication of a rescue or breaking of the siege by outside forces."

And so, two days before Pegasus was launched from Ca Lu, the Marines at the combat base undertook their first offensive strike of the siege. It was to be a revenge raid.

Bravo Company had lost more than 50 dead and 135 wounded to enemy shelling, and 25 of its men still lay in the crescent-shaped killing ground south of the combat base. The company had been mauled, yet few of its men had even seen the North Vietnamese. The dark mood of Bravo grunts would poison Marine morale unless the company had a chance "to settle an old score."

The first offensive action at the combat base would be a punishment raid against the North Vietnamese who had ambushed Lieutenant Jacques' patrol.

The battalion commander and his staff worked for a month to plan the attack. Nine artillery and mortar batteries would fire support missions every inch of the way, with jet bombers and the 175mm guns multiplying the shielding shrapnel. Captain Kenneth W. Pipes and Bravo Company would advance within a moving double-box of protective fire all the way to the target.

At 0800, the men of B Company rose from the concealing slopes of a draw and crossed the Poilane Plantation road under cover of heavy fog. Volleys of artillery shells threw up gouts of red earth just seventy-five yards ahead of them, and on both flanks. Four 106mm recoilless rifles and six heavy machine guns poured direct fire into the enemy positions. The Marines fixed bayonets. When the artillery boxes collapsed behind the enemy bunker line to cut off reinforcements, Bravo Company charged over the same ground that had claimed the lost patrol.

Suddenly, the fog lifted.

Enemy mortarmen quickly launched dozens of shells, and one of the first landed in the middle of Bravo's command group. The radio observer was killed instantly, and so was the forward observer for the heavy mortars. Captain Pipes took a fragment through the upper arm that lodged in his chest two inches from his heart.

Pipes stayed on his feet, and urged his men forward. In the early planning for this attack, the battle maps had been sectioned into general fire zones that were designated by fruit names—Apples, Oranges, Grapes. With the forward observers dead, it was impossible to make fine adjustments in the supporting fire; Pipes cradled the radio in his good arm, pressed the "Talk" button, and told the guns to "Fire Apples," or "Fire Grapes."

Bravo Marines swarmed into the enemy trench lines, pinning down the defenders with machine gun and automatic rifle fire while fellow Marines seared and blasted each North Vietnamese bunker with flame throwers, grenades, and satchel charges. "The men carried out their grisly work for over three hours," the Marine history recorded, "and by noon the trench-works had become a smoking tomb for 115 North Vietnamese."

The dead Marines of the lost patrol were recovered where they fell, their wallets, watches, rings, and dog tags undisturbed.

Bravo's raid was celebrated at Khe Sanh as "a brilliant feat," and "the only really successful attack against the enemy."

A cable arrived from Saigon bestowing a Meritorious Unit Commendation on Pipes' Marines:

"Officers and men of Company B, 1st Battalion, 26th Regiment, United States Marine Corps, deserve highest praise for aggressive patrol action north of Khe Sanh on 30 March. Heavy casualties inflicted on a bunkered and entrenched enemy force indicated typical Marine ésprit de corps and professionalism.

"Well done."

It was signed:

General William C. Westmoreland, COMMUSMACV.

In the early days of April, the battalions of the 1st Air Cavalry Division moved closer to the combat base—once landing as close as five hundred yards from the perimeter wire.

The cavalrymen found an awesome ruin, "a wasteland of interlocking craters." "By now," a Marine historian wrote, "the verdant green hillsides, once the site of the best coffee plantations in Indochina, had been pounded into a red orange moonscape."

General Tompkins, whose roots were in rural South Carolina, had described Khe Sanh in January as a beautiful place where the forest was full of game and the streams were full of trout. Now, he said, "the place was absolutely denuded. The trees were gone . . . everything was gone. Pockmarked and ruined and burnt . . . like the surface of the moon."

The first Americans into Khe Sanh Village found a shattered ruin without a sign of life—and bomb craters big enough for entire houses. "The ville was all rubble, bodies, nothing. . . ."

General John Tolson could hardly wait to put his division to more useful work. The 1st Air Cavalry was trained and equipped for heavier duty than a Potemkin relief operation.

The Marines showed the same fixed-grin enthusiasm. As far as they were concerned, "the enemy threat had been squelched weeks before Pegasus had gotten off the ground." They "had not been rescued from anything."

Still, even with the enemy gone, the charade had to be carried through to the end.

On April 8, air cavalrymen completed a sweep of Route 9 and met a Marine company from the combat base. Some of the soldiers and Marines mugged for the television cameras and still photographers, but most just "shrugged indifferently."

On April 9, for the first time in forty-five days, not one enemy shell fell on the combat base.

On April 11, General Westmoreland, who had flown to Washington especially for the occasion, stood on the White House lawn with President Johnson to announce the formal link-up of Colonel Lownds' 26th Marines and the roadbuilders of the 11th Marine Engineer Battalion. Route 9 was open to traffic, he declared.

Westmoreland told the story of the battle of Khe Sanh in considerable detail. It was, in a way, a summing up of his years in Vietnam. He was coming home soon, and this would be his last great battle. His report was written in tons; it described a battle of superlative feats and numbers—of war the American way.

Every branch of American arms had played a vital role in the victory, the general said proudly, beginning with the Marines' "heroic defense."

The combat engineers had performed a "herculean task" by replacing nine bridges, constructing seventeen bypasses, and rebuilding eight miles of roadway to reopen Route 9 in less than two weeks.

The resupply effort, Westmoreland said, "stands as the premier logistical feat of the war."

Marine and Army artillery had distinguished themselves by firing 158,891 shells during the siege—answering every enemy shell with more than ten. The Air Force made 9,691 fighter bomber attacks at Khe Sanh, the Marines 7,078, and the Navy 5,337—delivering 39,178 tons of bombs, rockets, and napalm, contributing their share to what Westmoreland called, with satisfaction, "one of the heaviest and most concentrated displays of firepower in the history of warfare."

"The key to success," Westmoreland asserted, "the big gun, the heavyweight of firepower, was the tremendous tonnage of bombs dropped by B-52"—75,000 tons in 2,602 sorties.

Westmoreland had been more critical in February when the North Vietnamese buildup seemed immune to the bombing. Furthermore, recent battlefield interrogations had turned up persuasive evidence that the B-52 missions had been compromised.

North Vietnamese Army Lieutenant Le Thanh Dong, a thirty-three-year-old officer who had surrendered in mid-March, told his captors that he had gotten warnings up to twenty-four hours before a B-52 strike. He credited foreign agents who, he said, sent timely information through the Central Security Service in Hanoi.

Captain Nguyen Cong Tan, who had commanded a North Vietnamese intelligence operation before he defected, claimed he had been aware of take-off times and targets for B-52 missions. Four other captives claimed in separate interviews that their units had received the tentative coordinates of B-52 raids, and warned to move if they were in a target area.

One high-ranking North Vietnamese officer said he thought it was "ludicrous" to use the big bombers to support troops in combat. "The extreme measures used to insure that American troops will not be on the receiving end are so elaborate that the element of surprise is completely lost," he said.

In late March, Hanoi Radio broadcast a poem it said had been written by troops at the Khe Sanh front:

> The Yanks have modern B-52s
> Of which they make a bugaboo
> But woe to the GIs
> When we opened fire
> On the front of Highway Nine.
> How they wept and cried!
> And us, clean-shaven,
> We asked them after each battle:
> What can cause more trouble
> Our cannon or your B-52?

Captain Phan Van Hong, who had commanded enemy infantry at Khe Sanh, told American interrogators that he had received "frequent, timely, and accurate warnings" of B-52 raids either by telephone or radio "at least two hours before the strike."

But the formal relief of the siege and the unchallenged success of Operation Pegasus was a time for celebration—not for questions or doubts. In General Westmoreland's final summary, the B-52 strikes were "decisive," and they eclipsed any other element in the battle.

Westmoreland told the pilots and crews of B-52 bombers on Guam: "Without question, the amount of firepower put on that piece of real estate exceeded anything that had ever been seen before in history by any foe, and the enemy was hurt, his back was broken, by airpower . . . basically the fire of the B-52s."

"It was a battle won by you," Westmoreland told the bomber crews, "and exploited by the 1st Air Cavalry Division of the United States Army, and the Marines."

• • •

THE SUN CAME out at Khe Sanh. The enemy shelling ceased, the airfield was reopened to C-130s, and Colonel Lownds turned command of the regiment over to his replacement.

Now was the time to compose the recommendations for honors and medals: a Navy Cross for Colonel Lownds, a Presidential Unit Citation for the 26th Marine Regiment, and, for Westmoreland, elevation to Chief of Staff of the U.S. Army.

It was almost over.

11.

One More Time

Captain William Dabney stood on the crest of Hill 881 South in the chill midnight darkness, watching men with rifles stumble past in the gloom. It was the first few minutes of Easter Sunday, April 14. The Marines were moving out early to reach jumpoff points for a dawn assault on 881 North.

There was symmetry—and irony—in fighting the last battle on Hill 881 North.

India Company had opened the siege here on January 20 when it bumped into the infantry screen for an enemy rocket regiment. For eighty-four days, India had stared at the mountain's misted slopes, dueled with its snipers, and counted the thousands of rockets that lifted from its summit and sides.

India wouldn't be going today; the company would provide direct fire support to the Third Battalion. This time, three companies would go instead of three platoons—600 men instead of 185.

Dabney wouldn't be going, either. He had been relieved a few hours before, and placed on the promotion list for Major. Colonel Lownds was also gone; he had turned the 26th Regiment over to Colonel Bruce Meyers on April 12.

Like Bravo Company's foray, the Easter Sunday attack was to be a punishment raid—a chance to strike directly at an unseen enemy, to settle an old score.

Few of the young Americans who crouched in the bombed

wasteland at the foot of 881 North this Sunday morning in April knew that other Americans had crouched in the same place twice before in the last year.

Forty-nine weeks earlier, two Marine battalions had attacked this same hill—and suffered the heaviest casualties of the war in the Hill Fights. During the battle, a prominent Bru leader named Anha tried to tell the Marines about a tunnel that ran through the mountain. Anha's father had been foreman on the plantation of Madame Bordeauducq, and Anha had been like a brother to Felix Poilane. He knew about the tunnel—really a warren of caves—because many of the Bru people had hidden their precious kettles there.

A Marine major, who thought Anha was Vietnamese, had brushed the information aside.

News of the heavy Marine losses swept quickly through the Bru hamlets the next day, and dominated conversations in the village. Carolyn Miller and her husband had visited the Poilanes that afternoon, and found Felix particularly upset by reports that more than one hundred Marines had died. He expressed his regret to the Millers, countrymen of the fallen soldiers, and then he asked:

"Why don't they ask for guides from the local people?

"They probably thought that after all that bombing it would be safe to go up, but any Bru person could have told them that the mountain is full of caves. The North Vietnamese undoubtedly just retreated into the caves until the bombing was over, and were there to meet them when they sent in ground forces."

The French plantation owner was treated with cold suspicion during these tense weeks of combat, and he did not feel he could offer suggestions to the Americans—and be believed.

Captain Dabney had not known about the caves when he took India Company up 881 North on January 20.

The 600 Marines waiting for dawn on Easter Sunday morning didn't know about the caves, either.

The Americans would retire from Hill 881 North, from the Khe

Sanh Plateau, from I Corps, and from Vietnam without ever learning that North Vietnamese Army troops moved *below* this battlefield—in tunnels and caves secure from heavy bombing.

• • •

THE MEN OF the Third Battalion looked ragged as they crouched in the tall grass, waiting for the signal to move out. They were tired, dirty, hollow-eyed, and some showed huge body sores—souvenirs of trench life with too little water. They'd been living on combat rations for months. Many wore ripped or rotting uniforms, although in some units there were more replacements than veterans. India Company, for example, had placed 167 dead or wounded men on medical evacuation helicopters during the siege—out of a roster strength of 185 men.

The new colonel helicoptered to 881 South where he could personally supervise the final attack of the Khe Sanh campaign. He had doubled the normal prep fires for this operation, adding the 1st Air Cavalry Division's eight-inch guns and 155 howitzers to the usual Khe Sanh mix of Marine mortars, 105s and 155s and the Army's 175s. Marine fighters put bombs, rockets, and napalm on specific backslope targets. The Marines on Hill 881 South fired directly over the heads of the attackers, leading them up the slopes with massed direct-fire volleys from eight 106mm recoilless rifles, two 105 howitzers (the third had been destroyed by an enemy shell) and six .50 caliber machine guns salvaged from downed helicopters.

Several times, when the Marine force paused to consider the proper attack against a line of trees, the eight recoilless rifles simply blew away the tree line.

The attack kicked off at 5:40 A.M., and scout dogs gave first warning a half hour later. Brisk firefights broke out on the facing slope as enemy outposts gave warning, but the Third Battalion was not to be denied.

"Moving behind a wall of steel," the Marine history recorded, "the battalion clawed its way through the defenses . . . stormed the hill, swarmed over the crest, and killed anyone who stood in the way."

Some of the Marines were seized by a bayoneting frenzy that not even their officers could restrain.

A group of North Vietnamese, shell-shocked by the heavy bombardment, ran insanely from bunker positions to open ground. The assault companies were ordered to halt while air and artillery finished off the cluster of terrified soldiers, but a handful of Marines plunged in with bayonets. Their company commander apologized on the battalion radio net: "Sir, I can't stop them. . . ."

The Marines mopped up small pockets of resistance into the early afternoon, killing and counting 106 North Vietnamese, and declared at 2:28 P.M. that Hill 881 North was in friendly hands.

As the new regimental commander and Dabney watched from 881 South, a Marine shinnied up a tree whose limbs had been sheared away by shellfire, gripped the trunk with his knees, and tied a United States flag to the topmost splinters.

When he had climbed down, the Marines turned and struggled back down the steep slopes of 881 North. Casualties had been "surprisingly light" this time: six dead and thirty-two wounded.

Marines from the assault companies were staggering with fatigue when they arrived atop Hill 881 South just as night came. The battalion commander was there, and his executive officer, to slap each man on the back and congratulate him for a job well done.

"They were near exhaustion, filthy, bearded, ragged," recalled the commander, Lieutenant Colonel John C. Studt. "Some wore bloody battle dressings.

"But they were loaded with captured NVA weapons, and they were all grinning."

• • •

A C-130 PROVIDER landed on the combat base airstrip this Easter Sunday, blowing a tire in an old shellhole and slamming into a forklift. Only one man was killed: Felix Poilane, who had thumbed a ride on the first available flight to Khe Sanh to see what he could save of his plantation.

• • •

THE NEXT MORNING, at 8 A.M. on April 15, the U.S. Command announced that Operation Pegasus had been concluded and that all objectives had been achieved: Route 9 reopened, the enemy routed, the siege relieved.

Pegasus, like the defense of Khe Sanh, American officers told news reporters in Saigon, could be counted as one more outstanding success of American arms in Vietnam.

It was almost over.

12.

THE CURTAIN FALLS

The Marines had hoped to close the combat base as soon as the revenge raids were completed, but on April 15 Westmoreland vetoed the plan. The base had become too much of a symbol to abandon abruptly; at least a thousand Marines would have to stay to show the flag.

The 26th Marine Regiment, however, was free to go, and on April 18 it was airlifted from the combat base. The regiment had been there when the fight began on January 20, and it had been there when the siege was declared over on April 8, and it had been in at the finish, with flamethrowers and bayonets on 881 North. General Tompkins had the 3rd Marine Division's brass band on the tarmac when the regiment arrived at Quang Tri City; the first thing the dirty Marines heard as they marched down the ramps was "a stirring rendition of the Marines' Hymn." Every man, by order of the commanding general, got a hot shower, a clean uniform, and a big steak dinner before nightfall.

The Army had already left Khe Sanh.

As soon as the cameras recorded the ritual handshake that confirmed the "relief" of the Marines, General Tolson turned the 1st Air Cavalry Division toward the A Shau Valley, where he was sure he could find action. The 101st Airborne Division went, too, and the 3rd ARVN Airborne Task Force. Pegasus only brushed Khe Sanh with its wings.

The combat base had become a liability, and an embarrassment, even before the middle of April.

It could be shelled by unshellable enemy guns, it was plagued by foul weather, and it had failed spectacularly to block enemy movement into South Vietnam.

"We are no longer stopping any invasion," one Marine officer said in the last days of the siege. "In fact, from the tops of the bunkers we can see Communist trucks moving along Route 9. . . .

"It looks like a little Los Angeles freeway."

General Tompkins was especially upset by North Vietnamese disdain for American fighter bombers.

"Right to the end, they drove lighted trucks, with headlights, and the vaunted A-6 [Intruders] could no more catch them than I can fly," Tompkins said. "As far as interdicting the North Vietnamese lines of communications, U.S. airpower was almost completely zero."

The new airfield and fortified base at Ca Lu offered an attractive alternative to Khe Sanh: it was out of range of the guns in Laos, closer to friendly lines, and no where near as fog-cursed.

But it would not be easy to abandon Khe Sanh.

The combat base had been portrayed for months as a critical strongpoint—as "the crucial anchor of our defenses along the demilitarized zone." Maps prepared in Washington showed how the base blocked five avenues of infiltration. Without Khe Sanh, American military authorities had warned, the end of the line would be turned and enemy divisions would "pour down Route 9" to attack Quang Tri and Hue.

The focus of General Westmoreland, official Washington, and the news media on the battle at Khe Sanh had made it "the most famous military engagement of the Vietnam War, even though it has not yet taken place."

America had come to care for the young Marines who uncomplainingly carried out a difficult task—"the little band of defenders," as President Johnson had pictured them, "holding the pass at Khe Sanh."

General Westmoreland was attentive to the vibrations in the political threads from Washington, and he knew he could not simply shut down the base and walk away.

The problems were political—not military.

At the very core of the U.S. decision to stand and fight at Khe Sanh had been "an unwillingness to grant the enemy a psychological victory by giving ground." It was even more difficult to step back now that the enemy threat had loomed so large at Khe Sanh—and now that the hills had been blooded again.

Generals Rosson and Cushman, the highest-ranking Army and Marine officers in I Corps, had urged abandonment, and Westmoreland's chief of operations, General John Chaisson, agreed: "From the military standpoint, there's no doubt it's the desirable posture."

But General Westmoreland was extremely sensitive to public opinion in the United States, and he worried that abandonment might be misunderstood by many Americans.

Moving to Ca Lu would mean dismantling the combat base, tearing up the airstrip and then breaking up the road, completely undoing the work of Pegasus.

"When this is to be done, how this is to be done, and how this is to be handled, from, shall I say, the public relations standpoint, is what makes this a rather sticky problem," Chaisson told admirals and generals in Honolulu in May.

"One thing we feel quite strongly that we can't buy," Chaisson said, "is the enemy one morning sitting on top of Khe Sanh. . . .

"We just can't afford that type of play on his part."

It was especially important that the discussions about abandoning Khe Sanh not become public before May 23, when President Johnson was scheduled to honor the 26th Marines for their defense of the combat base and the hills. In formal ceremonies in the Cabinet Room of the White House, the Commander in Chief personally put into Colonel Lownds' hands a Presidential Unit Citation—a proud new banner to hang with the regiment's flag and battle standard, and then he solemnly shook the hand of Sergeant Major Agrippa W. Smith, representing the enlisted men who had served at Khe Sanh. Once again the story of the siege was told, and the valor of Marines recounted. For President Johnson, especially, it seemed a fitting conclusion to a battle upon which "the eyes of history itself" had looked.

It was almost over.

The few Marine units still at Khe Sanh were busily firing shells into the hills to use up the last stocks of ammunition when General Westmoreland made his final swing through I Corps a few weeks later.

He reviewed the final plans for shutting down the combat base, and agreed with Generals Rosson and Cushman that it should be razed promptly. But, he added, they must wait until after June 11 and let the new commander of U.S. forces in Vietnam, General Creighton W. Abrams, choose "the optimum time" for closing the base.

On the morning of June 17, just six days after Westmoreland left Vietnam, the Marines began slashing sandbags, blowing up bunkers with plastic explosive, filling in trenchlines with bulldozers, and peeling up the pierced steel plates of the airstrip. All supplies, equipment, ammunition, vehicles, building beams, and airfield matting were to be trucked out, the order read, "[and] everything else buried by bulldozer, burned, or blown up."

It was imperative that no identifiable landmark remain that could become the centerpiece for a North Vietnamese propaganda film.

When the combat base had been reduced to an unrecognizable red blur on the cratered landscape of the plateau, the Marines backed down Route 9—blowing up the new bridges, destroying the new bypasses, and triggering landslides under the new roadway until the highway was once again a shattered ruin from Khe Sanh to Ca Lu.

The pullout proceeded in complete secrecy to avoid a public relations disaster in the United States. The North Vietnamese still observed Khe Sanh from the face of Co Roc, and could see quite clearly that the Americans were destroying their fortifications and disappearing down Route 9. Americans did not know about the pullout because news reporters were forbidden to write about it by the U.S. Command.

John S. Carroll of the *Baltimore Sun* went considerably out of his way during a late-June tour of I Corps to see the famous Marine base one more time. He was astonished to discover that the bunkers had been blown up and the airfield destroyed—and the Marines were already packed up to move to Ca Lu. Carroll raced back to Saigon to write what he believed to be one of the more important stories of the war: Khe Sanh was being abandoned.

Carroll's story set off precisely the kind of public questioning and criticism that General Westmoreland and his staff had feared.

In Washington, President Johnson was not available for comment. Mr. Johnson had not been involved in any way, Press Secretary George Christian told reporters; the decision to abandon Khe Sanh had been solely a military decision.

General Westmoreland explained carefully that the decision to abandon Khe Sanh had not been made by him, but by General Abrams.

In Saigon, General Abrams explained that he had acted on the recommendation of Generals Rosson and Cushman.

In Paris, the spokesman for North Vietnamese affairs, Nguyen Thanh Le, told a news conference:

"The United States military commanders once decided to defend the base at all costs. They are now forced to retreat from the base. The high command pretends the retreat was ordered because the base is unessential now."

Smarting from the criticism, the U.S. Command in Saigon acted swiftly. Brigadier General Winant Sidle, chief of information for MACV, called John Carroll before him, reprimanded him for endangering the lives of American troops by reporting on military movements in progress—and suspended his MACV identification card.

A formal communiqué was issued: the huge increase in American troop strength in the northern two provinces and the extraordinary helicopter assets of the 1st Air Cavalry Division had given the U.S. command much greater flexibility in dealing with enemy threats. With vastly enhanced mobility, and with enemy forces poised for assault at new and different targets, it no longer made sense to have powerful U.S. forces "tied to specific terrain"—like the Khe Sanh Combat Base.

"Therefore, we have decided to continue the mobile posture we adopted with Operation Pegasus in April. The decision makes the operation of the base at Khe Sanh unnecessary."

It was over.

Body Counts

During testimony before a special committee of the United States Congress in November of 1970, Colonel David Lownds and General Rathvon Tompkins disagreed for a moment on the exact number of Marines killed at Khe Sanh.

One hundred ninety-nine, said Lownds.

Two hundred five, countered the general.

Yes, the colonel remembered quickly, it was 205. But it was important for the congressmen to understand, he continued, that the number represented all Marines killed on the Khe Sanh plateau from November 1, 1967 to April 1, 1968—the duration of a larger military operation named Scotland—and not just those lost at the combat base during the siege.

Two hundred five dead in such a lengthy battle is a reasonable, acceptable, justifiable number as the military measures losses in combat, and it has come to be accepted as the true accounting of the cost for victory at Khe Sanh.

Two hundred five dead represents only three percent of the Marine force at Khe Sanh, and when compared to the estimated losses of the North Vietnamese, no other battle of the war produced a more satisfying body count/kill ratio for American forces than the siege of Khe Sanh.

Yet 205 is a completely false number.

John Wheeler, a veteran Associated Press correspondent who

spent more time at Khe Sanh than any other reporter, discovered the lie in late February. Wheeler saw more men being killed or wounded than were being reported by the Marines. One day he walked over to Charlie Med to look at the records and talk with the surgeons. When his personal count exceeded the "official" number by 100, Wheeler closed the books and walked away. He never believed the numbers again.

The Reverend Ray W. Stubbe, a Lutheran chaplain, estimated that 475 Marines were zipped into green plastic body bags during January, February and March at Khe Sanh.

The chaplain was a kind of Pepys for the combat base, writing down every report and rumor in his diary, and wandering from the somber intelligence briefings in Colonel Lownds' command bunker to the soup counter at "Howard Johnson's" in the village, from the drawing room of the Poilane plantation to the morgue room of Charlie Med. In the endpapers to his unpublished book, the chaplain lists the name, rank, serial number, and date of death of 441 Americans for whom he offered prayers during the siege.

The official number of 205 does not include the Marines who died in the Easter Sunday attack on Hill 881 North; these deaths were counted in Pegasus' totals.

Nor does the official number include the lost comrades of the "bloody, filthy, vacant in the eyes" survivors of the horror at Lang Vei, where ten Green Berets were killed or missing in action.

Three hundred sixteen CIDG soldiers—South Vietnamese and Bru montagnards and Hré Montagnards—had also been lost in the flames of Lang Vei, but they were not included in the official list of dead.

And how dearly did the 33rd Laotian Elephant Battalion pay for its brief appearance on the stage at Khe Sanh? Overrun by tanks, panicked into flight to Vietnam, caught in the battle for Lang Vei, disarmed at the gates of the combat base, and trapped on the most heavily bombed battlefield of the war, the Laotian battalion surely lost hundreds from its long columns of disheartened soldiers, and women, and children.

Robert Ellison isn't one of the official 205. The twenty-three-year-old photographer had just scored a professional triumph: *Newsweek* magazine had purchased a whole portfolio of his color shots of Khe Sanh. His picture of an explosion in the combat base ammunition dump would be on the cover. Ellison was on his way back to Khe Sanh on March 6, lugging a case of beer and a case of soda pop for new-found friends at the combat base, when enemy fire ripped through his plane and it crashed—killing everyone aboard.

Ellison had hitchhiked his ride—civilian journalists could almost always find a loadmaster who would let them aboard at the last minute—and so his name did not appear on the passenger manifest; thus he has never been counted among the official casualties of Khe Sanh.

But then none of the forty-nine Marines, Air Force crew, and Navy corpsmen killed in the March 6 crash are counted in the official statistics of the Siege of Khe Sanh, either; their plane struggled on one engine long enough to crash outside the formal map boundaries of Operation Scotland, and the bodies were not recovered until much later, after the books had been closed.

The official number of dead does not include any soldiers from the 37th ARVN Ranger Battalion, which absorbed the only enemy attacks on the combat base perimeter, and which was pounded by the same shells and rockets that hurt the Marines. Deeply distressed by the deaths of many of their wives and children in the Tet fighting, the ARVN Rangers had nevertheless won the respect of Marine officers with their aggressive tactics and commitment to the fight. Their sacrifices at Khe Sanh appear nowhere in the official record of the siege.

Two hundred five dead does not include casualties from the Special Forces' compound on the southwest perimeter of the combat base. Nearly 500 South Vietnamese and Montagnard irregulars under Green Beret control guarded the main gate from this position, and also conducted short patrols to seek intelligence from the Bru; their dead and wounded are not part of the official number.

And what ever happened to First Lieutenant Le Van Quoc, left standing at the gate after his long night of personal heroism?

Of all the Allies on the Khe Sanh Plateau—"the friendlies," as they came to be known in the special language of the Vietnam war—the Bru people suffered the heaviest losses. During the emergency evacuation of civilians at the start of the siege, the South Vietnamese province chief in Quang Tri City had specifically excluded the Bru people.

Three thousand Bru tried to walk out on Route 9 in late January, when the road was considered impassable, but only 1,643 made it to Cam Lo, including a sixty-year-old man who had carried his crippled wife the whole way. In March, the Marines airlifted 1,432 Bru to safety.

Most of the Montagnards had to seek shelter on a plateau where there was no shelter.

"The amount of firepower put on that piece of real estate," Westmoreland had boasted, "exceeded anything that has ever been seen before in history." The general sternly preached "the sanctity and sacredness of the civilian who was on the Vietnam battlefield through no fault of his own," but Niagara's deluge could hardly be selective.

On one occasion, U.S. fighter bombers attacked a column of Bru civilians who were being forced by North Vietnamese soldiers to carry boxes and equipment along Route 9. The pilots regretted killing the Bru, but "the immediate situation dictated an attack to prevent the movement of supplies."

Chaplain Stubbe estimated that 5,000 Bru were killed during the battle at Khe Sanh, but none appears on the official list of 205 dead.

Father Poncet is not there either. The young French priest with the sparkling eyes had been evacuated from the village to a place of safety: Hue. During Tet, the priest and M. Linares were walking near the Perfume River when a burst of rifle fire knocked them down. Linares had been in the car when Papa Poilane was executed on Route 9; now he rose to his hands and found himself unwounded again. Father Poncet was dead.

And the official number does not include the fifty-one Marines, forty-six Army cavalrymen, and thirty-three ARVN paratroopers who were killed during the relief mission, Operation Pegasus.

Because the bookkeeping methods for body counts were determined by the military operations in which the fatalities occurred, and because the operations at Khe Sanh changed names from Scotland to Pegasus to Scotland II to Charlie, the official count of American dead in the siege stopped on April 1—forever fixing the number at 205.

Marines who kept the combat base open when public relations required it, and Marines who shut the base down when military good sense prevailed, did not qualify for a Presidential Unit Citation and were not counted among the official dead in the Battle of Khe Sanh.

• • •

AND WHAT ABOUT the North Vietnamese?

"My staff estimated the North Vietnamese lost 10,000 to 15,000 men in their vain attempt to restage Dienbienphu," Westmoreland wrote several months later. "[We] lost two hundred five."

Colonel Lownds was convinced that two whole divisions of the North Vietnamese Army had been destroyed, and anyone who looked at the cratered terrain around Khe Sanh knew the enemy's losses must have been terrible. "The most reasonable estimate," said a U.S. Army general, was 10,000 killed or seriously wounded.

All of the numbers were estimates, and some were wild guesses;

heavy clouds and dense ground fog made precise counts impossible. Seventy-eight bodies were counted after the North Vietnamese attack on February 29, for example, but the Marines believed they had "wiped out an entire regiment."

The official body count for the Battle of Khe Sanh was 1,602 North Vietnamese dead—buy not even the Marine commanding general believed it especially when he heard that only 117 rifles and 39 crew-served weapons had been captured. Field reports with such wide disparities in bodies and weapons, General Tompkins declared, were "a bunch of poop."

Captain Dabney put it even more harshly:

"Most body counts were pure, unadulterated bullshit. Generals manipulated a 'good kill' by flip-flopping numbers, and a certain dishonesty was bred. All of us knew that the staff was not coming out to count the bodies in front of our lines."

General Tompkins thought the whole concept of measuring success in war by body counts was "ludicrous, absolutely ludicrous," but he played the game because it was expected of him.

"They'd report something . . . anything, and I'd just shove it on," Tompkins said. "I didn't give a damn what they were saying [about body counts]. It was a system going on; it was required by Saigon."

General Tompkins was not alone; six out of every ten American generals who served in the Vietnam war believed that official body counts were "often inflated."

The exaggeration of enemy death tolls was exposed most baldly during a military briefing in the White House for President Johnson's Wise Old Men. It was late in March, when the conservative counselors were beginning to wonder if the cost exceeded the prize in the Vietnam war. A military officer, trying to show how dramatically the war had turned around since February, reported that 45,000 enemy soldiers had been killed in the Tet Offensive—a staggering setback for any army.

United Nations Ambassador Arthur Goldberg remembered

that American forces in Vietnam had experienced a ratio of seven wounded for every man killed, and he asked the officer what enemy strength had been at the beginning of the offensive. Between 160,000 and 175,000, the officer replied. Was the enemy's wounded-to-killed ratio much different than the American ratio, Goldberg wanted to know. It ran about three and a half to one, the officer said.

But that was impossible, Goldberg exclaimed. It meant the enemy had no more effective forces left on the battlefield!

"A long and devastating silence followed."

Judgments

By any military standards, Khe Sanh was a clear United States victory . . . a textbook example of what the military calls "occupying terrain by firepower." Air Force enthusiasts call it history's first victory of air power over ground forces.

—*U.S. News and World Report, May 6, 1968*

As far as interdicting the North Vietnamese lines of communications, U.S. airpower was almost completely zero. Right to the end, they drove lighted trucks, with headlights, and the vaunted [night-flying bombers] could no more catch them than I can fly.

—*General Rathvon McC. Tompkins,*
Commanding General of the Marines at Khe Sanh

By pinning down and by decimating two North Vietnamese divisions, the few thousand Marines and their gallant South Vietnamese allies prevented those divisions from entering other major battles such as Hue and Quang Tri.

—*President Lyndon B. Johnson*

One of the reasons why General Giap did not attack Khe Sanh [is] that he did not want to awaken in the American people an overriding emotion of patriotism in support of the war.

If, during a favorable break in the weather, when American air power would have been hampered, and before the Marines were well dug in (they were never so well entrenched as the French at Dienbienphu), the death and capture of more than 5,000 Marines might well have incited such a response from the United States. . . .

Besides, Khe Sanh proved to be a superb diversion for the Tet Offensive.

—*Sir Robert Thompson, British military analyst*

In Hanoi, General Giap was smugly satisfied with his handiwork. He had never had any intention of capturing Khe Sanh. His purpose there all along had been to divert U.S. attention and resources. And it had accomplished its purpose magnificently.

While the rest of the world watched the extravaganza at Khe Sanh, Vo Nguyen Giap, perhaps one of the world's most brilliant generals, looked elsewhere.

—*Dave Richard Palmer, American military analyst*

There were two enemy divisions around Khe Sanh and part of a third waiting in the wings—15,000 to 20,000 men—facing one reinforced American regiment of about 6,000 men.

The one South Vietnamese and four American battalions [at Khe Sanh] represented only one-sixtieth of the 299 U.S. and Allied combat battalions in Vietnam.

How could anyone legitimately question who was tying down whom?

—*General William C. Westmoreland*

What Giap wants is to control the population of South Vietnam. American opinion is concentrated on Khe Sanh, while political commissars are speaking in the public squares of every small village, and even in Saigon itself.

—*Major Jean Pouget, veteran of Dienbienphu*

Khe Sanh was one more American effort in a chimerical series to create a battle of Dienbienphu, one that American firepower would "win." It bespoke a low estimate of Giap's tactical judgment.

—*Robert B. Asprey, American military historian*

Dienbienphu, Dienbienpu, look, it's not always true that history repeats itself.

Khe Sanh didn't try to be, nor could it have been, a Dienbienphu. Khe Sanh wasn't that important to us. Or it was only to the extent that it was important to the Americans—in fact, at Khe Sanh their prestige was at stake.

Because just look at the usual paradox that you will always find with the Americans: as long as they stayed in Khe Sanh to defend their prestige, they said Khe Sanh was important; when they abandoned Khe Sanh, they said Khe Sanh had never been important.

Besides, don't you think we won at Khe Sanh?

I say yes.

—*General Vo Nguyen Giap*

Khe Sanh will stand in history, I am convinced, as a classic example of how to defeat a numerically superior besieging force by coordinated application of firepower.

Khe Sanh [was] one of the most damaging, one-sided defeats among many that the North Vietnamese incurred, and the myth of General Giap's military genius was discredited.

—*General William C. Westmoreland*

The most important battle of the war.

—*General Lewis W. Walt, U.S Marine Corps*

Khe Sanh was an unsound blow in the air.

—*General Victor H. Krulak, U.S. Marine Corps*

Khe Sanh has won a large place in the history of the Vietnam war as an inspiring example of American and Allied valor.

One day, the victory over the siege may be judged a decisive turning point that finally convinced the enemy he could not win.

—The Washington Star, June 9, 1968

The absurdity of Khe Sanh will rate a book by itself. Holding it, relieving it, and evacuating it were all regarded as victories.

—Sir Robert Thompson

We have curtailed the tide of Communist aggression and prevented the overrunning of the Republic of Vietnam. In over three years, the enemy has not won a single major military victory. . . . In the first six months of 1968, the Communists lost an estimated 170,000 men.

Large portions of the countryside have been secured and a major segment of the population brought under government control and protection. Many miles of roads and waterways have been opened. We have made great strides in developing self-sufficient Vietnamese armed forces.

By virtue of their understanding, discipline, combat proficiency, and humanitarian actions, our troops have earned the respect of the Vietnamese people. . . .

Although a serious Communist challenge remains, the Republic of Vietnam is growing steadily stronger. The foundations we have laid are soundly constructed and, with firm resolve, an independent and viable nation should emerge.

—General William C. Westmoreland,
Report on the War in Vietnam, June 1968

Acknowledgments

In addition to the authors and correspondents and military personnel whose contributions are acknowledged in the Notes, I am especially grateful for the lively interest of Carolyn Miller, an eyewitness in Khe Sanh whose love for the Bru still glows; for the steady hand of Joseph P. Davison, mapmaker, who uniquely combined the skills of a professional cartographer and an artillery officer, of Rollie Krichbaum, who read the manuscript in its penultimate draft; for the willing assistance of John T. Dyer Jr., Curator of Art at the Marine Corps Museum, and the cheerful competence of the Marine Corps Library's professional staff, which made me welcome for weeks; for the hospitality of my aunts Doris Baster and Nada Poole, who opened their house and hearts to me during research trips to Washington, D.C.; and for the encouragement and help of my wife, Ellen, whose patience made it possible.

NOTES

Authors and book titles are given here in the clearest abbreviated form. Complete bibliographical details are cited in Sources.

1. The Curtain Rises

In stiff manila folders in a back room of the U.S. Marine Corps library in the Navy Yard, in Washington, D.C., are daily, weekly, and monthly Situation Reports, copies of radio messages, intelligence summaries, cable traffic, casualty totals, and even penciled personal notes from every Marine unit that fought at Khe Sanh. These are the bones of the story of the siege, and they were first put together by Marine Captain Moyers S. Shore II, in *The Battle for Khe Sanh.*

Shore was under unique pressure; both the Commandant of the U.S. Marine Corps and the Chief of Staff of the U.S. Army looked over his shoulder as he worked. His book was designed specifically to rebut criticism of the decision to stand and fight at Khe Sanh—and of the way the fight was fought.

Shore's work is flawed by the many official approvals it had to win before publication, but the captain had worked hard to collect the memories and the views of every important player. These records include letters, notes, transcripts of interviews, observations, dissents, and even first drafts of Shore's book annotated by officers who served at Khe Sanh. They are invaluable, but uncatalogued, and in Shore's notes and in mine they are labeled "Comments."

William Dabney, now a lieutenant colonel in the Marine Corps, shared his memories and views during interviews in October and November of 1978 and January of 1980.

A final valued source for this chapter, and for all the siege, was Ray W. Stubbe's Chaplain at Khe Sanh, Volumes I and II (a typed manuscript, 1,504 pages, dated 1971, in the Marine Corps library). Stubbe's rambling diary is chock-full of eyewitness accounts, wild rumors, and official reports on everything from the weather, the rats, and the Bru to enemy intentions, regimental briefings, and rising casualty tolls.

PAGE

10 trout as big as salmon: Tompkins, *Oral History*, p. 48.

13 the Hill Fights: Shore, pp. 10–16.

13 "We're coming after you!": Stubbe, p. 118.

14 no . . . target . . . had been so heavily bombed: *Marines in Vietnam—1967*, p. 125; Shaplen, *Road from War*, p. 137.

14 "no NVA, no trees, no nothin' ": Stubbe, p. 120.

15 "We . . . came back with half [our men]": *Congressional Record—House*, May 22, 1967, pp. 13381–82.

15 "well-equipped . . . well-uniformed, well-fed": *Electronic Battlefield*, pp. 80–81.

18 "all the resources of the Navy, Marine Corps, and Air Force": Pearson, p. 30.

22 "In other words, they bag 'em.": Chaisson, *Oral History*, p. 154.

22–26 This account of the attack on 881 North comes from Shore, and Dabney, but also from the hand-written accounts of radio operators, enlisted men, and officers who nominated the dead lieutenants for medals. These eyewitness accounts are attached to the formal "Award Recommendation" forms on file with the Department of Navy. Sergeant Jessup won the Silver Star for his heroism. The Navy Cross was awarded posthumously to platoon leaders Tom Brindley and Michael Thomas.

26 a . . . tradition more sacred than life: *Small Unit Actions in Vietnam—Summer, 1966*, p.94.

27 The official history is Shore's work, *The Battle of Khe Sanh*.

2. Westmoreland

The details of Westmoreland's personal history come from his autobiography, *A Soldier Reports*, and from *Westmoreland: The Inevitable General*, by Ernest B. Furgurson. For an understanding of the art of being a general, I am grateful to Maureen Mylander's *The Generals*.

I attended many of Westmoreland's briefings in Vietnam in 1967 and 1968, and twice interviewed him at length as he traveled by jet around the country. I was present at the battles of Con Thien, Loc Ninh, and Dak To, but I am also indebted to the official reports and numbers published by military sources, especially Westmoreland's *Report on the War in Vietnam*.

PAGE

29 Westmoreland . . . moved . . . past West Point classmates: Furgurson, p. 290.

30 "the . . . best . . . army in the world": Graff, p. 98.

31 a campaign for the presidency: Furgurson, p. 333.

31 "at the snap of a finger": Furgurson, p. 214.

31 plane . . . reeked of monkey shit: Westmoreland, *Soldier*, p. 27.

31 the first perfect . . . "compleat general": Mylander, p. 64.

32 "to evoke an image of cascading shells": Westmoreland, *Soldier*, p. 339.

32 Checker . . . onto the board: Westmoreland, *Report*, p. 160.

33 "daring amphibious hook": Westmoreland, *Soldier*, p. 204.

33 "chimerical": Westmoreland, *Soldier*, p. 113.

34 a jumble of generals: Westmoreland, *Report*, p. 83, and Kahin and Lewis, pp. 131–75.

34 Big Minh playing tennis: Westmoreland, *Soldier*, p. 63. Some Vietnamese complained that Westmoreland tended to have greater confidence in Vietnamese who spoke good English regardless of their military or political skills: see Tran Van Don, p. 152.

34 ARVN: Westmoreland, *Soldier*, p. 59–70.

35 nozzles . . . of disabling gas: *Soldier*, pp. 46–47.

35 "trying to push spaghetti": Charleton, p. 135.

35 talked . . . with Sir Robert Thompson: Furgurson, p. 296, and *Soldier*, p. 100.

36 "The critical importance of the little plateau was immediately apparent": Westmoreland, *Soldier*, p. 336.

36 "rules": *Soldier*, pp. 40–48, and Furgurson, pp. 296–300.

37 "forego dissent": Mylander, p. 211.

37 another six months: *Soldier*, pp. 63–65.

38 "was not . . . going to fall on my sword": *Soldier*, p. 77.

39 drinking . . . coup leaders under the table: *Soldier*, p. 99.

40 In January 1965: This short history of the early war years is from Westmoreland's accounts in *Soldier* and *Report*, and from the summary in Halberstam, *Brightest*, pp. 544–79.

41 "We must be prepared for a long war": *Soldier*, p. 139.

42 "field-marshal psychosis": *Soldier*, pp. 115–16. See also Halberstam, *Brightest*, p. 248.

42 "Full speed ahead types": Furgurson, p. 313.

42 "The Influence of Public Opinion": Furgurson, p. 200.

42 "a forceful player who knew what he wanted": Halberstam, *Brightest*, p. 576.

42 "the win phase": *Soldier*, p. 142.

43 "a Caucasian arrogance": Halberstam, *Brightest*, p. 541.

44 "firepower, mobility, and flexibility": *Soldier*, p. 150.

44 "the first team": Halberstam, *Brightest*, p. 541.

44 A thumbed copy of . . . *Street Without Joy: Soldier*, p. 277.

44 France had been able: The account of Groupement Mobile 100's dying comes from Fall, *Street*, pp. 185–250, and Fehrenbach, pp. 414–15, 475.

47 "medical problems": *Report*, pp. 269–70.

49 "Are we fighting the Russians?": *Soldier*, p. 23.

49 "Good God, . . . our cause is lost!": Samuel Eliot Morison, *The Oxford History of the American People* (New York: Oxford University Press, 1965), p. 225.

50 "I hoped . . . would extend the nation's staying power": *Soldier*, p. 295.

50 "a bolt of ribbon wins many battles": *Soldier*, p. 304.

50 "mail from home . . . and hot meals": *Report*, p. 147, and *Soldier*, p. 269.

52 "Courvoisier, at $1.80 a fifth": Herbert, p. 130.

52 But firepower: Firepower statistics and technological advances come from Westmoreland's *Report* and *Soldier*, and from the excellent *Air War—Vietnam*, by Frank Harvey. Lewallen, and Littauer, also provided helpful information.

53 "expensive in dollars but cheap in life": Graff, p. 82.

53–60 Westmoreland seeded: Nearly all of the material in this section is drawn from the Department of the Army study, *Cedar Falls-Junction City: A Turning Point*, by Lieutenant General Bernard William Rogers, henceforth *Cedar*. Jonathan Schell wrote about this same operation in *The Village of Ben Suc*.

55 "They were human moles": *Soldier*, p. 55.

55 "scorched earth": *Soldier*, p. 40.

56 "the people are strongly xenophobic": *Soldier*, p. 53 and 152.

56 "the village of Ben Suc no longer existed": *Cedar*, p. 41.

57 "even a crow . . . will have to carry lunch": *Cedar*, p. 73.

57 "What we need . . . is more bombs": Ellsberg, p. 234.

57 "Think big": *Cedar*, p. 15 and 83.

59 "[Your] commanders disgraced themselves": *Cedar*, p. 135.

60 "Viet Cong units have the recuperative powers of the phoenix": Halberstam, *Brightest*, p. 464 (citing *Pentagon Papers*).

60 "I never thought it would go on like this": *Brightest*, p. 633.

61 "the count . . . erred on the side of caution": *Soldier*, p. 273.

61 "Any American commander . . . would have been sacked": *Soldier*, p. 25.

61 "uncommonly adept at slithering away": *Soldier*, p. 100.

61 "vastly more desirable . . . fight in remote areas": *Report*, p. 132.

62 "Digging the guerrillas out": *U.S. Marines*—1966, p. 8.

62 "Rattling around the . . . border held nothing good for our side": Marshall, *West*, p. ix.

63 "If we avoided battle, we would never succeed": *Soldier*, p. 150.

63 "if considerably more American troops can be obtained": *Soldier*, p. 227–28.

66 decoy: Marshall offers several extraordinary examples of North Vietnamese soldiers sacrificing themselves to set up Americans for the kill; the Khe Sanh battle would provide more.

67 "A sense of despair": *Pearson*, p. 94.

67 "We are very definitely winning": "End of the Vietnam War in Sight?" *U.S. News and World Report*, August 12, 1967 and September 11, 1967.

67 "never-ending searches": *Soldier*, p. 207.

67 Con Thien: The story of Con Thien is from Pearson, and from *Soldier*.
68 "It was Dienbienphu in reverse": *Soldier*, p. 204.
68 "We killed some . . . as they came over the top": Interview at Loc Ninh.
69 lost . . . at A Shau: The driest account of the fall of A Shau appears in Kelly, *U.S. Army Special Forces*, pp. 92–95.
69 Loc Ninh: The story of Loc Ninh comes from newspaper accounts of the period; Hay, *Tactical Innovations*, pp. 42–56; Kelly, *Special Forces*, pp. 127–33; and my own reporting.
71 "you made it look too easy": Hay, p. 56.
71 "I have doubts he can hang on": "In a Military Sense, the War is Just About Won," *Washington Star*, Nov. 7, 1967.
71 Sgt. Vu Hong: Albright, *Seven*, p. 87.
71 camp at Dak To: The story of Dak To comes from newspaper accounts of the period, the author's reporting, and Hay, pp. 78–96.
71 "You can ring a bell": Chaisson, *Oral History*, p. 127.
72 "It looked like Charlie had . . . nuclear weapons": Bernard Weinraub, "Tense Dak To G.I.s Hunt Elusive Foe," *New York Times*, November 17, 1967, p. 1.
73 "a classic example of allied superiority": Hay, p. 78.
73 "Is it a victory?": Chaisson, p. 121.
73 "The NVA is sucking . . . American forces away": quoted in Peter R. Kann, "Value and Price in Battle of Dak To," *Wall Street Journal*, Nov. 28, 1967, p. 1.
73 "entice the Americans close to the . . . border and bleed them without mercy": Warner, *Certain Victory*, p. 134.
74 "A unit might be 'lured' ": *Soldier*, p. 147 and 194.
74 "A boxer faces problems": *Report*, p. 133.
74 "The war *was* going well": *Soldier*, p. 315; *Report*, p. 135.
75 "delusion": Soldier, p. 235.
75 President Johnson had received: The uncertain, changing mood of the people in the United States is captured best in Oberdorfer, *Tet!*, pp. 77–114.
76 "I *was* confident": Soldier, p. 22.
77 "the advantage of nearby sanctuaries": *Report*, p. 138.
77 "there was no way Giap could win": *Soldier*, p. 405.
77 "we are definitely winning this war": Stewart Alsop. "Will Westmoreland Elect Johnson?" *Saturday Evening Post*, Jan. 13, 1968.
77 "many frustrations": *Soldier*, p. 261.
78 "the instrument of his army's downfall": *Soldier*, p. 261.
78 "I had no illusions": Soldier, p. 339.

3. In the Time before the War

For details about civilian life in Khe Sanh, I am especially indebted to Carolyn Miller who worked with her husband for six years at Khe Sanh to create a written

Bru language so the Montagnards could read the New Testament. The Millers spent nearly fourteen years in Vietnam learning the spoken vocabulary of the Bru, writing down the words, training literacy teachers, helping the mountain people learn to read and write—and all the while, translating the New Testament into Bru. War drove them from Khe Sanh, but they continued their work for seven more years in Banmethuot, a city hundreds of miles to the south. The Millers and their five-year-old daughter were captured in the final North Vietnamese offensive of 1975, and they spent a difficult eight months in captivity. Mrs. Miller wrote about the ordeal in *Captured!* (Christian Herald Books, Chappaqua, N.Y., 1977). The Millers now live near Kota Kinabalu, in East Sabah, Malaysia, where they have undertaken another language project.

Some information about the early years at Khe Sanh was also gleaned from a tale told by Francois Pelou, a French news correspondent in Vietnam, as recorded by Oriana Fallaci in *Nothing, and So Be It*, pp. 224–28.

PAGE

89 "If I were General Giap": Shaplen, *Road from War*, p. 94.

89 "not a shot . . . fired in anger": *U.S. Marines—1966*, pp. 82–83, and Shaplen, *Road from War*, pp. 93–100.

90 "it would be too isolated": Chaisson, *Oral History*, pp. 371–74.

90 "you . . . haven't lost a damn thing": *U.S. Marines—1966*, p. 109.

90 "with a shoe in your tail": *U.S. Marines—1966*, p. 109.

91 "someone will be hurt": Miller letters.

92 "setting out honey to attract flies": Fallaci, *Nothing*, p. 226. Hill Fights: *Marine Corps Operations—1967*, p. 124.

92 "The NVA are excellent troops": Stubbe, p. 131.

93 the Lang Vei . . . camp: Albright, *Seven*, pp. 109–110, and Stubbe, pp. 122–23.

93 Jeane Dixon: Stubbe, p. 169.

93 airfield had been badly damaged: Nalty, *Air Power*, p. 8.

94 "one horrendous ambush": Tompkins, *Oral History*, p. 17.

94 a strike into Laos: Nalty, p. 104.

94 "most magnificent bunker you ever laid eyes on": Tompkins, *Oral History*, pp. 26–27.

95 "something mysterious about those wretches": Tompkins, p. 34. (Army and Marine officers were stunned by the opulence of Green Beret team houses—which often featured excellent furnishings, a wet bar, refrigerators, movie projectors, and whole libraries of paperback books and pornographic movies. The Green Berets figured that since they lived closest to death, they might as well live highest on the hog.)

96 "Khe Sanh . . . remembered in American history": Stubbe, p. 589.

96 "We don't have our eyes!": Stubbe, p. 634.

97 "I'm getting worried": Tompkins, *Oral History*, p. 16, see also Simmons, *Marine Corps Operations*—1968, p. 295.

97 "We're going to Laos": Stubbe, p. 684.

98 "[We] had to play this thing very delicately": Charleton, p. 143.

98 "Things are picking up": Stubbe, p. 800.

98 Khe Sanh Village: The picture of Khe Sanh Village on the eve comes from Stubbe, and from Miller letters.

99 "a spy for them": Miller letter.

99 "very tempting for the Viet Cong": Fallaci, *Nothing*, p. 225.

101 "If I ever had to pay protection money": Miller letter.

102 six men appeared: the killing of the NVA officers: In *Comments*, Marine Major Harper L. Bohr Jr. asserts that a regimental commander was *not* among the dead, but he still believes one of the bodies was Chinese—"too big and too non-VC looking."

103 "hostile units . . . materializing . . . south of the DMZ": Nalty, p. 14; Major Jerry E. Hudson in *Comments*; and Pearson, p. 29.

103 "an undeniable opportunity": Pearson, p. 30. (Chaisson, *Oral History*, p. 374, says: "We didn't think they'd have the Guts to mass a couple of divisions—to take a chance on what we could do them, even through cloud cover, with bombing.")

104 "very hazardous business": *Electronic Battlefield*, p. 89.

104 "They're going to attack": Stubbe, p. 734.

105 "It was essential that the hills . . . remain in the hands of the Marines": Shore, p. 31.

105 Captain Daloney: preparations at Khe Sanh: Shore, pp. 32–33; Stubbe, Tompkins, Nalty and Pearson.

107 truck traffic inside . . . Laos: Pearson, p. 30.

108 the agonized scream of someone hurt: *Electronic Battlefield*, p. 34.

109 the movie schedule: Stubbe, p. 753.

4. "Here they come!"

PAGE

110 First Lieutenant La Than Tonc: The extraordinary gift of Lieutenant La Than Tonc emerges from military writings as one of the most spectacular intelligence coups of the Vietnam war. The story, with new details in every telling, appears in Westmoreland's autobiography, in General Tompkins' interviews with the Marines' oral history researchers, in Shore (pp. 39–45), and even years later in testimony before Congress (*Electronic Battlefield*). Once again the Reverend Ray Stubbe was writing everything down in his diary; he even talked with the two sergeants who interrogated the defector.

The North Vietnamese defector would have been instantly shredded by flechette rounds if he had sneezed as he walked toward the jittery Marines; he lived to tell a story that influenced U.S. military movements and thinking for months.

110 he seemed so *eager*: *Comments* (Lt. Col. James Wilkinson).

111 "We had nothing to lose": Stubbe, pp. 771–72.

111 "a detailed description of the coming offensive": Shore, p. 39.

113 "He . . . gave a wealth of information": Swearengen, "Siege," p. 24.

114 "the enemy will soon seek victories": *Soldier*, p. 319.

114 "reminiscent of Dienbienphu": Kelly, "U.S. Watches," *Washington Star*, January 21, 1968.

115 pounded Hill 861: Shore, pp. 39–41; Swearengen; *Comments*; and Stubbe, pp. 780–81.

117 In a colossal explosion: Most Marines who served at the combat base measured time from "when the ammo dump went." The story is vividly told in nearly every source.

118 "extreme combat fatigue": *Comments* (Major Kenneth W. Pipes, who was commander of Bravo Company).

119 they could not find the enemy guns: Shore, pp. 43–44.

120 "We were never able to silence the [enemy guns]": *Electronic Battlefield*, p. 83.

121 lost ninety-eight percent of his ammunition: Nalty, p. 25.

121 "critical, to say the least": *Comments*.

5. "I DON'T WANT ANY DAMN DINBINFOO"

President Johnson's declaration to the Joint Chiefs of Staff about "Dinbinfoo" was captured in Texan phonetics by Michael Herr, in *Dispatches*, p. 105.

The influence of the 1954 battle on American military planning, thinking and deployment throughout the 1960s is evident in the sources cited below. The fixation of the President and Westmoreland on Khe Sanh comes from Johnson's *The Vantage Point*, Doris Kearns' *Lyndon Johnson and the American Dream*, and Westmoreland's *Report* and *Soldier*. For military details in this chapter and in others, I relied in part on two publications of the armed services: *The War in the Northern Provinces, 1966–1968*, by Lieutenant General Willard Pearson, and *Air Power and the Fight for Khe Sanh,* by Bernard C. Nalty.

PAGE

123 Captain Larry Budge: Furgurson, p. 14.

124 Everyone . . . thought about Dienbienphu: Herr, *Dispatches*, pp.99–100.

124 "Your rifles had better be clean": Ellsberg, p. 288.

125 "we don't want any Dienbienphus, not one": Marshall, *Monsoon*, p. 233.

126 The President . . . had become insecure, fearful: Kearns, p. 256.

126 "the Communists are preparing for a maximum military effort": Johnson, p. 371.

127 "intend to reenact a new Dienbienphu": Schandler, p. 86.

127 "Kamikaze tactics": Johnson, p. 379.

128 sand table thoughtful guesses . . . : "How the Battle for Khe Sanh Was Won," *Time*, April 17, 1968.

128 too costly . . . helicopters: Nalty, p. 56.

128 the Laotians were gone: Bits of the Laotians' sad story can be found in Shore, *Comments*; and Albright, *Seven*.

129 "casualties [would be] too numerous" Nalty, p. 25.

129 "a guaranteed one thousand casualties—fast": This was the consensus of Marine officers at Khe Sanh, determined by Associated Press correspondent John Wheeler, who spent much of the siege at Khe Sanh. Interview, August 1978.

129 Dabney . . . lost twenty more: records of Third Battalion, 26th Marines.

129 "create another Dienbienphu": Westmoreland letter to Commandant of the U.S. Marine Corps, *Comments*.

130 "unalterably opposed": Nalty, pp. 68–70.

130 "There is no doubt": the emphases are in the original Chaisson, *Oral History*, p. 134.

131 Sharp suggesting he withdraw: Nalty, p. 68.

131 "knew the terrain intimately": Tompkins, *Oral History*, pp. 19–20.

131 One Nine: Shore, p. 48.

132 "We're surrounded": Stubbe, pp. 803–4.

133 "show of strength": Westmoreland cable to Sharp, January 22, 1968.

135 "Give me some . . . stouthearted men": Dabney interview.

135 head count: Stubbe, p. 815.

137 A surprise landing: Schandler, p. 89, and Oberdorfer, p. 173.

137 war with North Korea: The compounding tension of these days in early 1968 may have been captured best in the Chronology of *Tet!*, pp. 337–51. Don Oberdorfer's daily, sometimes hourly, catalogue of events gives the pell-mell pace of the times.

138 "I couldn't stand it any more": Kearns, p. 271.

139 "We'll just go on bleeding them": Westmoreland speech to editors of the Associated Press, cited, in Simmons, *U.S. Marines—1967*, p. 123.

139 "Khe Sanh commands the approaches": *Report*, p. 162.

140 "I believed we could do all these things": *Report*, p. 163.

140 "the only logical thing to do": *U.S. Marines—1968*, p. 296.

140 It was the only time: Others say that President Johnson called Westmoreland, and even Lownds, by direct telephone, but Westmoreland asserts this was the only time he ever talked to the President from Saigon.

141 The President asked tougher questions: Max Frankel caught Mr. Johnson's hands-on approach to the Khe Sanh battle in "White House: Ultimate Command Post," *New York Times*, February 10, 1968, p. 1.

141 Every day, Westmoreland: Oberdorfer, p. 172, and Nalty, p. 17.

141 Westmoreland . . . could no longer trust the Marines: *Soldier*, p. 342, and Pearson, p. 66, and especially Chaisson, pp. 229–30.

141 "The most unpardonable thing . . . ever": Tompkins, p. 82.

141 Pegasus Operation: Pearson, p. 34, and Nalty, p. 107.

141 "various bits of . . . disturbing intelligence": *Soldier*, p. 318.

142 ARVN Ranger 37th Battalion: Shore, p. 51. Tran Van Don asserts in *Our Endless War* that slights such as this had enormous impact on ARVN morale.

142 "I don't want any damned Dienbienphu": The President's declaration was first reported by *Time* in the first week of February 1968.

143 Maxwell Taylor . . . came back worried: Schandler, p. 88, and Nalty, p. 17. It was a widely held military opinion. Gen. Matthew B. Ridgeway, for example, believed that defeat was "the almost invariable fate of troops invested in an isolated fortress." (cited in Asprey, p. 805.)

143 similarities between Dienbienphu and Khe Sanh: O'Neill, *Strategy*, p. 14.

143 "None of us was blind": *Soldier*, p. 337.

144 The French, he decided: *Soldier*, p. 337.

145 "I knew Khe Sanh was different." *Soldier*, p. 338.

145 "Why would the enemy give away his major advantage?": *Soldier*, pp. 320–21.

145 "[We] might be able to do . . . what the French [couldn't]": Nalty, p. 22.

145 " 'sending a message' to Hanoi . . . tactical nuclear weapons": *Soldier*, p. 338.

146 Pegusus was underway: Pearson, pp. 13–14.

147 the largest air strike of the war: Nalty, p. 82.

147 Westmoreland . . . accomplishment: *Soldier*, and Nalty, p. 27, and *Marines—1968*, p. 294, and *Comments*.

148 "turkey shoot": "History Book Battle," *U.S. News and World Report*.

6. Giap

Vo Nguyen Giap remains an elusive figure a quarter century after his triumph at Dienbienphu—even after his years of war leadership against the United States. The only lengthy conversation with him to appear in English is in Oriana Fallaci's *Nothing and So Be It*, but this was a recollection/reconstruction of an audience he gave to a group of French women Communists—not a sit-down interview. Some of Giap's remarks are so out of character, and some are so hauntingly like remarks he made to others years before, that this remembered pastiche must be approached warily. Still, in a world of paucity, it is a source.

Bernard Fall, and Jules Roy, and Douglas Pike, and Wilfred Burchett offer pieces for a portrait of Giap, and Robert J. O'Neill, who taught history in the Royal Military College of Australia, tried to put them all altogether in *General Giap: Politician and Strategist*.

Giap's journalism and his academic papers seem to have disappeared from history. Some, of course, were seized and destroyed by the French secret police.

What survives are his military writings—musings on the art of war, manuals on infantry tactics, assessments of the French and American forces he faced. Reading these turgid tracts, it is easy to imagine a dour, stiff, unimaginative dullard, and to wonder how the bright, young student writer of the 1930s became the plodding dogmatist of the 1960s.

Then I came across "Unforgettable Months and Years," a piece Giap wrote in 1970 to celebrate Ho Chi Minh's eightieth birthday. It was a revelation. The article was beautifully written, with an eye for color and detail, an affection for people, and especially a love for history. Here was the Vo Nguyen Giap who had impressed teachers at the prestigious Quoc Hoc School in Hue. It's an extraordinary document, and I tried to locate the Vietnamese woman who translated it—just to see if American military translators had stiffened Giap's prose. My letters were unanswered.

Giap has all but vanished from the world stage. Frank Snepp, in *Decent Interval*, reported Giap was so sick in 1975 ("decrepit and ravaged by Parkinson's disease") that he no longer directed North Vietnamese military affairs.

PAGE

149 bold strike into . . . South Vietnam: North Vietnam's preparations for invasion were noted by almost every visitor to Hanoi from 1965 on, including Harrison Salisbury, Wilfred Burchett, Mary McCarthy, and others.

149 "Beethoven-like": Giap, *Banner*, p. vii.

149 "Volcano Under the Snow": O'Neill, *General Giap*, p. 17, insists it should be "ice-covered volcano."

149 300,000 soldiers . . . at home: Littauer, p. 188, says 270,000, but notes that Giap had 450,000 in the reserves.

150 "soldiers of the just cause": it was a name taken by Vietnamese guerrillas in the seventh century A.D., Burchett, *Catapult*, p.18.

151 two muskets . . . fourteen flintlocks, and a Chinese pistol: These weapons are listed in Giap's own writing and in other sources, but Burchett, *Catapult*, p. 122, asserts that on the eve of the raid he received "one American machine gun with 150 cartridges, six fire bombs and a case of time bombs."

151 Giap . . . knew the history: Vietnam's history of invasion and resistance comes from a wide variety of sources, notably Buttinger, Fall, Lamb and McAleavy (see Sources).

152 "use the jungle like a weapon": Bloodworth, p. 244.

153 "an abundance of tropical diseases": Burchett, *Catapult*, p. 27.

153 Tran Hung Dao had written: Pettit, p. 358.

153 "a perpetual struggle . . . with invaders": *Catapult*, p. 11.

154 the Death of a Thousand Cuts: MacAleavy, p. 52.

155 "Giap is still beautiful like a girl": O'Neill, *Giap*, p. 20.

157 "We forgot we were only thirty-four human beings": from a 1964 newspaper article published in Hanoi; cited in Giap, *How We Won*, p. 7.

157 "made without cocks": Lancaster, p 425.

157 "women are against regulations": Langer, p. 113. See also Miller, *Captured!*, in which the North Vietnamese cadre is described as "morally almost puritanical."

158 "even if the . . . mountains go up in flames": Giap, "Unforgettable," p. 16.

158 Archimedes Patti: Charleton, *Many Reasons*, p. 3.

159 "no longer scattered like . . . sparrows": Giap, "Unforgettable," p. 71.

159 "one inch of ground . . . one citizen": from Jean Lacoutre's preface to Giap, *Banner*.

159 angry crowd . . . Hanoi: McAlister, p. 267, and Lancaster, p. 148.

160 "you probably . . . will not succeed": Tran Van Don, p. 143.

160 white duck suit . . . trilby hat: O'Neill, *General Giap*, pp. 45–46.

160 met again in Dalat: O'Neill, *General Giap*, p. 41, and preface to Giap, *Banner*.

160 The rest of 1946: Fall, *Two Vietnams*, pp. 101–130, and O'Neill, *General Giap*, pp. 45–46.

162 Giap spent 1946–1950: O'Neill, *General Giap*, p. 52.

162 political officer: Kinnard, p. 64, discusses the supremacy of the political officer, but more detailed information can be had in Pike, *Viet Cong*.

163 "a whole ideological struggle" cited in Fall, *Two*, p. 114.

163 "Without the people": from Giap, *Banner of People's War*.

163 "the soul of the Army": Fall, *Two*, p. 343.

163 held Dong Khe: Fall, *Two*, pp. 110–111.

164 Civil War in the United States: Morison, *The Oxford History of the American People*.

164 26th Regiment: Samuel Eliot Morison, *The Two-Ocean War* (Boston: Little, Brown and Co., 1963).

164 "Comrades, forward!": Roy, p. 105.

164 American bombers destroyed: the bomb statistics: Department of Defense Target Summary, cited in Van Dyke, p. 26.

166 One thousand civilians died . . . every week: a McNamara memo to President Johnson, cited in Littauer, p. 48.

166 500,000 worked at bomb repair: Van Dyke, p. 44.

166 "It is a sacred war": Salisbury, p. 75.

167 U.S. losses: Littauer, p. 41, argues that in early 1968 the United States was losing one plane for every forty sorties. See also Van Dyke, pp. 60–70, and Thompson, No *Exit*, p. 96, and *Visions of Victory*, p. 32.

167 "We would welcome them": Burchett, *Catapult*, p. 42.

168 "in the end it is you that will tire": Ellsberg, p. 30.

168 "Prepare for the Worst": Burchett, *Vietnam North*, p. 7.

168 "The enemy will pass slowly": Fall, *Two*, p. 113.

168 "I'm the one who usually gives the orders": Burchett, *Vietnam North*, p. 120.
169 Task Force Delta: *U.S. Marines—1966*, p. 85.
170 "ass in the grass": Herbert, p. 139.
170 "His forces remain insufficient": Giap, *Big Victory*, p. 86.
170 "We cannot compare our weapons": *Visions*, p. 84.
170 "They are greenhorns": Burchett, *Vietnam North*, p. 124.
171 "eat soup with forks": *Visions*, pp. 137–38.
171 "morale of American soldiers is lower than grass": *Visions*, p. 138.
171 the one-year tour: discussed in many sources, including Mylander, p. 79, and Palmer, *Summons*, p. 97.
171 "grueling, protracted war of attrition": *Visions*, p. 40.
171 "have a good fighting method": Giap, *Big Victory*, p. 86.
171 "our answer to the B-52s": Langer, pp. 158–59.
172 "you can see the worried expressions": Harvey, p. 10.
173 "an unshakeable conviction that their cause was just": Martin, *Reaching*, p. 219
173 "you need time. . . . Time": Fallaci, *Nothing*, pp. 84–86.
173 Giap counseled patience: Oberdorfer in *Tet!* and Palmer in *Summons* argue that Giap was the driving force for the Tet Offensive, but Kinnard (p. 65) believes that Giap opposed a go-for-broke offensive, and urged a protracted war strategy. Sullivan in *Winter-Spring Offensive*, and McGarvey in *Visions of Victory* also paint Giap as a reluctant dragon—as do his own military writings in the fall of 1967. I believe the evidence shows that Giap did not think a surprise attack would drive America out of the war—that years of warfare would still be required.
174 "prolong the war": *Visions*, p. 17.
174 "We are in no hurry": "The Enemy Strategist," *New York Times*, March 8, 1968.
175 "the puppet army . . . impotent": Giap, *Big Victory*, p. 31.
176 "Our soldiers . . . fear no sacrifices": Giap, *Big*, p. 91.
176 "sharp, shrewd . . . drops of black light": Fallaci, *Nothing*, pp. 77–78.
177 "Surprise is very important": Giap, *How We Won*, pp. 53–54.

7. The Tet Offensive

The clearest and most thoughtful study of the enemy's 1968 Tet offensive, and especially its impact on America, is Don Oberdorfer's *Tet!* I am indebted in this and successive chapters to his research and reporting. Peter Braestrup's *Big Story* is essential for an understanding of the period between January and April of 1968. Lieutenant General Willard Pearson's *The War in the Northern Provinces*, especially the chapter "The Bleak Picture" (pp. 29–65), was very helpful. And Herbert Y. Schandler, in *The Unmaking of a President*, wrote an insider's view of the powerful political and economic forces working on President Johnson.

The U.S. Navy library in Washington, D.C. keeps a dozen, perhaps sixteen, thick volumes of Xeroxed newspaper clippings, literally thousands of articles that were clipped from American newspapers in the late 1960s, pasted on paper, duplicated, and published at the Pentagon as a twice-daily digest on Vietnam war journalism. In the grey seas of print in these volumes are many dramatic snapshots of the war, and especially of Tet.

Finally, I was in Saigon during the Tet Offensive and heard Westmoreland assess the meaning and impact of the enemy attacks from the steps of the U.S. embassy. I twice traveled the length of South Vietnam to see the results of the surprise offensive, and my own notes have a place in this chapter.

PAGE

179 the scene in the Situation Room: *Tet!*, pp. 18–19.

179 Westmoreland stood: my notes, and *Tet!*, p. 34.

180 492,000 American servicemen: Schandler, p. 343.

180 "It did not occur to us": *Report*, p. 158.

181 "about to run out of steam": my notes.

181 "dismay and incredulity": *Soldier*, p. 332.

182 "By the skin of our teeth": Chaisson, p. 214.

182 "We did not expect": my notes.

182 a collective gasp of astonishment: *Tet!* tells the story best.

182 "maximum effort": Johnson, p. 385.

183 "We should be prepared": Schandler, p. 88.

183 "seriously imperiled": *Report*, p. 158.

183 "nuclear weapons or chemical agents": Schandler, p. 88.

183 an honest evasion of truth: See George C. Wilson, "No A-Arms Requested for VN, U.S. Says," *Washington Post*, Feb. 10, 1968, p.1; or Joseph C. Goulden, "U.S. Denies A-Weapon Plan, But Keeps Viet Option Open," *Philadelphia Inquirer*, Feb. 10, 1968. p. 1; or John W. Finney, "Anonymous Call Set Off Rumors of Nuclear Arms for Vietnam," *New York Times*, Feb. 13, 1968, p. 1, among others in *Newspaper Files*.

183 "the enemy could drive us back": *Soldier*, p. 350.

184 the first through-trip . . . in years: *Report*, p. 182.

184 twenty-five bridges and eleven culverts: *Operations of U.S. Marine Forces in Vietnam, January, 1968*. Fleet Marine Force, Pacific. p. 63.

184 The logistics situation turned critical: Pearson, p. 58.

184 "a high measure of surprise": *Marine Corps Operations—1968*, p. 3.

184 Quang Tri City: Pearson, p. 55.

185 fighting . . . in Hue: This account is drawn from Don Oberdorfer's excellent account in *Tet!*, and from Pearson, Braestrup, and my own notes.

186 116,000 fled their homes: *Report*, p. 160.

187 from the *north*: Pearson, p. 62.

187 Tolson . . . fuel shortages: Braestrup, p. 239.

187 "beans, bullets, and gasoline" and the 1st Cav at Hue are from Pearson, pp. 29–65.

188 "Their presence . . . previously unsuspected": Pearson, p. 49.

188 8,000 died: *Soldier*, p. 328.

189 Whispers of discontent: "General Westmoreland Shift Held Unlikely," *Washington Post*, Feb. 6, 1968, p. 4.

189 "complete confidence in your judgment": *Soldier*, p. 336.

189 "I desperately need reinforcements": The message traffic between Wheeler and Westmoreland is in *Soldier*, pp. 352–56. See also Schandler, p. 98, and Johnson, pp. 386–91.

190 rockets near . . . [Wheeler]: Both Schandler, pp. 98–100, and Westmoreland, *Soldier*, p. 354, tell the story and suggest it influenced Wheeler.

190 "second wave of attacks": *Soldier*, p. 356. (General Chaisson briefed reporters in Saigon on Feb. 22 with the same information. Author's personal notes.)

190 "heightened risk": Johnson, pp. 386–91.

190 "in the rack": *Soldier*, p. 354.

190 with substantial reinforcements: *Soldier*, p. 354, and Johnson, p. 386.

191 Wheeler reported: Johnson, p. 390, and Schandler, Oberdorfer, *Soldier*, and Braestrup, pp. 433–64.

191 a wrenching reassessment: The mood, and the accelerated pace of events of this time, are captured best in *Tet!*, especially pp. 241–46, and analyzed again in Braestrup's *Big Story*.

191 "A tidal wave of defeatism": Palmer, *Summons*, p. 201.

192 "General Westmoreland is confident he can hold": Johnson, p. 391.

8. Bitter Little Battles

These accounts of combat come from Marine Corps files, unit chronologies, and especially Shore, pp. 64–71.

PAGE

193 a thick, wet fog: *Comments*.

194 sensors . . . targeting was guesswork: Nalty, p. 93.

195 applauded themselves: Captain Baig called it "general euphoria" in testimony before Congress, *Electronic Battlefield*, pp. 83–89.

195 till 861 Alpha: Shore, pp. 64–66, and Stubbe, p. 948.

197 Lang Vei: the story of Lang Vei comes from many sources, but primarily from the excellent account by John A. Cash in Albright, *Seven Firefights*, pp. 120–27, and Shore, pp. 66–68.

197 Luong Dinh Du: Stubbe, p. 972, and *Seven*, p. 112.

198 "Be prepared to execute the contingency plans": from the First Battalion/26th Marines' Command Chronologies, January to March, 1968; and *Comments*.

198 On January 14: Nalty, p. 32.

200 "built to take a regiment": Stubbe, p. 971.

204 The Marines said no: Shore, pp. 67–68, and *Seven*, p. 129.

204 "They told me to get out": Braestrup, p. 327.

204 message . . . to Westmoreland: *Soldier*, p. 340.

205 Gen Tompkins passes word Negative: This penciled note is in a folder marked "26th Marines—Messages," in the Marine Corps library.

207 "was a failure": *1968 Summary*. HQUSMACV. Office of Information, Saigon. 1969.

208 "Maybe it's a spade": Herr, p. 161.

208 "One of Westy's best days": *Tet!*, pp. 189–90.

208 Radio Hanoi was boasting: AP dispatch, A120, Feb. 9, 1968.

208 "I grew more and more shocked": *Soldier*, p. 342. See also Chaisson, *Oral History*, p. 230.

209 A Company: from Shore, pp. 69–70; Pearson, p. 75; Stubbe, p. 1025, and records of the 26th Marines.

210 losses . . . "light": *Electronic Battlefield*, p. 86.

210 mob: Shore, p. 69; *Soldier*, p. 341; Wheeler, AP dispatch, Feb. 8, 1968.

211 "mostly old men, women, and children": Nalty, p. 66.

211 "I don't know what we'll do": from George E. Esper's AP dispatch (AP-A032), Feb. 9, 1968.

212 "we are not . . . going to be defeated": *Soldier*, p. 328.

9. Life in the V-Ring

The chapter title comes from a piece written by John Wheeler, the Associated Press correspondent who spent more days and nights at the combat base than any other journalist. A basement flood had turned clippings of his original dispatches into goo, but Wheeler willingly shared his memories and his hospitality in New York City in August, 1978. The microfilm library at Associated Press provided the original Wheeler reports from Vietnam.

Other descriptions of the base during the siege come from Shore's *The Battle of Khe Sanh*, Braestrup's *Big Story*, the brooding black and white photographs of David Douglas Duncan in *I Protest!*, Stubbe's *Chaplain at Khe Sanh*, and Michael Herr's *Dispatches*, pp. 86–166. Herr does not always put the right unit on the right hill, and he sometimes confuses dates or minor facts, but no other writer more perfectly captured the mad pace and contradictions of the Vietnam war. Herr writes with his nerve ends, and his book is an important contribution to understanding the war.

PAGE

214 "It hangs, hangs": Herr, p. 108.

214 "like a shanty slum": cited in Braestrup, p. 308. Herr wrote "like a Colombian slum" in *Dispatches*, p. 106.

215 U.S. Air Force was confident: Nalty, p. 24.

216 "The airstrip seemed . . . bedeviled by fog": Nalty, p. 9.

216 "Why I Defected to the Viet Cong": Miller letter.

216 "a severe obstacle": Guay, "The Khe Sanh Airlift."

217 "Zero, zero, day after day": *Electronic Battlefield*, p. 90.

217 not supposed to be in Vietnam: Nalty, p. 12.

217 February 10, a Hercules: Shore, p. 76; Nalty, p. 43.

218 "too valuable to be risked": Nalty, pp. 36–38.

218 LAPES mission: Shore, pp. 76–78, and Nalty, pp. 51–52. (Nalty says the first LAPES delivery was Feb. 16.)

220 "hello Momma": "CBS Evening News," Feb. 15, 1968. (The Marines would later claim they delivered forty-three tons of mail to Khe Sanh during the siege—fourteen pounds of letters and packages for every man at the base.)

220 parachuted supplies: Shore, p. 79, and Nalty, p. 47.

221 "Thank God, Jesus Christ": Herr and Braestrup and many others wrote about this mad dash, but this is from Lewis M. Simon's AP dispatch (AP070-854A), Feb. 27, 1968.

221 The airlift . . . unexpected problems: Nalty, pp. 42–50.

221 "Theoretically . . . six times as much as the French": Nalty, p. 42

222 "days, weeks": Herr, p. 109.

222 Masters asked repeatedly: Nalty, p. 55.

222 One of every ten: Wheeler, AP dispatch, A075-953A, Feb. 9, 1968.

222 bunker materials: Shore, p. 55.

223 "They worked nine to four": Perry, "Dusty Agony."

223 "digging your own grave": Lewis M. Simons' *AP* dispatch, AP007-1228P, Feb. 10, 1968. See also "Marines Find Flaws," *New York Times*, Feb. 22, 1968, p. 1, and Herr, p. 105.

224 Nothing . . . could stop the . . . shells: Shore, p. 57.

224 reconnaissance company: Wheeler, "Morale," AP, dispatch A075-953A, Feb. 9, 1968, and especially Duncan, *I Protest!*, and Donnelly, "Draw Noose," *Newsweek*.

224 it was "The Eyes": Herr, p. 87.

225 Lownds: Wheeler, AP dispatch, A075-953A, Feb. 9, 1968.

225 "Thanks to a small army": Shore, p. 93.

225 "utterly insensible": Herr, p. 144.

226 "The blade is . . . poised"; "The General's Biggest Battle": *Time*, Feb. 16, 1968, p. 19.

226 "Can we hold this place": Wheeler, AP dispatch, A034-634A, Feb. 5; and Simons, AP dispatch, A007-1228P, Feb. 10, 1968.

226 "we're here to stay": *Washington Post*, Feb. 5, 1968, cited in Braestrup, p. 508.

226 "That's the way it is": Simons, AP dispatch, 007-1228P.

226 "they pick just the right . . . terrain": Shaplen, *Road*, p. 117.

226 "You don't fight this fellow rifle to rifle": Littauer, p. 52.

227 Schweinfurt: Martin Caidin, *Black Thursday* (Ballantine Books, N.Y., 1960), p. 22.

227 B-52: Nalty, p. 82, and *USAF*, p. 157.

227 ten fighter bombers: *USAF*, p. 52 and 225; Shore, p. 94.

227 bombers had been diverted: Nalty, pp. 61–62.

228 150 targets a day: Pearson, p. 76; *USAF*, pp. 218–25, and *Electronic Battlefield*, p. 88.

228 artillery: Shore, pp. 93–112.

228 enemy shells: *Comments* reports that during Operation Scotland, the combat base and the hill outposts took 898 60mm mortar shells, 2,895 82mm mortar shells, 326 120mm mortar shells, 185 recoilless rifle shells, 1,743 artillery shells, 1,249 rockets (which differs very sharply from Captain Dabney's estimate of 5,000 rockets from Hill 881 North alone), and 3,612 "unknown" shells, for a total of 10,908 enemy shells.

229 Dienbienphu . . . 45,000 shells: Keegan, p. 89.

229 Allied outpost . . . 14,000 rounds: "History Book Battle," *U.S. News and World Report*, pp. 43–44.

229 "barrage": "Plight of Khe Sanh Called Not So Dire," *Washington Post*, March 3, 1968, p. A20.

229 "continuous roll of thunder": Davis, Kenneth S., *Experience of War* (Doubleday and Company, Inc., Garden City, N.Y., 1965), p. 159.

230 "dreary, dirty, miserable war": Chaisson, *Oral History*, pp. 329–30.

230 "I'll know someone is lying": Wheeler, AP dispatch, 002-108P, Feb. 12, 1968.

230 "peck, peck, peck": Simons, AP dispatch, 070-854A, Feb. 24, 1968.

231 "This ain't the Marine Corps I know": Simons, 070-854A.

231 On 881 South: Most of this account of life and death on the hilltops, especially on Hill 881 South, comes from Shore and from author's interviews with William Dabney.

232 Pineapple Chunk: Shore, p. 98.

232 The dental patient: Shore, p. 82.

233 "It's now or never": Wheeler, "Wound," AP dispatch, 027-304P, Feb. 21, 1968.

233 "pure hell": Althoff, "Helicopter Operations," pp. 47–49.

234 "psychological breakdowns": Dabney interview. See also Wheeler, "Hills," AP dispatch, 011-157P, March 1, 1968.

234 "If it wasn't for the Gaggle": Shore, p. 89.

235 "we would never have surrendered": Dabney interview.

235 "prettiest waterfalls I've ever seen": Shore, p. 89.

235 flag ceremony: Shore, pp. 1–2.

236 The enemy was hurting: Dabney interview.

237 pet snipers . . . Luke the Gook: Shore, p. 116 and Herr, p. 125, and Perry, "Dusty Agony."

237 "I think those North Vietnamese are nervous": from a Feb. 5, 1968 *Washington Post* article, cited in Braestrup, p. 308.

237 "Let's kill our seven each": Arnett, Peter, "Khe Sanh," *AP* 089-1047A, March 7, 1968.

238 If the North Vietnamese had poisoned: Nalty, p. 105, and Thompson, *No Exit*, p. 69.

238 "never, never . . . Never": Tompkins, *Oral History*, p. 40.

238 Westmoreland . . . surprised: *Soldier*, p. 347.

238 February 23: *Marines—1968*, p. 301.

238 expected . . . heavier: Nalty, p. 14, provides a list of the guns and rocket launchers that U.S. intelligence had expected to arrive at Khe Sanh.

238 men from Bravo Company: Shore, pp. 122–123, *Comments* (especially Captain Pipes), and author's interview with John A. Cicala Jr.

239 "trolling along": Tompkins, *Oral History*, p. 31.

240 "Is anyone else alive?": Wheeler, AP dispatch, 080-954A, Feb. 27, 1968.

240 "immediate emergency": Nalty, p. 62.

240 seismographic equipment: *Soldier*, p. 346.

241 The B-52s made their first: *USAF*, p. 157, and Nalty, pp. 83–86.

241 Nalty, p. 86, says 492 B-52 missions, not 589 missions.

241 "One hiccup": Wheeler interview.

241 "a string of volcanos": *Comments*.

241 "God . . . they don't even care": Arnett, AP dispatch, 089-1047A, March 7, 1968.

242 "like long, thin arms": *Comments* (Lt. Col. W.J. White).

10. The False Finish

In addition to the *Newspaper Files* and *Command Chronologies*, the essential sources are Oberdorfer's *Tet!*, especially "America the Vincible," p. 237–77, and "The Shock Wave," pp. 157–96, and Braestrup's *Big Story*, particularly "Khe Sanh: Disaster in the Making?" pp. 256–34. I do not always agree with Braestrup's conclusions, but his collection, organization, and analysis of *all* the important news accounts of the Tet period are awesome.

PAGE

243 The whole world was watching: Braestrup, p. 256.

243 "near-Gettysburg proportions": Jerry Greene, "Johnson Turns the Dotted Line Into a Hot Spot," *New York Daily News*, Feb. 6, 1968.

244 "No single battle of the Vietnam War": "The General's Biggest Battle," *Time*, Feb. 16, 1968.

244 "We do not doubt the outcome": Oberdorfer, pp. 193–94.

244 "That's what we get paid for": Perry, "Dusty Agony."

244 "What if those gooks . . . are *really* out there?": Herr, pp. 113–14.

245 the last day of February: Shore, pp. 124–25; *Electronic Battlefield*, p. 87; Pearson, p. 77. This small attack, staged by about three platoons of North Vietnamese soldiers (according to *Comments, Associated Press*, and *Newsweek*), slowly grew to a company-sized attack (according to Lownds in *Electronic Battlefield*, p. 87) to an enemy battalion (in Pearson, p. 77), to "at least a regiment" according to fire support officers in *Comments*, until finally, in the official Marine history, p. 124, it becomes "a heavy attack against the base, [possibly] the main prong of the Communist offensive." The larger estimates are based on sensor reports and stories from the Bru, who were said to have seen piles of bodies along Route 9.

246 "This was not their best effort": Arnett, AP dispatch, 089-1047A, March 7, 1968.

246 "just another probe": "Waiting," *Newsweek*, March 11, 1968, p. 58.

246 C-123 Provider: *U.S. Marines—1968*, p. 303.

246 fewer than a dozen trenches: Perry, "Dusty Agony," and Swearengen, "Siege." p. 28.

247 anti-aircraft fire . . . "unsophisticated": Guay, "The Khe Sanh Airlift."

247 "a vital link": *Comments*.

247 "Khe Sanh was a trap": English, *Oral History*.

248 "there must be, some good sound reason for being there": Shoup, David M. Testimony to Committee on Foreign Relations, 90th Congress, 2nd sesson, March 20, 1968.

248 "Perhaps our generals prepared for the wrong battle": "ABC Evening News," Feb. 5, 1968.

248 "Maybe Khe Sanh is just a feint": *Newsweek*, Feb. 12, 1968. Palmer, *Summons*, pp. 175–76, argues persuasively that Khe Sanh was a diversion. On February 11, the North Vietnamese declared on Hanoi Radio that the buildup at Khe Sanh had been a feint (*Visions*, p. 53).

248 "illogical": my notes from a Feb. 14, 1968 briefing.

248 the enemy had turned his attention: Roberts, Gene, "U.S. Command Sees Hue, not Khe Sanh, as Foe's Main Goal," *New York Times*, March 7, 1968, p. 1. The rising doubts about enemy intentions were also caught in "Khe Sanh: U.S. Girds for Red Blow," *U.S. News*, Feb. 26, 1968, pp. 29–30.

248 "between 6,000 and 8,000 men": Johnson, p. 405.

249 206,000 additional American soldiers: The impact of Westmoreland's troop request is explored in many studies, especially Schandler and Braestrup, but it is measured best in Oberdorfer, pp. 269–73.

249 "very heavy fighting": Buckley, "Westmoreland Asserts."

249 "lost the cream of his army": *Report*, p. 135. See also Oberdorfer, pp. 185–86, and *Soldier*, p. 321.

250 "Nobody in Saigon": *Soldier*, p. 321.

250 "They got so damn hysterical": Nalty, p. 104. Charleton, p. 128–30, also discusses the psychological impact of Tet.

250 Military assessments: Chaisson had already described how close Saigon came to chaos in the first days of Tet; Palmer, *Summons*, p. 103, asserts Tet was an intelligence failure comparable to Pearl Harbor or the Battle of the Bulge.

251 "we'd have had a catastrophe": Johnson, p. 417.

251 "The doors were left wide open": Thompson, *No Exit*, p. 142.

251 "even 525,000 American troops were not enough": O'Neill, *The Strategy of General Giap*, p. 16.

251 "would have required literally millions of men": *Soldier*, p. 147.

251 Ridgeway said: Halberstam, *Brightest*, p. 142; see also Ridgeway's Memoirs, cited in *U.S. News and World Report*, Jan. 3, 1966.

252 the war strained: Schandler, p. 53; and Thompson, *No Exit*, p. 58.

252 The fear of Chinese intervention: Littauer, pp. 35–37 is especially good, but Johnson, Graff (p. 137) and Shoup also discuss it in detail.

252 "to kill the tree by plucking leaves": Palmer, *Summons*, pp. 94–95. See also Report, pp. 291–93.

252 monthly average: Kinnard, pp. 94–95.

253 threshold of pain: Oberdorfer is best, beginning at p. 238; see also Schandler, pp. 138–46.

253 "The American people would never forgive me": Johnson, p. 408.

254 Westmoreland . . . brief to the Commander: Johnson, pp. 416–17.

255 meticulously prepared: Nalty, p. 96, and Shore, pp. 132–34.

255 "attempted repeat of Dienbienphu an abject failure": *Soldier*, p. 347.

256 Westmoreland felt betrayed: *Soldier*, p. 410.

257 Tolson . . . knew it was a charade: Stubbe, p. 1239, says Tolson's intelligence chief believed Khe Sanh was a diversion for the Tet attacks on Hue. See also Tompkins, *Oral History*, p. 80.

257 "a life more similar to rats than human beings": *Comments*.

257 Marines . . . "not sufficiently prepared": Touhy, William, "Marines' Leaders Disappoint U.S. Command," *Washington Post*, March 3, 1968.

257 Westmoreland . . . considered resigning: *Soldier*, p. 262.

258 "I want . . . no implication of a rescue": *Comments*.

258 Bravo grunts: Shore, pp. 128–30, and *Comments*.

260 "a wasteland": *Comments*.

260 "red orange moonscape": *U.S. Marines—1968*, p. 303.

260 "absolutely denuded": Tompkins, *Oral History*, p. 48.

260 "The ville was all rubble": Stubbe, p. 797.

260 "the enemy threat had been squelched": Shore, p. 137.

260 Westmoreland . . . to Washington: *Soldier*, p. 347.

261 "heroic defense": Shore, pp. vi–viii.

261 "premier logistical feat of the war": *Report*, p. 172.

261 "one of the heaviest . . . displays of firepower in the history of warfare": *Soldier*, p. 339. (The numbers are from Shore, and *Report*, and Nalty, p. 105.)

261 "The key to success": *Report*, p. 171, and *USAF*, p. 157.

261 evidence that the B-52 missions had been compromised: John S. Carrol, "Reds Claim Forewarning of B-52 Raids," *Baltimore Sun*, March 20, 1968, p. 2. (See also footnotes below.)

262 "surprise is completely lost": Burchett, *Vietnam North*, p. 141.

262 Hanoi Radio . . . poem: AP dispatch, A031, March 30, 1968, cited in Braestrup, p. 149.

262 "frequent, timely, and accurate warnings": Nalty, p. 88.

(NOTE: In July of 1981, the Federal Bureau of Investigation arrested a former U.S. Air Force warrant officer, George Helmich Jr., and charged him with espionage for the Soviet Union. Between 1963 and 1965, the FBI said, Helmich sold top secret decoding equipment to the Soviet Union—equipment capable of unlocking the electronic doors on the black boxes inside B-52s, unscrambling the codes, and identifying the targets. U.S. intelligence had worried about critical leaks in the B-52 bombing program, but believed security could be assured by cutting the South Vietnamese out of the selection and approval of specific targets. If the charges against Helmich are proved true, then his espionage may have helped enemy forces at Khe Sanh avoid the full power of the strategic bombers.)

263 "his back was broken by . . . B-52s": *USAF*, p. 157.

263 "It was a battle won by you": Nalty, p. 88.

263 honors and medals: Shore, pp. 141, 145–46.

11. One More Time

This account of the last Marine attack on Hill 881 North comes from the brief battlefield summaries called Situation Reports; from *Shore*, pp. 141–43; and from the battalion commander who supervised the assault: Lt. Col. John C. Studt, "Battalion on the Attack," *Marine Corps Gazette*.

PAGE

265 Anha tried to tell the Marines: Carolyn Miller letter. See also Corson, *Consequences*, where Anha is elevated to "the hereditary king of the Bru," a completely false title.

265 "Why don't they ask for guides?": Miller letter.

266 167 dead or wounded . . . of 185: Studt, "Battalion."

267 "Sir, I can't stop them. . . .": Shore, p. 142.

267 "they were all grinning": Studt, *Battalion*, p. 44.

12. The Curtain Falls

PAGE

269 Westmoreland vetoed: Nalty, p. 100.

269 The 26th . . . Regiment: Shore, p. 144.

270 "like a little Los Angeles freeway": Beverly Deepe, "U.S. Military Seeks Khe Sanh Offensive," *Christian Science Monitor*, March 26, 1968.

270 "U.S. airpower was almost completely zero": Tompkins, *Oral History*, p. 24.

270 "the crucial anchor of our defenses": Asprey, p. 1281.

270 "pour down Route 9": Neil Sheehan, "5,000 U.S. Marines Face 20,000 of Foe," *New York Times*, Feb. 23, 1968.

270 "the most famous military engagement of the war": Clayton Fritchey, "Khe Sanh: Like Waiting in the Electric Chair," *Washington Star*, March 11, 1968.

271 "an unwillingness to grant the enemy": Sheehan, "5,000 Marines."

271 "a rather sticky problem": Chaisson, *Oral History*, pp. 149–50.

271 the White House: Shore, pp. 145–46.

272 "the optimum time": Shore, p.149.

272 "buried . . . burned, or blown up": *U.S. Marines—1968*, p. 311.

273 John S. Carroll: "Report," *Atlantic Monthly*, October, 1968, and author's interview.

273 "The high command pretends": *U.S. Marines—1968*, pp. 311–12.

274 "the operation of the base at Khe Sanh unnecessary": Ibid.

Body Counts

PAGE

275 One hundred ninety-nine . . . Two hundred five: *Electronic Battlefield*, p. 95.

275 John Wheeler: author's interview.

276 441 dead Americans: Stubbe, beginning on p. 1440. Stubbe (pp. 798–800) also reports that thirteen American helicopter pilots, fourteen American

helicopter crewmen, and seventy-four Vietnamese soldiers died in a landing zone ambush not far from Khe Sanh Village on January 21. The sole survivor was an Army major named Tommy Stiner who worked his way through enemy patrols for thirteen hours, stumbled into the Marines' mine fields, and was shot by a Marine sentry before being rescued. The story appears nowhere else.

277 Robert Ellison: the author was one of many news correspondents who tried to back track Ellison when he was reported missing.

278 the Bru: Stubbe, p. 1222 and pp. 1084–87; and Shore, p. 127.

278 "The amount of firepower . . . exceeded anything . . . in history": *USAF*, p. 157.

278 "sanctity and sacredness": Chaisson, *Oral History*, p. 299.

278 "the immediate situation dictated an attack": Nalty, p. 66.

278 Father Poncet: Miller letter.

279 Pegasus: Shore, p. 143.

279 "My staff estimated": *Soldier*, p. 347.

279 Colonel Lownds was convinced: *Electronic Battlefield*, p. 95.

279 "most reasonable estimate": Nalty, p. 103.

280 "wiped out an entire regiment": Swearengen, "Siege," p. 27.

280 the official body count . . . 1,602: Shore, p. 131, and *Comments* for the count of weapons.

280 "a bunch of poop": Tompkins, *Oral History*, p. 40.

280 "pure, unadulterated bullshit": Dabney interview.

280 "ludicrous, absolutely ludicrous": Tompkins, p. 40.

280 "often inflated": Kinnard, p. 72.

281 "A long and devastating silence": Halberstam, *Brightest*, p. 653.

Judgments

PAGE

283 "U.S. airpower was almost completely zero": Tompkins, *Oral History*, p. 24.

283 By pinning down and by decimating two North Vietnamese divisions": Stubbe, p. 1234.

284 "Khe Sanh proved to be a superb diversion": Thompson, *No Exit*, pp. 68–69.

284 "General Giap was smugly satisfied": Palmer, *Summons*, p. 172.

284 "How could anyone legitimately question who was tying down whom?": *Soldier*, p. 339.

284 "What Giap wants is to control": Edward Mortimer, "Veterans of Dienbienphu Appraise Khe Sanh," *Washington Post*, Feb. 14, 1968.

285 "Khe Sanh was one more American effort": Asprey, p. 1282.

285 "don't you think we won at Khe Sanh?": Fallaci, *Nothing*, pp.85–86.

285 "Khe Sanh will stand in history": *Soldier*, pp. 336–37.

285 "The most important battle of the war": Lewis W. Walt, "Khe Sanh—The Battle That Had to Be Won," *Reader's Digest*, August, 1970.

285 "an unsound blow in the air": Krulak, *Oral History*, p. 7.

286 "The absurdity of Khe Sanh": Thompson, *No Exit*, p. 142.

286 "viable nation should emerge": *Report*, pp. 292–93.

Sources

Asprey, Robert B. *War in the Shadows*, Vol II. Garden City, New York: Doubleday, 1975.

Bloodworth, Dennis. *An Eye for the Dragon*. New York: Farrar, Straus & Giroux, 1970.

Braestrup, Peter. *Big Story: How the American Press & Television Reported and Interpreted the Crisis of Tet in Vietnam and Washington*. Garden City, New York: Anchor Press/Doubleday, 1978.

Brandon, Henry. *Anatomy of Error*. Boston: Gambit, 1969.

Browne, Malcolm. *The New Face of War*. Indianapolis, N.Y.: Bobbs-Merrill, 1968.

Bunting, Josiah. *The Lionheads*. New York: Popular Library, 1972.

Burchett, Wilfred G. *Vietnam North*. New York: International Publishers Co., Inc., 1966.

———. *Vietnam: Inside Story of the Guerilla War*. New York: International Publishers Co., 1965.

———. *Catapult to Freedom*. London: Quartet Books, 1978.

———. *Grasshoppers and Elephants: Why Vietnam Fell*. New York: Urizen Books, 1977.

Buttinger, Joseph. *A Dragon Defiant*. New York: Praeger, 1972.

Charleton, Michael and Moncrief, Anthony. *Many Reasons Why*. New York: Hill and Wang, 1978.

Christian, George. *The President Steps Down*. New York: Macmillan, 1970.

Corson, William R. *Consequences of Failure*. New York: W. W. Norton, 1974.

———. *The Betrayal*. New York: W. W. Norton, 1968.

Duncan, David Douglas. *I Protest!* New York: The New American Library, 1968.

Duncan, Donald. *The New Legions*. New York: Random House, 1967.

Ellsberg, Daniel. *Papers on the War*. New York: Simon & Schuster, 1972.

Emerson, Gloria. *Winners & Losers*. New York: Random House, 1976.

Fairbairn, Geoffrey. *Revolutionary Warfare & Communist Strategy*. London: Faber & Faber, 1968.

Fall, Bernard B. *Street Without Joy*. Harrisburg, Pa.: The Stackpole Company, 1961–64.

———. *Last Reflections on a War*. Garden City, N. Y.: Doubleday & Co., 1967.

———. *The Two Vietnams*. Revised edition. New York, Washington and London: Frederick A. Praeger, 1966.

———. *Hell in a Very Small Place: The Siege of Dien Bien Phu*. New York: Vintage Books, 1968.

Fallaci, Oriana. *Nothing and So Be It*. Garden City, N. Y.: Doubleday & Co., 1972.

Fehrenbach, T. R. *This Kind of War*. New York: Giant Cardinal Edition, 1964.

FitzGerald, Frances. *Fire in the Lake*. Boston: Little, Brown & Co., 1972.

Furgurson, Ernest B. *Westmoreland: The Inevitable General*. Boston: Little, Brown & Co., 1968.

Gavin, James M. *Crisis Now*. New York: Random House, 1968.

Gellhorn, Martha. *A New Kind of War*. Manchester, England: A Guardian Booklet, 1966.

Giap, Vo Nguyen. *People's War, People's Army*. Hanoi: Foreign Languages Publishing House, 1974.

———. *How We Won the War*. Ypsilanti, Michigan: RECON Publications, 1976.

———. (and Van Tien Dung). *Banner of People's War*. New York: Praeger Publishers, 1970.

———. *Unforgettable Months and Years*. Translated by Mai Van Elliott. Data Paper: Number 99, S.E. Asia Program, May, 1975, at Cornell University, Ithaca, New York.

———. *Big Victory, Great Task*. New York: Frederick A. Praeger, 1968.

Glasser, Ronald J. *365 Days*. New York: Bantam Books, 1971.

Goulden, Joseph C. *Truth is the First Casualty*. New York: Rand McNally & Co., 1969.

Graff, Henry. *The Tuesday Cabinet*. Englewood Cliffs, New Jersey: Prentice-Hall, 1970.

Greene, Felix. *Vietnam! Vietnam!* Palo Alto, Calif.: Fulton Publishing Co., 1966.

Harvey, Frank. *Air War—Vietnam*. New York: Bantam Books, 1967.

Hassler, Alfred. *Saigon, U.S.A.* New York: Richard W. Baron Publishing, 1970.

Hefley, James and Marti. *No Time for Tombstones*. Harrisburg, Pa.: Christian Publications, 1974.

Herr, Michael. *Dispatches*. New York: Alfred A. Knopf, 1977.

Johnson, Lyndon Baines. *The Vantage Point*. New York: Holt, Rinehart & Winston, 1971.

Halberstam, David. *The Making of a Quagmire*. New York: Random House, 1964.

———. *The Best and the Brightest*. New York: Random House, 1972.

Herbert, Anthony B. (with James T. Wooten). *Soldier*. New York: Dell Publishing Co., 1973.

Just, Ward. *To What End*. Boston: Houghton, Mifflin Co., 1968.

Kahin, George McTurnan and Lewis, John W. *The United States in Vietnam*. Delta Publishing Co., 1967.

Kearns, Doris. *Lyndon Johnson and the American Dream*. New York: Harper & Row, 1976.

Keegan, John. *Dien Bien Phu*. New York: Random House, 1974.

King, Edward L. *The Death of the Army*. New York: Saturday Review Press, 1972.

Kinnard, Douglas. *The War Managers*. Hanover, N. H.: University Press of New England, for the University of Vermont, 1977.

Knoebl, Kuno. *Victor Charlie*. London, England: Pall Mall Press, 1967.

Kovic, Ron. *Born on the Fourth of July*. New York: McGraw-Hill Book Co., 1976.

Lamb, Helen B. *Vietnam's Will to Live*. New York & London: Monthly Review Press, 1972.

Lancaster, Donald. *The Emancipation of French Indochina*. New York: Octagon Books, 1974.

Lane, Allen, ed., *Prevent the Crime of Silence*. Reports from Sessions of the International War Crimes Tribunal Convened by Bertrand Russell. London: Penguin Press, 1971.

Langer, Paul and Zasloff, Joseph J. *North Vietnam and the Pathet Loa, Partners in the Struggle for Laos*. Cambridge, Mass.: Harvard University Press, 1970.

"Lessons from the Vietnam War." Report of a Seminar Held at the Royal United Service Institute, February 12, 1969, Whitehall, England.

Lewallen, John. *Ecology of Devastation: Indochina*. Baltimore, Maryland: Penguin Books, 1971.

Lewy, Guenter. *America in Vietnam*. New York: Oxford University Press, 1978.

Littauer, Raphael and Uphoff, Norman. *The Air War in Indochina*. Boston: Beacon Press, 1972.

Lucas, Jim G. *Dateline: Vietnam*. New York: Award Books, 1964 & 1965.

Marshall, S.L.A. *West to Cambodia*. New York: Cowles Book Co., 1968.

———. *Battles in the Monsoon*. New York: William Morrow & Co., 1967.

———. *The Soldier's Load and the Mobility of a Nation*. Washington, D.C.: The Combat Forces Press, 1950.

———. *Ambush*. New York: Cowles Book Co., 1969.

Martin, Earl S. *Reaching the Other Side*. New York: Crown Publishing, 1978.

McAleavy, Henry. *Black Flags in Vietnam*. New York: Macmillan Co., 1968.

McAlister, John T., Jr. *Vietnam: The Origins of Revolution*. Garden City, N. Y.: Doubleday & Co., 1971.

McCarthy, Mary. *Vietnam*. Middlesex, England: Penguin Books, 1967.

———. *Hanoi*. New York: Harcourt, Brace and World, 1968.

Mecklin, John. *Mission in Torment.* Garden City, N. Y.: Doubleday & Co., 1965.

Miller, Carolyn Paine. *Captured!* Chappaqua, New York: Christian Herald Books, 1977.

Millet, Allan R., ed. *A Short History of the Vietnam War.* Bloomington, Indiana: Indiana University Press, 1978.

Mulligan, Hugh A. *No Place to Die.* New York: William Morrow and Co., 1967.

Mylander, Maureen. *The Generals.* New York: Dial Press, 1974.

Oberdorfer, Don. *Tet!* Garden City, N.Y.: Doubleday & Co., 1971.

O'Neill, Robert J. *General Giap: Politician & Strategist.* Cassell Australia Ltd., 1969.

———. *The Strategy of General Giap Since 1964.* Canberra, Australia: Australian National University Press, 1969.

Palmer, Dave Richard. *Summons of the Trumpet.* San Rafael, Calif.: Presidio Press, 1978.

The Pentagon Papers; The Secret History of the Vietnam War. New York Times Edition. New York: Bantam Books, 1971.

Pettit, Clyde Edwin. *The Experts.* Secaucus, New Jersey: Lyle Stuart, 1975.

Pike, Douglas. *Viet Cong.* Cambridge, Mass.: The M.I.T. Press, 1966.

Raskin, Marcus G. and Fall, Bernard B., eds. *The Vietnam Reader; a Collection of Essays and Original Documents.* New York: Random House, 1965.

Rottmann, Larry; Barry, Jan; and Pacquet, Basil T., eds. *Winning Hearts and Minds; War Poems by Vietnam Veterans.* New York: McGraw-Hill, 1972.

Roy, Jules. *Battle of Dien Bien Phu.* New York: Pyramid Books, 1966.

Sack, John, *M.* New York: The American Library, 1967.

Salisbury, Harrison E. *Behind the Lines—Hanoi.* New York: Bantam Books, 1967.

Schandler, Herbert Y. *The Unmaking of a President: Lyndon Johnson and Vietnam.* Princeton, New Jersey: Princeton University Press, 1977.

Schell, Jonathan. *The Military Half: An Account of the Destruction in Quang Ngai and Quang Tin.* New York: Vintage, 1968.

———. *The Village of Ben Suc.* New York: Alfred A. Knopf, 1967.

Shaplen, Robert. *Time Out of Hand.* New York: Harper & Row, 1969.

———. *The Road from War: Vietnam 1965–70.* New York: Harper & Row, 1970.

Snepp, Frank. *Decent Interval.* New York: Vintage, 1977.

Steinbeck, John, IV. *In Touch.* New York: Dell Publishing, 1968.

Tanham, George K. *Communist Revolutionary Warfare.* New York: Frederick A. Praeger, 1961. Revised 1967.

Terzani, Tiziano. *Giai Phong! The Fall & Liberation of Saigon.* New York: St. Martin's Press, 1976.

Thompson, Sir Robert. *Peace is Not at Hand.* New York: David McKay Company, 1974.

———. *No Exit from Vietnam.* New York: David McKay Company, 1969.
Thorne, David and Butler, George, eds. *John Kerry and Vietnam Veterans Against the War; The New Soldier.* New York: Collier Books, 1971.
Tran Van Don. *Our Endless War.* San Rafael, Calif.: Presidio Press, 1978.
Van Dyke, Jon M. *North Vietnam's Strategy for Survival.* Palo Alto, Calif.: Pacific Books, 1972.
Visions of Victory. Analytical Introduction by Patrick J. McGarvey. Hoover Institute on War, Revolution and Peace, Stanford University, 1969.
Walt, Lewis W. *Strange War, Strange Strategy.* New York: Funk & Wagnalls, 1970.
Warner, Denis. *The Last Confucian.* Baltimore: Penguin Books, 1964.
———. *A Certain Victory.* Kansas City: Sheed, Andrews and McMeel, 1978.
Webb, James. *Fields of Fire.* Englewood Cliffs, N.J.: Prentice-Hall, 1978.
West, F.J., Jr. *The Village.* New York: Harper & Row, 1972.
West, Richard. *Victory in Vietnam.* London: Private Eye Productions, 1974.
Westmoreland, General William C. *A Soldier Reports.* Garden City, N.Y.: Doubleday & Co., 1976. (*Soldier*)
Windchy, Eugene G. *Tonkin Gulf.* Garden City, N.Y.: Doubleday & Co., 1971.

Military and Government Sources

Albright, John; Cash, John A.; and Sandstrum, Allan W. *Seven Firefights in Vietnam.* Office of the Chief of Military History, U. S. Army, Washington, D. C., 1970.
Berger, Carl, ed. *The U. S. Air Force in Southeast Asia, 1961–73.* Office of Air Force History, Washington, D. C., 1977. (*USAF*)
Clapp, Lt. Col. Archie J. *The Marines in Vietnam, 1954–73.* History and Museums Division, Headquarters, U. S. Marine Corps, Washington, D. C., 1977.
"Comments," Uncatalogued letters, annotated manuscripts, and commentaries on Capt. Meyer Shore's *The Battle for Khe Sanh*, by participants. (*Comments*)
Command Chronologies. The daily accounts of battle and routine for each battalion and for the Twenty-sixth Marine Regiment. On file at the U. S. Marine Corps Library, with original radio messages, maps, situation reports, and other primary material.
Ewell, Lt. Gen. Julian and Hunt, Maj. Gen. Ira A., Jr. *Sharpening the Combat Edge: The Use of Analysis to Reinforce Military Judgement.* Dept. of the Army, Washington, D. C., 1974.
Guay, Lt. Col. Robert, USMC. *The Khe Sanh Airlift.* January 31, 1969. A lecture and slide presentation analyzing air logistical requirements.
Hay, Lt. Gen. John H., Jr. *Tactical and Material Innovations*, Dept. of the Army, Washington, D. C., 1974.

Hearings of the Electronic Battlefield Subcommittee of the Preparedness Investigations Subcommittee of the Committee on Armed Services, U.S. Senate, 91st Cong., 2nd sess., November 18, 19, and 24, 1970. (*Electronic Battlefield*)

Kelly, Col. Francis J. U.S. *Army Special Forces, 1961–1971*. Dept. of the Army, Washington, D.C., 1973.

Marine Corps Oral History Collection Catalog, History and Museums Division. Headquarters, U.S. Marine Corps, Washington, D.C., (*Oral History*)

Mc Christian, Maj. Gen. Joseph A. *The Role of Military Intelligence, 1965–67*. Department of the Army, Washington, D. C., 1974.

Nalty, Bernard C. *Air Power and the Fight for Khe Sanh*. Office of Air Force History, U.S. Air Force, Washington, D.C., 1973.

Newspaper files. Thousands of newspaper clippings on the Vietnam War, organized roughly by date, in twelve or more bound volumes in the U.S. Naval Library, Washington, D. C. This twice-daily digest of morning and afternoon papers (it often included transcripts of television, radio and wire service reports) was prepared to keep Pentagon officials aware of every detail of American media coverage of the Vietnam war.

Pearson, Lt. Gen. Willard. *The War in the Northern Provinces*, 1966–68. Department of the Army, Washington, D. C., 1975.

Rogers, Lt. Gen. Bernard William. *Cedar-Falls-Junction City: A Turning Point*, Dept. of the Army, Washington, D. C., 1974.

Shore, Capt. Meyers SI, III. *The Battle for Khe Sanh*. Historical Branch, 6-3 Division, Headquarters, U.S. Marine Corps, Washington, D. C., 1969.

Shoup, David M. Testimony to the Committee on Foreign Relations, 90th Cong., 2nd Sess., March 20, 1968.

Shulimson, Jack. *U.S. Marines in Vietnam, 1966; An Expanding War*, (Working Draft). History and Museums Division, Headquarters, U.S. Marine Corps, Washington, D. C., April, 1978.

Sullivan, Cornelius D. *Winter-Spring Offensive in the Vietnam War: Its Conduct and Higher Direction*. The Center for Strategic Studies, Georgetown University, Washington, D. C., November, 1968.

U.S.M.A.C.V. 1968 Summary, Office of Information, Saigon, 1969.

Westmoreland, General William C. *Report on the War in Vietnam* (as of June 30, 1968). Washington, D. C., Government Printing Office, 1969.

———. Speeches: South Carolina General Assembly (April 26, 1967); Testimony to Armed Services Committee (November, 1967); Joint Session of Congress (April 28, 1967); Press Club, Washington, D. C. (November 21, 1967); and *Associated Press* Managing Editors (Spring, 1967).

Whitlow, Cpt. Robert H. *U.S. Marines in Vietnam, 1954–1964*. History and Museums Division, Headquarters, U.S. Marine Corps, Washington, D. C., 1977.

Selected Military Articles

Althoff, Lt. Col. David L. "Helicopter Operations at Khe Sanh," (Interview), *Marine Corps Gazette*, vol. 54, no. 5 (May 1969).

Caufield, Maj., M. P. "India Six," *Marine Corps Gazette*, vol. 53, no. 7 (July 1969).

Collins, Col. John M. "The Vietnam War in Perspective," Strategic Research Group, National War College, Washington, D.C., 1972.

Davis, Maj. Gen. R.G. and Jones, Lt. J. L., Jr. "Employing the Recon Patrol," *Marine Corps Gazette*, vol. 54, no. 5, (May 1970).

Hammond, Lt. Col. J. W., Jr. "Combat Journal," *Marine Corps Gazette*, vol. 52, no. 7, (July 1968).

Kipp, Robert M. "Counterinsurgency from 30,000 Feet: B-52s in Vietnam," *Air University Review*, XIX, no. 2, (January–February 1968).

Serong, A. P. "The 1972 Easter Offensive," *Southeast Asia Perspectives*, 10, (Summer 1974).

Simmons, Brig. Gen. Edwin H., USMC. "Marine Corps Operations in Vietnam, 1967," *Naval Review*, 1969.

———. "Marine Corps Operations in Vietnam, 1968," *Naval Review*, 1970.

Studt, Lt. Col. John C. "Battalion on the Attack," *Marine Corps Gazette*, vol. 54, no. 7 (July 1970).

Swearengen, Maj. Mark A. "Siege: 40 Days at Khe Sanh," *Marine Corps Gazette*, vol. 54, no. 4, (April 1975).

Turley, Lt. Col. G. H. and Wells, Capt. Mr. R. "Easter Invasion," *Marine Corps Gazette*, vol. 57, no. 3, (March 1973).

Selected Articles

Alsop, Stewart. "Will Westmoreland Elect Johnson?" *Saturday Evening Post*, January 13, 1968.

Arnett, Peter. "Viet Red Drive Challenges U.S. Military Assumptions," *Baltimore Sun*, February 7, 1968.

Baldwin, Hanson W. "The Enemy's Armory Goes Modern," *New York Times*, March 3, 1968.

———. "Khe Sanh Disturbs Many in Marines," *New York Times*, March 14, 1968.

Braestrup, Peter. "Copters Run Constant Risks to Supply Khe Sanh Outposts," *Washington Post*, March 5, 1968.

Buckley, Tom. "U.S. Cuts Estimate of Foe's Strength," *New York Times*, November 25, 1967.

———. "U.S. Troops Face Point-Blank Fire; Near Top of Hill," *New York Times*, November 22, 1967.

———. "Offensive Is Said to Pinpoint Enemy's Strengths," *New York Times*, Feb. 2, 1968.

———. "Westmoreland Asserts 'Very Heavy Fighting' is Ahead," *New York Times*, March 11, 1968.

Carroll, John S. "Reds Claim Forewarning of B-52 Raids," *Baltimore Sun*, March 20, 1968.

"Cavalry Charge to Khe Sanh by Road and Chopper," *Life*, April 19, 1968.

Coffey, Raymond R. "The Scene in Vietnam: Gloomier and Gloomier," *Chicago Daily News*, March 7, 1968.

———. "Viet 'Progress,'" *Chicago Daily News*, January 10, 1968.

Deepe, Beverly. "U.S. Military Seeks Khe Sanh Offensive," *Christian Science Monitor*, March 26, 1968.

"Drawing the Noose?" *Newsweek*, Feb. 5, 1968.

Duncan, Donald. "Khe Sanh," Life, vol. 64, no. 8, February 23, 1968.

"End of Vietnam War in Sight?" *U.S. News & World Report*, September 11, 1967.

Evans, Rowland and Novak, Robert. "Policy Makers and Generals Worry Over Massive Buildup at Khe Sanh." *Washington Post*, January 31, 1968.

Farrer, Fred. "Dak To Called Start of Great Defeat for Commies," *Chicago Tribune*, November 23, 1967.

"Force at Khe Sanh," *New York Times*, January 26, 1968.

Frankel, Max. "White House: Ultimate Vietnam Command Post," *New York Times*, February 10, 1968.

"General Westmoreland Shift Held Unlikely," *Washington Post*, February 6, 1968.

"General Says U.S. Can Hold Khe Sanh," AP. *New York Times*, 25 March, 1968.

"General's Biggest Battle, The," *Time*, February 16, 1968.

"General's Illusions, The," *St. Louis Post-Dispatch*, February 27, 1968.

Gould, Jack. "U.S. is Losing War in Vietnam, N.B.C. Declares," *New York Times*, March 12, 1968.

Greene, Jerry. "Johnson Turns the Dotted Line into a Hot Spot," *New York Daily News*, February 6, 1968.

Harwood, Richard. "The War Just Doesn't Add Up," *Washington Post*, September 3, 1967.

"History Book Battle: The Red Defeat at Khe Sanh," *U.S. News & World Report*, May 6, 1968.

"How the Battle for Khe Sanh was Won," *Time*, April 17, 1968.

Just, Ward. "Khe Sanh: Holding the End of the Line," *Washington Post*, January 31, 1968.

Kann, Peter R. "Value and Price in Battle of Dak To," *Wall St. Journal*, November 28, 1967.

Kelly, Orr. "The Enemy in Trouble—18 Months and No Big Victory," *Washington Star*, November 8, 1967.

———. "In a Military Sense, the War is Just About Won," *Washington Star*, November 7, 1967.

———. "Loc Ninh Emerging as Significant Fight," *Washington Star*, November 21, 1967.

———. "U.S. Watches Buildup Near Outpost," *Washington Star*, January 21, 1968.

"Khe Sanh: U.S. Girds for Red Blow," *U.S. News & World Report*, February 26, 1968.

"Khe Sanh: 6000 Marines Dug in for Battle," *Life*, February 9, 1968.

Lescaze, Lee. "Dak To Battleground: The Enemy's Choice," *Washington Post*, November 25, 1967.

———. "Reds Edging Closer to Base at Khe Sanh," *Washington Post*, January 24, 1968.

Martin, Robert P. "Million Americans Soon in Vietnam?" *U.S. News & World Report*, March 18, 1968.

"Man on the Spot," *Newsweek*, February 19, 1968.

Mohr, Charles. "Khe Sanh and Dien Bien Phu: A Comparison," *New York Times*, March 7, 1968.

Mortimer, Edward. "Vets of Dien Bien Phu Appraise Khe Sanh," *Washington Post*, February 14, 1968.

Perry, Merton. "The Dusty Agony of Khe Sanh," *Newsweek*, March 18, 1968.

Potter, Phillip. "U.S. Ready for Showdown with Viet Reds at Dak To," *Baltimore Sun*, November 15, 1967.

Roberts, Gene. "U.S. Command Sees Hue, Not Khe Sanh, as Foe's Main Goal," *New York Times*, March 7, 1968.

"Sees Hanoi Needing a Victory," *New York News*, September 5, 1967.

Sheehan, Neil. "5,000 U.S. Marines Face 20,000 of Foe," *New York Times*, February 23, 1968.

Taylor, Frederick. "The Eve of Battle," *Wall Street Journal*, February 15, 1968.

Touhy, William. "Marines' Leaders Disappoint U.S. Command," *Washington Post*, March 3, 1968.

Walt, Lewis W. "Khe Sanh—the Battle That Had to be Won," *Reader's Digest*, August, 1970.

Weinraub, Bernard. "Tense Dak To G.I.s Hunt Elusive Foe," *New York Times*, November 17, 1967.

———. "U.S. Aides Say Khe Sanh Will be Held at All Costs," *New York Times*, February 9, 1968.

Wilson, George C. "U.S. Bombing of Two Vietnams Tops Its World War II Drop in Europe," *Washington Post*, December 3, 1967.

Index